To Rio
A river of joy, laughter and love. The most wonderful gift I could ever imagine.

To Stephen Ghysels
Whose boundless curiosity and humor have helped me stay the course towards my goals while keeping me laughing and living in a balanced, healthy way.

To Dr. Marilyn Ravicz
When I was asked as a young child in elementary school and again as a young woman in graduate school to name the figure, whether contemporary or historical, I admired most for qualities such as courage, a devotion to helping others, intelligence, and generosity of spirit, in both cases my answer was immediate and simple: my mother.

To Dr. Robert Ravicz
Wise and loving, a wonderful father who bestowed on his daughter the courage to follow her dreams.

Contents

I am thankful to all of the women who have allowed me into their lives to share their pains and their joys, their courage and strength is truly amazing. I am also thankful to those men who care more about human beings than about keeping a tight grip on all of the chips so that they inevitably win the game.

In addition, we owe much to the people who have dedicated their lives to discovery and study to improve our mental, spiritual, and physical well-being in a world of chaos. Finally, I must thank Richard Ravicz, a solid, supportive elder brother, and Tanyo Ravicz, the most talented, brilliant writer I know, whose dedication to his craft served as a model to me in my efforts.

Introduction

Few living in our technologically driven, hectic world would question the importance of stress management. However, some might question the need for yet another book on stress management. If you're in this group, you might even add that you don't have the time to read about—let alone practice—stress-management techniques! The truth is, you can't afford to ignore the recent research and discoveries that are providing vital information about stress that you *can* incorporate into your life. You can improve your sense of challenge and excitement, and your ability to maintain a healthy, flexible life balance. The traditional idea of stress management to reduce, or at a minimum to "deal" with stress is outmoded. What is essential for you to learn is that there are actually two types of stress. Negative stress (*distress*) is what most of us refer to when we're "stressed out." New evidence, however, shows that *prostress*, my term for positive stress, can promote physical and mental health. In this book, stress management involves taking a look at the impact of both negative and positive stress on your mental and physical well-being. You will be taught practical, effective techniques to reduce distress and increase prostress.

A second question regarding the necessity of this book: Why the focus on stress and *women*? What does one's sex have to do with how he or she perceives, experiences, or reacts to stress? As you will learn, a great deal.

Positive stress, or prostress, involves pleasure, growth, challenge, and excitement. Imagine for a moment the following example: You're going mountain climbing. You've done this before on a number of mildly difficult mountains. This time you're venturing to conquer a mountain rated more difficult, but you're confident. You've prepared well, and you believe your abilities and body strength are on par with the risk and demands. You're excited and anticipating the climb—you have to admit that you're feeling slightly nervous as you take your first few steps but shortly the thrill of the challenge dominates. Pretty soon, you're looking up, scanning the face of the mountain for the best place to continue your ascent. You're visualizing different possibilities and then making your move. Although you're unaware of it, your anxiety is gone, replaced by *energy* and exquisite *focus*. You scan, plan, and make your move— again and again. The rhythm takes over and you are lost in the flow of your movements. You feel assured and confident. Even though it's been over one and a half hours, you've been so absorbed with the mountain and your movements, that it seems only minutes have passed. You can't believe it when, with muscles straining, you've reached the last few steps, and then you're there. You're at the top, you met your goal, you answered the challenge that you'd set for yourself. You feel proud and powerful. You feel like you can tackle anything now and start making plans for embarking on life's next "difficult climb."

Although stress does not spare anyone based upon gender, a growing body of evidence is highlighting sex differences in the stress phenomenon. Stress is a process and not a simple stimulus-response dynamic as previously proposed. The fact that stress involves a complex interactive process is the first central point of this book. Gender comes into play in a variety of ways and produces differences between the male and female experience of stress.

- Women and men are exposed to different stressors.

- Women and men create different stressors.

- Women and men perceive stressors differently.

- Women and men use different coping techniques to deal with stress.

- Negative stress (distress) can have different consequences on women and men (psychological and physical).

Because of my training and work in clinical psychology, I've had the opportunity to work with many women, both individually, as clients, as well as with larger numbers of women through stress management and related workshops I've designed and conducted. The interaction of stressors in our many female roles (as employee, mother, wife, woman, caretaker, volunteer worker, social coordinator and friend, to name a few), together with the fact that most of us either ignore or are unaware of the real extent and damaging potential of negative stress in our lives, have convinced me (and the many women I've informally polled) of the need for this book. Most of the stress research to date has focused on men, and it's essential to redress the dearth of knowledge applicable to women. Not only have I gathered crucial information about women and stress through clinical work and research, but I'm also intimately familiar with this complex dance myself. In terms of women and the workplace and stress, I gained an important perspective both through obtaining an MBA from a competitive program and from working in various industries occupying positions from low "wo"man to upper "wo"man on the totem pole. Returning to graduate school a second time after I was married, I worried that it was "too late" to start another career and was sometimes overwhelmed by the female-related stressors. Like most women in our culture today, I've experienced getting more and more pieces of the pie placed on my plate as my responsibility. Writing this book is a perfect example: I was simultaneously completing my doctoral program, working full time, running seminars, and having a baby—among other things! There's no question that I would've been unable to accomplish these things as the former stress-mess I had been. The techniques included in this book have been invaluable in allowing me to grow, experience balance in my life, and actually enjoy the road as I travel it, bumps, divergences, uphills, and downhills. Sure, sometimes I relapse into a bout of the hurry and worry sickness; however, I couldn't live the life I do now, so full, flexible, and balanced, without using the tools presented in this book.

So, my endeavors in the business and academic worlds, my research, and practical experience with women in a variety of therapeutic and consulting formats, and most importantly, my being a woman "in the trenches," I've learned much about the dynamics of stress especially relevant to women. I have explored the wheres, whys, and hows of negative stress. I have come to realize the absolute need for prostress, and what types of stress-management (or "self-management") techniques are most effective in reducing distress. It is this body of knowledge that you will hopefully find informative, and enjoyable, because it is without a doubt, critical in improving your life quality.

How This Book Works

At some points, it will be necessary to include discussion of empirical evidence, technical terminology, and historical background from various subjects. Part 1 of this book examines how and why women experience and perceive stress differently than men. The nature of our roles as employees, mothers, wives, friends, and as women in general exposes us to certain gender-specific stressors. More importantly, the *interaction* of such roles underlies the likelihood of a woman's experience of negative stress. Men and women experience events such as marriage or holidays differently. Women have many difficult, distressful responsibilities linked with those events, like arranging the marriage or preparing holiday meals. So later in the book when you're thinking about prostress activities to include in your daily life, watch out for those events with "hidden" negative stressors.

Physiological differences between men and women can also explain differential gender responses to negative stress in the form of physical disorders such as coronary heart disease and autoimmune disorders, as well as psychological disorders such as depression and anxiety. Other dynamics affecting a woman's experience of stress include self-esteem, social support, the emphasis on female weight and appearance, coping mechanisms, and personality characteristics such as optimism, hardiness, and the drive toward excellence and achievement.

The importance of prostress for our health and well-being is the second central point of this book. It's time we realize that stress isn't strictly a negative phenomenon. In fact, depending upon how you perceive a potential stressor, you can either suffer or benefit from the stress process. Prostress, its potential benefits on your mental and physical health, and how to increase the level of prostress in your life will be discussed in detail.

With the understanding of the female stress process provided in part 1, you'll move on to part 2 which will provide you with effective, tailored ways to manage, cope with, and even benefit from stress. This portion presents mental and physical stress-management techniques to help you develop and practice new stress-management skills. These methods have been proven successful within the area of stress management, and I've used them with many women at stress-management seminars, who have found them highly effective in increasing their sense of control over their health, happiness and lifestyles. As you work through part 2, you'll acquire the tools to reduce the negative stress and boost the prostress in your life. Imagine climbing out of the hole of distress-induced hopelessness and helplessness into which many of us have unwittingly buried ourselves.

A holistic perspective is essential in discussing stress and serves as the third central point of this book. As philosophers and practitioners of centuries ago knew and scientists are recently beginning to "rediscover," the mind and body are inextricably linked, and changes and experiences impact both. How and even whether one experiences stress is affected by the functioning of mind and body. Likewise, stress exerts its impact on both mind and body. The exercises presented in part 2 will show you how stress-management techniques are based upon the fact that both mind and body are affected by stress and show how both must be used to combat the sneaky side of negative stress.

The exercises and fill-ins are very powerful in getting you to participate and learn while receiving reinforcement from actually tracking your progress. This type of active participation and tracking is much more effective than passive absorption of suggestions and instructions.

As you read this, remember that while stress is inevitable, negative psychological and physical consequences are not. You can use these techniques to find the optimal level of stress for you. Let us embark upon a journey to take control over stress with the realization that we are not helpless victims but that we can actually grow and thrive from our challenges.

Part I

Understanding Stress

1

What Is Stress?

From the amount most of us probably read about stress and stress management, you would think we'd all be experts in these subjects by now. However, judging from the huge personal and societal costs of stress, something is wrong with the curriculum! This book will go far in redressing this situation, especially for women, so that you truly can be competent, stress-optimizing, self-management leaders. I discuss and explore stress in a way that differs on several fronts from usual and older approaches. The most obvious difference, and the reason you're probably reading this book, is its focus on women and stress. Most of the research and work to date in the field of stress has focused on men. For a variety of reasons about which you will learn, women are exposed to different stressors, and perceive and experience stress differently. It's essential that these differences be examined and that you are given the tools needed to reduce your *negative stress*, or *distress*, and increase *positive stress*, or *prostress*. Indeed, stress is necessary for all of us, but any one woman can be experiencing too much or too little stress for her. Part 1 will familiarize you with female stress, and part 2 will provide the tools to help you obtain your optimal level of prostress.

The subject of stress has become extremely popular over the last several decades. Stress is blamed for physical and psychological illnesses, accidents, difficulties at work and home, drug and alcohol abuse, and a number of personal and societal problems. The pressured pace of our daily lives, cultural beliefs emphasizing achievement and success, the dissolution of families and social support networks, the demands from the many areas of our lives, and beliefs that much of our lives are out of our control cause us to experience negative stress (distress). Some experts suggest that the obvious solution to this stress in our lives is to simply eliminate it. This is neither possible nor healthy. Stress is an inevitable fact of life. The truth is that we need stress in order to grow and develop. Because we cannot abolish stress and sometimes even need it, are we doomed to live in a state of tension, discomfort, or ill health? Absolutely not! What we can do is to learn how to not only live with stress, but also benefit from it. First we need to understand "stress."

Stressors

Simply put, a stressor is any stimulus that causes stress. Even asking the question, "What is a stressor?" brings up an important distinction of this book as compared to other, particularly earlier, works. Traditionally, major life events such as divorce, marriage, job promotions, and completing school were considered stressors responsible for the harmful physical and psychological consequences of stress. For years, people were led to believe that the sheer *number* of these major life events determined their negative stress level and increased the likelihood of developing a physical illness. The problem with this traditional approach is that it isn't simply the number of such life events you experience that causes distress and illness. Instead, what matters is whether you see these life events and situations in a negative or positive way. I cannot overemphasize this essential discovery—that is, it is the *meaning you give* to a situation that determines whether you will interpret it as negative and consequently whether it will be psychologically or physically damaging. Once you grasp this realization and learn the techniques offered in this book, you'll gain a tremendous sense of control over your reactions, health, and life. While stress is unavoidable, distress is not!

Models of Stress

One of the earliest, most widely recognized researchers in the stress field was Hans Selye. Selye first developed an interest in this area in 1925 when he noticed that people seemed to show a single physical response pattern no matter what the stressor (Selye 1967). That means whether you are frightened by a bear or pleasurably thrilled by the plunging of a roller coaster, Selye asserted that your body would respond in the same aroused way. The following models of stress will explain further.

"You Always React the Same" Model

In 1980, Selye described stress as the general, *common response* to physical or psychological demands for surviving and achieving one's goals

Stimulus   ⟶   **Response**
(Stress, *or the general adaptation*
syndrome **)**

Selye's most important point is that even when the stressors you experience are quite different, your body's biochemical response is the same. So, a particular situation might cause one person to be afraid, another angry, and another excited. The link is that these three individuals all have the same physical reactions—he labeled this the *general adaptation syndrome*. However, experts now believe that everyone can have somewhat different physical reactions and that you can even learn to control these "automatic" physical changes. The implications of this discovery are huge. You can learn to control your responses to stress.

Your body's physical activation from exposure to a stressor is beneficial for a brief period of time. Problems arise, though, when the exposure and/or arousal continue. At this point, the initially adaptive response becomes a destructive one. You're subject to becoming a victim to what Selye calls the constant wear and tear of stress.

The Dual Nature of Stress

An important aspect of Selye's work is his pioneering idea that stress can be either negative or positive. This concept is central to stress optimization. This aspect of stress has been largely ignored by researchers and practitioners for years, but fortunately recent evidence strengthens Selye's findings. The dual nature of stress is invaluable to understanding and benefiting from stress and is discussed in depth in this book. Prostress (or "eustress," as Selye calls it) refers to the pleasant, challenging stress that offers fulfillment, growth, and arousal without the harmful consequences of negative stress. If you interpret stress positively, you won't have the long-term particularly harmful physical activation that coincides with experiencing negative stress or distress (Allen 1983; Edwards and Cooper 1988; Taylor 1991).

Remember, stress-linked, physical arousal doesn't necessarily indicate an increase in *negative* stress. Sometimes it indicates an increase in *prostress*. Arousal can be stressful, but if the stressor linked with this arousal is interpreted positively and handled actively, the stimulus can be energizing and challenging. Let's look at an example of my client Sharon who was given the chance to design a sales presentation. You will be reading more about her case later. But briefly, when she responded with positive thoughts about her chances for success and even about getting the opportunity to try, she felt challenged, excited, and energized. As you'll soon learn, not only does it appear that the physical arousal from prostress is less harmful than that of distress but it also seems there are even physical *benefits* from prostress motivation and arousal!

"You're All the Same" Model

A second model of stress focuses on the situation or stressor itself rather than on the responses. This model is similar to a common model often seen in magazines and books represented by the "Social Readjustment Scale," based on research by Holmes and Rache.

(Stimulus) Stress ⟶ Response

Just as there were problems with Selye's model, or the "You Always React the Same" model, there are also difficulties with this model. Let's call this one the "You're All the Same" model of stress. This view assumes that all people react in the same way to a particular stressor. This model doesn't allow for the fact that a particular situation can be quite stressful for one person and not at all stressful for another. Remember that whether or not you perceive something as a stressor depends on the *personal meaning* you give to it. You might respond to a stimulus as if it were a distressor, or you might experience it as a prostressor. Speaking in front of a room of people could produce *some* of the same physical changes in two people, but a trained confident speaker is more likely to be experiencing the pleasure and thrill of prostress, while a novice is likely to be absolutely terrified and distressed.

The "You're All the Same" model is indeed flawed. As mentioned, you may be familiar with one of the ways this approach was presented to the public. Perhaps at some point you completed a questionnaire, the "Social Readjustment Scale," found in older and even a few recent stress-management books or articles asking you to mark the major life events you had experienced in the past year. Then, you're told to add up the points of each event which you marked. The total number of points supposedly represent the total amount of stress you've experienced which predicts the likelihood of your becoming ill within a year. Obviously, this scale and the "You're All the Same" model are based on the idea that all major life events act similarly as negative stressors to everybody and increase the likelihood that one will become ill. The theory underlying this model is that major life events require you to adapt or change, with the assumption that change has a negative impact on your well-being. This model assumes that all of us who are exposed to certain events, whether retirement, vacation, marriage, or divorce, will interpret and value them in the same way. However, these events have quite different meanings and relevance for different people. Many people have experienced divorce as unexpected, heart wrenching, and completely devastating. Others may have been in a long-term difficult and unhappy marriage and may not have had such an overwhelmingly negative experience. Perhaps the divorce offered a sense of liberation, a release from an unhealthy situation, or the challenge of being independent again. The problem with this questionnaire and with the "You're All the Same" model in general is that it's the events we actively *perceive* as negative that lead to the harmful consequences of distress, not just events involving change. It isn't surprising that evidence shows only a weak link between these life events (*personally interpretable*) and health (Kanner et al. 1981).

"You Have a Choice" Model

Let's move on to the model of stress used in this book. This approach is more flexible and comprehensive than the two earlier models. It also acknowledges the fact that while environmental stressors can certainly influence you, you can also actively influence the quality and quantity of these environmental stressors. Let's call this the "You Have a Choice" model. Now you can see that you hold the ultimate responsibility—with the tools in part 2, you can learn how to use this truth in a way so as to greatly improve your happiness, pleasure with life, and mental and physical well-being.

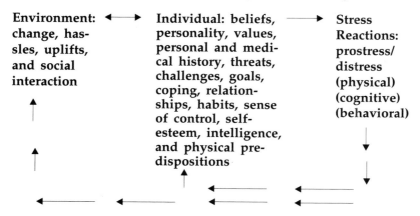

Environment: change, hassles, uplifts, and social interaction ←→ Individual: beliefs, personality, values, personal and medical history, threats, challenges, goals, coping, relationships, habits, sense of control, self-esteem, intelligence, and physical predispositions → Stress Reactions: prostress/distress (physical) (cognitive) (behavioral)

There are several things I would like to highlight in this model:

- As you can see, both the environment (situation) and the individual (biology and psychology) are active, causal forces in a complex system. Let us say that a potential stressor exists in the environment and may affect you, the individual (as seen with the arrow from environment to individual).

- However, your particular perceptions and thoughts affect how you see and think about this potential stressor. These processes determine whether you see this stressor as a distressor, a prostress or, or as relatively unimportant (as seen in the arrow from individual to environment) this shows the often ignored role of perception and beliefs in determining the positive or negative value and thus impact of the stressor.

- Besides being affected by your life experiences, your perceptions and thoughts are affected by your psychological and physical characteristics. The model shows that how you respond to stress (i.e., stress reactions) can 1) feed back to impact your coping techniques, beliefs, and habits (i.e., individual); and, 2) feed all the way back to affecting the environment by determining the kinds of situations and stressors you create.

The arrows leading from the "individual" and "stress reactions" back to the "environment" represent important parts of the stress process that are unique to the "You Have a Choice" model. For example, people known as "Type As" are described as competitive, irritable, rushed, intense, and obsessed with time. They have a tendency to perceive certain situations as threatening and distressing that others would not necessarily perceive this way. A colleague's offer to help out on a particular task might be interpreted by a Type A as a competitive taunting and perceived as, "You can't seem to be able to finish the job on your own and need my help to do it," or "If I help you, I'll get some credit for this too." A non-Type A would be more likely to perceive this sincere offer for what it is, accept it graciously, and experience relief rather than increased distress. This same example played out a bit further can be used to explain the feedback arrow from stress reactions all the way to environment. The Type A wanting all of the credit for herself and intent on proving her excellence in all spheres would turn down offers for help and end up struggling on her own. This pattern (stress reaction) of taking on ever-increasing amounts of work and being reluctant to accept assistance is typical of many Type As. By this behavior (stress reaction), they actively create more hassles, crushing deadlines, and frustrations. Basically, they end up making their environment increasingly negatively stressful and pressured. Type As also alienate peers and co-workers, which makes the environment even more threatening (both of these Type A stress reactions and their consequences are represented by the arrow from stress reactions to environment). This model, however, demonstrates a very different, positive dynamic as well. The feedback loop from stress reactions and individual to environment is seen in people who flourish through living on the edge and thrill-seeking. These people challenge themselves with situations offering prostress, such as mountain climbing, entering talent competitions, long-distance running, or by increasing the breadth of their jobs by requesting additional responsibilities or tasks.

So, the "You Have a Choice" model doesn't assume that stress is necessarily located in your situation/environment or within you. Instead, it comes from your appraisal of the situation as threatening, challenging, important, and the like. You may perceive a situation as important or interesting and as calling for some action on your part. If you feel you have the resources and abilities to meet the demands, you won't experience negative stress. The fit between the demands on one hand and the resources, and the abilities you believe you can offer to meet the demands (as perceived by you) on the other hand, largely determines how you'll experience the situation. Remember that the "You Have a Choice" model explains how certain people create more negatively stressful situations than others. Certain people, such as Type As, perfectionists, and overachievers, seek out or create distressful situations by overloading themselves with tasks and responsibilities, cutting off potentially stress-buffering social support, and believing that they must excel in everything that they do. Do any of these unhealthy, negative stress-boosting patterns sound a bit too familiar?

Daily Hassles

If it isn't the *number* of events, or the *type* of events that induce negative stress, what exactly is at the source of your stress? The answer is, it is a combination of your overall perception of stressors together with the *balance* of prostress and distress you create in your life. Therefore, you'll learn in this book how to adjust your beliefs (based on the "You Have a Choice" model), and create a healthier balance between positive, energizing stress and negative, debilitating stress. One of the first things to be aware of is the number of daily irritants in your life. It isn't only your major life events that you interpret negatively that are responsible for the harmful effects of stress, but also your daily "hassles." Kanner and his colleagues presented evidence in 1981 that daily minor irritants actually have a *greater* harmful impact on our health than major life events. These daily stressors, or hassles, are actually better predictors of psychological and physical symptoms. You're likely to be all too familiar with hassles in your life. They include everyday distressing events such as driving in traffic, waiting in lines, worrying about your weight, having too many things to do, taking care of your home, losing things, dealing with demands from your children, other family members and friends, and having too much work or ambiguous job responsibilities. Can you relate to most, if not all, of these hassles in the list? I'm sure that you could add many other hassles to this list. Sometimes adding just one more item to your load can feel like it's going to be the final straw that will break your back. In Section 2 you will be given a form on which to list the hassles that are most disturbing and frequent in your daily life. These will serve as targets on which you can practice as you acquire your stress-optimizing skills.

Given your growing knowledge of stress, you may be asking, "So where does the balance come into play here?" Fortunately, there are positive, frequently occurring, or daily events called "uplifts" that serve to balance the hassles and increase the prostress in your life. These include good relations with your spouse, lover, children, or friends, completing a task, contributing in a meeting, playing a favorite sport, or meeting your responsibilities. The importance of having prostress in your life was clearly and cleverly shown by a study in which some people were told to engage in pleasurable uplifts and others were not. One month later, the people who had engaged in pleasant activities reported a higher quality of life and more pleasure than the people who hadn't been instructed to engage in any particular pleasant events. Another exciting discovery was made. The people with the most negative stress *before* the study who were told to engage in twelve prostress activities reported less psychological distress and greater pleasantness of experiences overall at the end of the study than people who had been dealing with *just as much negative stress before*, but who had been told to engage in only two or no prostress activities (Reich and Zautra 1981). The point to remember is that when you're experiencing a great deal of negative stress in your life, the number of prostress experiences you can include day-to-day to regain some balance is more important than ever. It's important for you to remember that daily hassles are central in determining your stress level (distress or prostress). Fortunately, this is the case, because there's a lot more we can do about the minor hassles and uplifts in our lives than about the major, generally unexpected, infrequent life events. You'll be learning just what you can do to tailor and optimize your personal stress management program in part 2.

Women and Stress Management

In my own stress management seminars and therapy, I have seen several types of women becoming involved in stress management. See if any of these types resonate with you. Most women can relate to at least one of these scenarios:

- **Affected by but unaware of negative stress' contribution to psychological and physical disturbances.** While these women report feelings of frequent discomfort, anxiety, and/ or depression, they are completely or largely unaware of the powerful role negative stress is playing in these problems. They might not even realize how much negative stress there is in their lives because they experience frequent, *seemingly* minor irritants or hassles that they discount. As you've learned, this type of negative stress can be more damaging to your health and well-being than distress from major life events or crises. She believes her life is no different from anybody else's and that she *should* be able to handle the minor stressors without so much distress.

- **Aware of and worried about physical and mental health.** These are her main concerns and she takes proactive steps to preserve them. This woman is generally more aware of the stressors and potentially harmful consequences of stress in her life than the first type of woman.

- **Recommended by others in her life, such as employers, friends or relatives to seek stress management skills.** I've had women initially attending my seminars because their bosses or other significant people pushed them to obtain help. These women are incredibly stressed out but can't target a specific area in their lives—it all seems overwhelming. I've been delighted to see that many of them end up strongly endorsing stress management and optimization.

- **Suffering physically.** Finally, there are those women who again might have little realization of the degree and impact of stress in their lives much like the first and third examples. However, they're suffering from any of a variety of physical problems that medical doctors or other experts believe are stress-induced. This type of woman might at first be skeptical of the need for stress management in her life. But, when she sees how relaxation, restructuring her thoughts, and other stress management techniques alleviate her pain or discomfort, she becomes another strong proponent of stress management.

It isn't surprising that many of the women with whom I have worked have been referred by their places of work. Job stress is a serious problem for both male and female employees, as well as for organizations themselves. If you work in a company, you've probably noticed that job-related stress reduces the effectiveness and efficiency of your department or group. It has been estimated that United States businesses lose anywhere from $50 to $80 billion annually due to stress. Negative stress that leads to decreased performance and productivity is manifested through physical disorders, accidents on the job, absenteeism, increased turnover, substance abuse, low morale, and a range of other problems.

Women and "Drivenness"

Women seem to be living the life of the proverbial hamster on a running wheel. We rush through our lives playing mother, wife, worker, volunteer, friend, peacemaker, and caretaker—the faster we run, the more we feel we have to do and the further behind we get. Not only do we have many roles to fulfill, but we add fuel to the fire by believing, 1) that we must excel at everything, and 2) that we must do as much as possible by ourselves. Why is this emphasis on achievement and accomplishment so powerful in our culture, and how and why does it affect women so strongly? Dr. Robert Hemfelt and his colleagues in their 1991 book, *We Are Driven*, go so far as to call this pattern the most prominent illness of the 1990s. They have labeled it *drivenness*, a pet term for compulsivity. They define it as an insatiable drive to do more and be more. Drivenness can lead to addictions, not only to substances such as alcohol and drugs, but even to work, fitness, perfectionism, attractiveness, helping others, earning money, running a perfect household, raising the perfect family, and many others. Do any of these patterns sound familiar to you? If so, it's very important that you read on to discover how you can change this type of unhealthy thinking and behaving.

While we may see our drive to excel and to always be available to others as solely positive and charitable, the true motivation may be rooted in deep feelings of inadequacy and shame. This sense of inadequacy and/or shame is particularly relevant to us as women and I've seen it over and over in the women with whom I work. It doesn't seem to matter how bright, talented, funny, or attractive we are, the feelings of being less-than and insecure run like a common thread through many of us. (This book, of course, may refer to a substantial proportion of women, but not every single one!) Why do these feelings exist in so many of us? They result from social forces, certain types of experiences and stressors, and overt and covert messages focused on us throughout our lives. You will learn much more about these harmful dynamics in later sections, as well as how to determine whether you are being driven by low self-esteem and fear of others seeing the "real you."

Prostress and Distress

Views of stress in the past have been largely negative. There is, however, a more realistic, accurate view of stress as being either potentially positive (prostress) or negative (distress). Whether it's positive or negative depends on how you evaluate the particular situation. For example, you might ask yourself, "Can I meet the demands of the situation?" "How important is this situation to me?" "Do I have experience in this?" "Do I have some control here?" "What might be the consequences of the situation?" If your answers are that you can meet the demands, that the situation is important to you, that you expect positive consequences and have some degree of control, it's likely that you'll experience prostress. Let's look back at the situation with my client Sharon who was briefly mentioned earlier. She had been working diligently in her job for about one year and was getting a bit concerned about opportunities for recognition and advancement in her division. Her boss had finally approached her and asked that she design a presentation for an important new sales pitch. If we knew how Sharon evaluated the situation by the above guidelines, we could have fairly accurately predicted her response. Did she think she was up to the challenge? Could she have some control over designing and presenting the sales pitch? Was the assignment important to her? Did she think she could design a successful sales pitch? If Sharon's answers had been "yes," she would have probably felt prostress—that is, excitement and a rush of creative juices to meet the challenge. Unfortunately, when a very anxious, tearful Sharon came to my office it was clear that she had ended up thinking negatively, telling herself that she was bound to make terrible mistakes and *forever* lose the chance for a promotion. Because of how she had perceived the situation, she experienced negative stress and the accompanying feelings of inadequacy, anxiety, and depression. Our work together consisted of having Sharon confront and realize the irrational, extreme nature of her beliefs and move on to the realistic, flexible prostress type of thinking, which allowed her to give a successful performance. Prostress and distress will be explained in more detail; for now just know that stress isn't always negative.

Mind-Body Connections

Stress is far from simple—it is a complex dynamic process involving both your mind and body. The growing fields of psychoneuroimmunology and mind-body medicine are evidence that our society and scientific community are finally beginning to accept that the individual as a whole must be considered in understanding and treating mental and physical disorders. As you know, your physical reactions to negative stress can be harmful to your body in and of themselves. Beyond this, your psychological responses to negative stress, such as anxiety, depression, frustration, and irritability, can also harm your body. Psychological stress affects and interferes with proper functioning of your immune, circulatory, and hormonal systems. Fortunately, the flip side of this is that your mind can be used to reduce the usual harmful consequences of negative stress. You can even use your thoughts and perceptions to improve your quality of life and reduce discomfort and pain when you are ill. The view that both your mind and body are impacted by stress (both negatively and positively), and that both must be used to manage and optimize stress gives you a more comprehensive and useful view than you'll find in other books about stress. You'll learn to determine in what areas of your life you're experiencing excessive distress and where and how your body manifests its common and unique responses to negative stress. You'll become familiar with how your cognitions (thoughts) lead to your perceiving a situation as either negatively or positively stressful. In part 2, you'll learn and actively rehearse techniques for monitoring and changing your body's dangerous physical and cognitive reactions. You will also learn when and how to expose yourself to the right kinds of challenging positive stressors.

Many of us spend countless hours and dollars trying to make our bodies look good. What we don't think about enough is that our bodies must be in good condition to react in the healthiest way to stress. Many behaviors that affect us physically, such as smoking, drinking, eating poorly, and not exercising are unhealthy, but you may not know they are double whammies because they greatly increase your negative stress levels. On the other hand, changing these behaviors improves your psychological and physical states. I'm not promising you a quick and easy fix. You weren't born a stress-mess nor did you become one overnight. I am reassuring you that if you really work at the exercises in part 2 and incorporate them into your lifestyle, you'll be able to achieve your personal optimal balance of stress by reducing your distress and increasing your prostress.

Stress and Your Body: The "Fight-or-Flight" Response

When you perceive a stressful situation, your body quickly goes through a number of changes. It's amazing how our physical bodies prepare for perceived threats by mobilizing and activating physical resources in a well-orchestrated, swift way. We've all experienced this stress response, whether it arises from slamming on our brakes to avoid an accident, or from being called on to contribute in a class or meeting. This so-called "fight-or-flight" response includes the following changes:

- Heartbeat increases to carry blood throughout your body and provide oxygen and nutrients more quickly to lungs, brain, and major muscles

- Blood pressure increases

- Breathing becomes shallow and quicker

- Muscles tense for action—especially the skeletal muscles of your back, shoulders, arms, jaw, face, thighs, and hips

- Blood flow to your extremities—like hands, fingers, and feet—decreases and they become colder

- Adrenaline and other hormones are released

- Perspiration increases

Many of these changes in your body result from activation of a part of your nervous system called the sympathetic nervous system. The sympathetic nervous system, together with the parasympathetic nervous system, make up the autonomic nervous system (ANS). For many years, it was believed that we had no conscious control over the ANS. That is, it was believed in our culture that we couldn't voluntarily change our blood pressure, heart rate, body temperature, and the like. Experts believed that mind and body functioned separately and independently. There has been enough significant evidence that negates this, and even Western medicine has had to incorporate and devise a number of techniques to cash in on the trend. If you listen to the nightly news you've probably been bombarded with advice on how to change your diet, take herbal remedies and vitamins, and alter your lifestyle to improve your health. The truth is that you can actually *directly* alter some functions of the "automatic" autonomic nervous system. In part 2, you'll learn how to gain control over the ANS and its responses to negative stress through biofeedback, relaxation, meditation, and other techniques.

Your Nervous System

Before we can understand how our bodies can respond in a healthy way to stress, we need to understand the two stress-related systems—the sympathetic and parasympathetic nervous systems—in a bit more depth. Your sympathetic nervous system is what *jump starts* your body into action when you swerve to hit a car drifting into your lane or dash to stop your toddler from touching the hot stove. On the other hand, your parasympathetic nervous system promotes *relaxation* and is in charge of maintenance activities, such as repairing tissues, nourishment, excretion, sleep, and rebuilding energy stores. While these two systems have different functions, there are important areas of overlap where the two should work cooperatively. Ideally, your sympathetic system rapidly activates your physical systems when you perceive a threatening stressor. When you perceive the threat to have ended, your parasympathetic system reduces the arousal and leads to the relaxation and rebuilding phase. What's essential in the functioning of these systems and in maintaining your health is that the two exist in balance. One of the keys to stress management is understanding and developing the harmonious functioning of these systems. This is just one of many examples in which you'll see the concept of balance as being integral and necessary to self and stress management.

The "fight-or-flight" responses described above are adaptive if you're in a truly life threatening or dangerous situation. In modern times, the problem is that our bodies and minds react in a negatively stressful manner to situations which, while they might be disturbing or troubling, are not life threatening. As you can see in the "You

Have a Choice" model, even harmless situations can lead to distress if they're interpreted unrealistically as threats. The result is that our bodies rev up to respond to a life-threatening situation and what do we do? Do we run away from a predator for five miles, or do we attack a ferocious animal intent upon destroying our young as our bodies evolved to do? Very unlikely, wouldn't you say? Today, what we usually end up doing is going back to our desks after an unpleasant stressful interaction with our unreasonable supervisor, trying to get back to work, and stewing to a juicy well-done for hours. Or, we may slam a door on our partner after having yet another typically stressful childish argument and end up sulking the night away in our bedroom.

Alternatively, we might become overly stressed from compiling minor hassles or irritations without knowing how to reduce and work out such negative stress. The result is that we pick up a drink, cigarette, or candy bar because we're so "stressed out." The problem with all of these reactions to stress is that our sympathetic systems remain on high alert. We haven't had the opportunity to physically discharge our tension and arousal and, as a result, the parasympathetic system can't reestablish harmony. This continuous state of arousal in which many of us spend too much time suppresses our immune system, causes muscular tension, irritability, anxiety, and generates headaches, ulcers, and a host of other physical problems.

The Possum Response

What might seem counterintuitive to you (unless you're aware of the central role of balance in determining health) is that problems also arise when the parasympathetic, or relaxation system, is excessively dominant. The "possum response" is what Phil Nuernberger calls this insufficiently researched area of overreaction of the parasympathetic system in response to discomfort or perceived threat. In his 1985 book, *Freedom from Stress*, he describes how asthma, some types of ulcers, suppression of the immune system, cancer, pathological depression, and hopelessness can all arise from overreaction of the parasympathetic system. While many of us respond to minor stressors in the typical way with excessive, prolonged sympathetic system arousal, others respond with the possum response, an unhealthy dominance of the parasympathetic system. Rather than becoming activated and preparing to fight or run, these people withdraw, roll over, and play dead. One of the ways a person might develop this type of response is through socialization. In women, this pattern is particularly relevant as we are often taught to be passive, accepting, and to avoid conflict (including stress) at all costs. Think about situations in your own life when you've been passive and avoided doing certain things just because you anticipated conflict and distress. Being polite or insecure, it was easier to leave it alone (the old, "If I ignore it, it doesn't exist" syndrome). Did this choice really end up decreasing negative stress? I would say, with a great deal of certainty, "No!" Avoiding situations and not acting in ways that maximize your well-being may work in the short run, but in the long run you'll end up feeling even more distressed than if you had been active and assertive in the first place.

The functioning and balance of the sympathetic and parasympathetic systems resemble the workings of a hot air balloon. When the sympathetic system "turns on" and arouses the body, it's like heated air giving the balloon the energy to lift off. As the air cools, or the parasympathetic system dominates, the balloon comes back to a slow descent and landing. If the hot air is insufficient or absent (i.e., the parasympathetic system is overactive or the sympathetic system is underactive), the balloon (you) can't get off the ground! On the other hand, burning fuel continuously to produce hot air and sustain energy will eventually deplete your fuel source. Likewise, those of us who habitually react with excessive, prolonged activation of the sympathetic system will inevitably burn out. These ideas are certainly not new and one sees them reflected in the philosophy of Chinese healing in antiquity. As Stephen Palos detailed in his 1972 book, *The Chinese Art of Healing*, the Chinese believe that there is a constant struggle within humans, just as within nature, between unifying but opposing forces. Many of you are probably familiar with the names of these opposing forces: the Yin and Yang. In Chinese cosmology, the yin is the feminine principle in nature and the Yang is the masculine principle in nature. For centuries, the Chinese have observed that when these forces are equally balanced, good health is the result. Likewise, one of the aspects of optimizing stress and in turn improving health depends on maintaining a balance within the body, such as between the sympathetic and parasympathetic systems.

2

Stress Isn't Always Your Enemy

Now that you're well aware of the dual nature of stress, you might be wondering about how outcomes of distress and prostress differ. Most stress research is stuck on studying the association between negative stress and physical and psychological problems. The evidence for this link is plentiful—distress has been linked with coronary heart disease (CHD), diabetes, degenerative diseases, speeding up the aging process, nonorganic abdominal pain, peptic ulcers, hypertension, depression, nervous disturbances, irritability, anger, and even increased incidence of cavities from saliva's increased acidity under stress! Negative stress also damages our health by interfering with eating, sleeping, and exercising or by causing increases in smoking, overeating, exercise addiction, fatigue, drinking alcohol, and abuse of and dependency upon illicit and prescription drugs. The following look at distress shows you how stress can be your enemy. Remember though, you can alter this path.

The Downside of Stress: Distress

Western medical science is finally taking a serious look at the mind-body linkage and is examining the associations between emotions and thoughts, the immune system, and the central nervous system. Your thoughts and emotions, together with your perception and experience of stress, impact your immune system and can either hamper or improve your health. The mind-body linkage is visible in ways beyond the impact of psychological factors on the immune system. Psychological distress also has damaging effects on other parts of the body, such as the circulatory and hormonal systems.

The Physical Consequences of Distress

You have undoubtedly heard a great deal about the association between stress and heart disease. Unfortunately, most of the research has focused on furthering the understanding of this linkage in men, while shockingly little attention has been paid to the high rates of heart disease in women. The reasons for stress increasing the likelihood of developing heart disease include: the triggering of cardiac arrhythmia; repeated elevations in serum lipids (i.e., cholesterol) and blood pressure; onset of myocardial lesions and the increased rate of damage to the coronary arteries. When you read chapter 7 on personality and stress, you'll read that these reasons are thought by many to underlie the high rates of heart disease in people, such as Type As, who react with excessive arousal to potentially stressful situations. Just as some personality factors are linked with heart disease, certain stressful events can be linked with developing heart disease depending on the meaning you give to these events. Some of these include marital problems, the sudden loss of self-esteem, interpersonal difficulties, and the recent loss of a loved one (Glass 1982). Several of these stressors occur more frequently in the lives of women than men, which will be discussed in more detail.

Distress and Cancer

There has also been much attention on the relationship between stress and cancer. Some experts believe that psychological stress is directly related to the onset of cancer. They point out that cancer rates are higher in people who are single, widowed, and divorced. Interestingly, levels of stress in single people are typically higher than in those who are married and people who are widowed and divorced have generally experienced an increase in distress (remember, though, that we cannot judge whether a situation is negatively or positively stressful unless we know how the person herself perceives the event—some women may in fact see themselves as better off on their own or with a divorce). While controversial, it is also believed that people who tend to develop cancer are those who don't express their emotions and experience internal turmoil and distress without having an outlet for such feelings. The internal distress and the energy going to suppress true feelings, hurt, etc., exhaust your physical resources. In turn, physical systems such as the immune system cannot function effectively and lose ability to resist anything from the common cold to the proliferation of cancerous cells.

We might think, "At least women come out ahead here because we've been allowed to express our feelings more than men." This conclusion is a half-truth. I am constantly surprised by the number of women I come across who, because they're taught overtly and covertly by society and family that they must be the caretakers, cheerleaders, and therapists for others, have ended up carrying out the hidden message that they have to deny, suppress, and ignore their feelings and desires to satisfy the needs and desires of *others*. Many women have also been taught to avoid expressing certain emotions like anger because it isn't "ladylike." When parents tell their little girls to do this, in effect they're invalidating the little girl's feelings. This leads to a disconnection with one's emotional life and a general emotional suppression. Others, while not consciously aware of it, repress and hide their feelings for fear that showing them would anger or disgust their partners and lead to abandonment or abuse.

The Psychological Consequences of Distress

Besides the damage negative stress can cause you physically, it's also associated with a variety of psychological problems, such as depression, anxiety, helplessness, eating disorders, and drug and alcohol abuse. Drug, alcohol, and food abuse are very difficult because they create negative and perpetual behavioral and physical problems that further increase psychological distress. As you may have experienced, when an increasing amount of your time and energy is dedicated, often in secret, to getting the next drink, drug, or binge, you have less time and energy available for the important parts of your life. Your family, job, friends, hobbies, and education can suffer as a result. Of course, women with these problems will try valiantly to deny this fact to themselves. In terms of physical changes, drugs, alcohol, and poor eating habits can lead to exhaustion, listlessness, gastrointestinal problems, tooth decay, and life-threatening illnesses. Obviously, these physical problems can disrupt your work, family, and relationships and send your distress level sky high. Although women with these disorders might seem like they have it all together for a while; eventually, the image inevitably crumbles.

Common "Quick Fix" Stress Relievers to Avoid

A great number of women turn to drugs, alcohol, and food as "stress relievers." They also help women to avoid dealing with reality and serve as ways to numb themselves from fears and insecurities. Many women claim they feel more outgoing, interesting, and attractive when under the influence. It's so hard to stop relying on these external substances because they give a "quick fix," or an instant boost to self-esteem and feelings of control. Unfortunately, when the high wears off, so do the illusory feelings of power and control. If you're someone who uses, you're probably all too familiar with the consequences: you are left feeling weaker, more helpless and hopeless, and more self-loathing than ever. Relying on external substances, objects, or people for self-esteem and to help cope with stressful situations, you end up increasing feelings of loneliness, sadness, anxiety, low self-esteem, and lack of control.

While I have worked with a number of women in this same situation, let's look at Jody, a client of mine who incorporated many of the dynamics of women abusing substances. Jody is a statuesque, attractive woman who came to me complaining of feeling numb, lacking self-direction, and a feeling of "selling out" to maintain a superficial, cheery facade that she called "prostituting." It turns out her family placed the ultimate importance on achievement, perfectionism, and, in women, beauty. She felt she could never live up to these values, and, of course, she never would, because they were unattainable and unrealistic. In order to gain the popularity she thought essential to her survival (because this would signal acceptance in her family), she turned to using drugs and alcohol. For a long time, they seemed the perfect way to help her ignore her distress, feel loosened up, friendly, and fun, and to suppress the thoughtful, sensitive aspects of her true self. Finally, partying was no longer fun as she became dependent on alcohol, lost her job, got several DUIs, ended up in an abusive relationship, and watched her life careening out-of-control. Through therapy, she eventually confronted her substance dependence and stopped using drugs and alcohol. This was a painful, difficult process because she described feeling like a newborn baby—completely vulnerable, not knowing what her feelings were, lacking any real sense of self, and lacking strategies to cope with stress. Jody asked herself and me many times what had become of the real, capable, sensitive, curious, and sincere girl she once felt herself to be? It took much effort to realize her own innate value, develop a cohesive self, assume responsibility, and overcome her need for external stress relievers.

In Jody's case, therapy was necessary to help her realize she was a strong, capable, desirable person, and to extinguish the negative, critical voices she had internalized from her parents and others. It's my hope that the techniques and information provided in this book will help you cope with the pressures in your life in a healthy, manageable way. However, I want to encourage you that if your background or experiences are such that you need further assistance in learning to value and understand your "self," and in being able to handle day-to-day responsibilities and stress, that you seek help from a therapist or other structured, helpful alternative. There is absolute gain and strength and no shame in this decision.

The Upside of Stress: Prostress

Prostress is your friend—it is the positive, psychological state you experience when you perceive a situation as challenging, potentially pleasurable in some way, and as offering positive consequences such as growth, desired change, or accomplishment of a goal. When we feel helpless and out-of-control in a situation, we experience distress. However, if we believe we can have some control over the situation, we're more likely to experience prostress. Remember that earlier beliefs about stress were that change, in and of itself, was negatively stressful. However, in this book and increasingly in the field of stress research in general, it's assumed that if you view change as offering growth and the chance to develop, you can approach it as a challenge rather than as a threat. Prostress represents a challenge and serves as a stimulus for positive development.

While there is a huge amount of information and writing on the problems caused by stress, there is relatively little on positive stress, positive emotions, and health. Mihaly Csikszentmihalyi has been one of the leaders in exploring this frontier. In his 1990 book, *Flow: The Psychology of Optimal Experience*, he describes a state very much like prostress that he calls "flow." You may have also heard the popular phrase, "being in the zone." These words describe prostress situations in which you experience challenge, control, skill usage, and optimal stimulation. These states are characterized by a sense of timelessness, accomplishment, joy, and a fading of self-consciousness. You can experience this with activities ranging from work, to simple sensual pleasures, to play. Artists and athletes alike frequently talk about finding themselves in the zone, at one with the activity, and experiencing intense calm and pleasure while being challenged to the upper limits of their abilities. This is prostress and it occurs when you are engaged in something in which your mind or body is challenged to the limits—this is optimal arousal. The situation is one you have chosen to pursue because of the promise of joy, thrill, growth, or resolution. Importantly, it is something you have actively made happen and so your mind is central in accurately assessing whether to enter into the challenge. Once you are engaged, your mind is so focused that anxieties have no place to reside. Your mind is stronger and more complex after any prostress experience.

Distress and prostress do not differ only on the basis of the quality of the experiences. They also differ on the basis of "quantity." Stress can be thought of as existing along a continuum of intensity, from the absence of stimulation to excessive stimulation. Some stress is necessary to sustain your basic life functions. As the level of stress rises to a certain point, your arousal and performance usually improve as well. This is why you might play a particularly great game of tennis during a competition or why you might perform better on an exam than on a homework assignment (as long as you aren't excessively anxious while taking the test). The presence of an optimal level of stress is experienced as a sense of challenge, pleasure, and fulfillment—that is, prostress. So, another way to differentiate between prostress and distress is to say that

- **Prostress** occurs *within your individual stress range* in which you feel an energizing, pleasurable level of activating stress.

- **Distress** occurs when there is either *too little* or *too much* stress-induced activation.

The latter kind of distress, arising from too much arousal, is probably what you think of first as stress when remembering your own experiences. Take a minute, though, to recall a situation, maybe a lecture or meeting, in which you were incredibly bored and absolutely unstimulated. This *lack of arousal* also leads to distress, as you can probably remember becoming increasingly fidgety (trying to increase stimulation), tense, and irritable.

How often you feel prostress is important to improving your physical, emotional, and mental health. You will incorporate this dynamic as you learn to use prostress in your life in part 2. For example, people were told to record their moods and levels of happiness at several points throughout the day for six weeks. The results indicated that the *frequency* of feeling fairly good rather than having a few highly intense periods of feeling good over one six week period was most important in determining positive mood and happiness (Larsen, Diener, and Cropanzano 1987). So, the small frequent pleasures you experience daily or weekly do two important things: they decrease the impact of negative stress *and* they contribute to your experience of prostress and happiness. In fact, just the *absence* of enough prostress can increase physical and emotional distress, lessening the satisfaction with your life. Feeling tired and distressed about your work and physical and mental well-being can understandably result when you're experiencing negative situations and conditions. But, this distress can even appear without such negative conditions just from the fact that you're not getting enough prostress in your life! What might really surprise you is that the lack of prostress in your life is sometimes more strongly related to a low level of satisfaction with your life than the actual presence of negative stress and negative situations. If you're not stimulated and challenged in life, you're probably going to feel more dull and complacent. Stress, therefore, isn't always your enemy—it can energize you!

Physical Consequences of Prostress

Prostress can actually improve your health. After experiencing a prostressor, your immune system actually demonstrates improved functioning while the opposite reaction occurs after experiencing a distressor. This fact helps explain why people who develop a minor illness, such as the flu or cold, often have experienced an increase in distressors and/or a decrease in prostressors just before getting sick. We're seeing an increasing number of these kinds of results stemming from the wave of research efforts in the currently popular field known as *psychoneuroimmunology*. This scientific study examines the effect of psychological factors on the immune system and is yielding many exciting discoveries with respect to holistic medicine and the mind-body linkage.

How does prostress improve health? While many questions are still unanswered, Jeffrey Edwards and Cary Cooper proposed in 1988 in their book, that prostress increases the production of anabolic hormones, HDL, or "good" cholesterol, and leads to other health-inducing biochemical changes. For example, during prostress, your body experiences a shift in the balance of hormones that can lead to physiological growth that can protect heart and other muscle tissue.

Actual physical changes were tracked during a study in which people were taught a technique for alternatively relaxing and activating their bodies. The activating part of the technique led to the increased levels of adrenaline and cortisol seen in the typical negative stress response. However, the people using this technique were in control of their arousal and relaxation and so actually described feeling emotionally *positive* states, including the well-being, self-assuredness, and euphoria characteristic of prostress. In fact, this technique has been used to improve physical problems, such as reducing hypertension, inflammation, and asthma (Machac, Machacova, and Hampi 1987). So, while prostress involves some of the same mechanisms of negative stress, such as activation and arousal, because of the psychological variations, the physical process differs and can improve rather than harm your health when you learn to control your relaxation and arousal process.

Deepak Chopra, the well-known doctor who unites the Eastern and Western traditions in his approach to preventing and treating illness, agrees that different emotional states produce different effects on the mind and body (Chopra 1993). Love, hate, and excitement all activate the body in a variety of different directions. We really shouldn't scoff at the cliché that laughter is the best medicine, because while you're laughing, your body is obviously in an aroused state. Following this, however, there's an overall healthy net decrease in your body's arousal and blood pressure. The positive state of mind associated with laughing positively affects your immune system by decreasing certain neuroendocrine hormones and stimulating killer cells central to preventing and combating disease. Laughter exercises your lungs, relaxes your diaphragm, increases the oxygen in your bloodstream, improves your mood, increases relaxation for more than half an hour afterward and, just as important for most of us, it doesn't even cost much! You can't truly laugh and enjoy yourself at the same time that you're feeling anxious and distressed—which would you prefer?

Psychological Consequences of Prostress

How does prostress affect you psychologically? One of the beneficial effects of prostress is that it improves your stress-coping efforts. In 1988, Jeffrey Edwards and Cary Cooper described three ways prostress can improve your coping abilities by acting as a

1. *Breather*, or break from ongoing stress that allows you to develop new problem-solving strategies.

2. *Sustainer* for your continued efforts to cope.

3. *Restorer* so that you feel reenergized or develop new resources.

Prostress also contributes to your mental and physical health by increasing your satisfaction and pleasure in life and with social interactions. In turn, this motivates you to maintain or develop a circle of social support. For years, it has been touted that having a strong social support network is a great distress-reducer. What's interesting to learn is that even if you really don't have such a good network, the mere fact that you *believe* you have support reduces the negative effects of stress (another example of the linkage between the mind-body functions).

One of the most important characteristics that determines whether you'll perceive an event as threatening or challenging is the degree of control you *believe* you have over it. You'll experience prostress and its benefits in situations when you feel involved, active, and believe you have some degree of control. In 1980, Alex Zautra and John Reich in their book provided the results of an enlightening study that pointed out this dynamic beautifully. Think carefully about the meaning of the following description. These two researchers compared people engaging in two different types of pleasurable activities: *positive origin events* were those in which the person was actively initiating and carrying out the pleasant event; *positive pawn events* were those in which the person, while experiencing a positive situation, was only a passive recipient. An example of a positive origin event might be your going out and making a new friend or learning a new sport (you make the effort), while an example of a positive pawn event might be your finding five or ten dollars on the ground (the event happened to you). The study's results showed that people who experienced the positive origin events, in which they had control and actively participated, reported a better quality of life and rated a variety of events as more pleasurable than those who experienced positive passive events. In fact, increasing the number of events that were pleasurable and positive but passive did *not* increase happiness or satisfaction. Of course, negative events were associated with lower quality of life and with psychological distress. In part 2, I will incorporate these findings and discuss how to choose and schedule positive events that demand your active involvement and control. This will both increase your prostress and boost your physical and emotional well-being.

Stress and Mind-Body Unity

Stress is both a psychological and physical phenomenon. How you experience stress and its effects involves both your mind and your body. While this idea is certainly not a new one, it didn't receive the attention and research efforts that it deserved in this culture for years. There is an ever increasing amount of research and evidence today showing that our beliefs and attitudes have an incredibly powerful effect on our physical and emotional states. In fact, thoughts, hopes, and expectations sometimes have a greater impact on the body than the physical elements usually thought to be most important. This fact was clearly illustrated in a long-term study that gathered data on medical students for eighteen years (Thomas and Duszynski 1974). While more than a hundred students were initially found to have high cholesterol levels, only fourteen eventually suffered from coronary heart disease (CHD). How did these unfortunate few differ from the others? The answer lies largely in the psychological characteristics of the students. It turns out that those who eventually suffered from CHD had reported higher levels of nervous tension, depression, insomnia, and anxiety than their associates *years earlier*. Those with equally high cholesterol levels who didn't develop CHD were calmer people who had reported lower levels of stress, anxiety, and depression. In later sections of this book, you'll find many other examples of the power of the mind over physical health (to produce both positive and negative changes) and learn how you can use it to improve your body's functioning.

Once we realize how mightily our minds impact our physical health, it's but a short step to recognizing that the mind can be used to *prevent* physical illness. This is another area our short-sighted medical-model based society has accorded shockingly little attention. As the burdens due to illness in our society increase and managed care companies become increasingly concerned about financial costs of medical treatment, this area will finally become the subject of much needed attention.

In essence, what all of this means for you is that not everyone exposed to stress inevitably becomes ill. You'll learn just what differentiates the people who do from those who do not. Some people pass through the most severely negatively stressful conditions and remain psychologically and physically healthy. How do they do it and how can you learn the techniques and tools they use to derive the same strength and benefits? This is certainly a central focus of this book and will prove invaluable to you as you continue on with your journey through life. The intent here though is not just to explore extreme situations but to learn to live our lives in a more positive, health-enhancing and enjoyable way day-to-day. We, as women, experience different stressors, perceive the same stressors differently, and respond differently to stressors. You really can learn to live your life in a kinder, gentler way that won't reduce your enjoyment or productivity. I know this latter is a concern because a number of the people with whom I've worked believe that if they don't keep up their relentless, frenetic pace, they'll fall more and more behind and eventually "lose." In actuality, most of my clients have told me with surprise that they've become more effective and efficient while dramatically improving the quality of their lives. I know of what they speak because it has worked for me and many women to whom I've been fortunate to pass this information.

3

Women's Health:
The Physical and
Psychological Benefits

When examining comparative health statistics between men and women, a strikingly obvious difference is our longer lifespan. We live approximately 10 percent, or seven years longer than men. Males have a head start early on with a higher ratio of male to female embryos, but greater male infant mortality and higher numbers of miscarriage and stillbirths begin to even out the score. This reversal pattern continues so that females far outnumber males by late adulthood. Why do we outlive men? The answer, of course, lies with women's greater adaptability and both our physical and mental states of being.

Women's Physical Health

We might come out ahead in terms of longevity but we don't necessarily do so with respect to overall health. Women suffer more frequently from chronic illnesses that inflict great suffering and are extremely costly. We have greater rates of consulting doctors, undergoing operations, using medications, and staying in hospitals. With respect to biology, research has focused on several causes of such gender differences. These include hormones, genes, and the interaction between the two. On the one hand, female hormones such as estrogen can have beneficial consequences. Estrogen and other female hormones seem to reduce the reactivity of our cardiovascular systems to stress and thereby might lower the rates of heart disease in women until menopause (Polefrone and Manuck 1987). In a strange but consistent twist, most of the studies of the role of estrogen in heart disease have been conducted on men! This isn't to say that heart disease poses no risk for women. Approximately 233,000 women die from coronary heart disease each year. It has been estimated that *up to two-thirds of medical doctors do not diagnose heart disease in women accurately*. This is because most studies on heart disease have been done on males and doctors are educated on the male model of heart disease. Thus, they aren't as likely to consider heart disease in women who come to them for medical attention. In addition, women can exhibit different symptoms than men when suffering from heart problems. For example, rather than "chest pain" we may experience what we call "indigestion" or "heartburn." Doctors can thus miss the diagnosis of heart disease. Furthermore, because there is less awareness and emphasis on heart disease in women, we are less likely to seek medical attention when experiencing symptoms. These dynamics may partially explain the *higher* mortality rates in women following heart attacks.

Autoimmune Diseases in Women

The same female hormones that protect us from certain problems also backfire sometimes. Estrogen has been linked with breast and uterine cancer and also seems to be associated with the onset of autoimmune diseases. Autoimmune diseases cause the immune system to backfire and attack the body's organs and tissues as if they were foreign invaders. Autoimmune diseases are much more prevalent in women than they are in men. One theory is that estrogen triggers the immune system to respond excessively. However, hormones don't tell the whole story. Genes also play a role—the general tendency to develop autoimmune diseases, though not necessarily any particular disease, can run in families. Women outnumber men by three to one in suffering from these conditions. For males to develop autoimmune disorders, a greater number of select genes from both parents must be transmitted.

You may be familiar with autoimmune disorders, whether you are suffering from one or know a friend or relative who is. Common types of autoimmune disorders include multiple sclerosis, lupus erythematosus, scleroderma, rheumatoid arthritis, and Graves' disease. The forms of lupus, a chronic disease involving inflammation of connective tissue, illustrate the most extreme example of gender bias with four out of every five cases being female. Scleroderma, excessive development of collagen in the body, and rheumatoid arthritis affect three times as many women as men, while multiple sclerosis affects twice as many women as men. Migraine headaches are sometimes included in the category of autoimmune diseases. Two other disorders that have begun to garner a great deal of attention and that occur far more frequently in women than in men are fibromyalgia and chronic fatigue syndrome. The etiologies of these disorders, that is, whether they are caused by viruses, sleep disorders, neurotransmitter deficiencies, information-processing problems, or immune system malfunctioning, are not yet clear. It's important to note that distress and other psychological factors are also involved with the onset and progression of these disorders. While initially women were told that such fatigue and pain was "in our heads," there's finally a growing consensus that these are true biologically based disorders. The depression so often associated with fibromyalgia is now rightfully deemed to be the *outcome* of suffering from this extremely painful, debilitating disorder rather than the cause. This certainly makes sense, doesn't it? The fact remains that negative stress can trigger and intensify episodes. For women then, because of the greater preponderance of these physical disorders, it's essential we learn techniques to reduce negative stress and increase prostress.

Also of import for women is the suggestion that certain personality characteristics are linked with the onset of diseases such as autoimmune disorders and cancer. This area of study is complex and very controversial. However, there is evidence that certain personality and behavioral characteristics are associated with illness or with difficulties in recuperating. As mentioned, one of the autoimmune disorders seen more frequently in women than in men is rheumatoid arthritis. Bernie Siegel, author of the 1986, *Love, Medicine & Miracles*, suggests that chronic rheumatoid arthritis is seen in people manifesting a lifelong pattern of self-denial. Many women end up adopting this pattern because of having been socialized to put their needs and wants after those of others.

There are also a number of biological functions and events specific to women that can be potent sources of distress. These include menstruation, pregnancy, postnatal depression, and other difficult psychological and physical consequences of childbirth, premenstrual symptomatology, and menopause. Not all of us go through the same physical experiences, and even those of us who do may experience them in completely different ways. Throughout this book, I ask you to remember that there are tremendous differences among women and how we experience and perceive situations and stress. I am exploring and clarifying general factors and experiences, any of which may or may not be relevant to you. It's your job to find those dynamics and elements that resonate with your experience to gain an improved understanding of these issues, and then to learn how to deal with them to diminish the drawbacks of negative stress.

I do want to briefly discuss how women are often treated by some medical doctors. Remember, this is again a generalization based on facts and many of you may have fine, direct relationships with your medical doctors. Because many doctors still seem to think that women's illnesses are more closely linked with psychological factors than those of men, they deal with us in a different fashion. In fact, it has been concluded that doctors may well give us shorter and more superficial explanations of our medical problems even though we tend to ask more questions. This is stressful and frustrating when we're rightfully attempting to educate ourselves about our problems but are met with resistance by doctors (Andersen 1993). As you'll soon learn, it's the people who challenge doctors and take matters into their own hands that fare better in remission from medical illnesses.

Women's Psychological Health

According to most data, women suffer more from psychological disorders than men. Women do tend to have more internalizing disorders, such as depression, anxiety, and eating disorders, while men more frequently exhibit externalizing disorders, such as delinquent and oppositional disorders and school problems. However, when disorders more typical to males, such as drug and alcohol abuse and antisocial personality disorder are considered in tallying the overall statistics, the differential rates of mental disorders among women and men become more similar. Before we take the statistics regarding mental disorders in men and women at face value, there are certain factors to consider. For instance, social and cultural gender factors—women are more likely than men to seek help, admit experiencing psychological difficulties, and to be diagnosed by professionals as suffering from psychological or psychiatric problems. Doctors label women's problems as psychosomatic (involving psychological factors) more often than men's and so prescribe psychotherapy rather than situational or structural changes that might help.

This discrepancy certainly isn't a modern phenomenon. The very word "hysteria" comes from the Greek word for womb—no "politically correct" terminology here! Hysteria was the term used to describe how women were expected to react to stressors (such as losing a husband); namely, with histrionic physical or emotional reactions.

Societal influences obviously lead to the appearance of greater rates of mental disorders in women than in men. Several recent large-scale studies have tried to clarify if there's really a gender difference in mental disorders given that women are *expected* to have more psychological difficulties and are more open about admitting problems. In 1987, Paul Cleary summarized findings from the Epidemiologic Catchment Area Studies that included 20,000 residents in various cities within the United States. It was concluded that women are at least two to three times as likely to suffer from depression as men.

Studies at the Medical University of South Carolina have used PET (positron-emission tomography) scans to examine brain activity of people experiencing different moods. Male and female subjects were asked to recall a sad event and rate the event on a sadness scale. The PET scans showed different brain activity in male and female subjects even when they reported events that were equal on the sadness scale. Women evidenced approximately *eight times more* blood flow in the front of the brain—the region involved during clinical depression.

Depression in Women

How we're socialized can also explain the increased depression in women. A survey of therapists conducted in the 1970s showed that so-called "healthy personality characteristics" were associated with the stereotypes of a healthy man in those days: active, independent, logical, and competitive. A healthy woman was described as being dependent, emotional, subjective, and easily wounded (Ruble 1983). Unfortunately, a 1983 repeat survey showed that even after all of the purported advances made by women, the stereotypes were still quite consistent with those of the 1970s. The so-called healthy female traits are the same ones that increase a woman's vulnerability to depression. Dr. Karen Johnson, in her 1991 book, *Trusting Ourselves: The Complete Guide to Emotional Well-Being for Women*, shows that focusing on others' satisfaction rather than understanding and satisfying your own wishes and needs is linked with depression. These are the very characteristics that society instills so very thoroughly and effectively into us as little girls, adolescents, young women, and older women.

Finally, let's look at the perception of an emotional loss, the inhibition of anger and aggression, the inhibition of action, and low self-esteem. Again, these are the very characteristics and emotions that we have more often than men. First, the emotional loss perceived by a woman can range from a single traumatic loss to frequent losses of emotional connectedness. Because relationships are so important to us, we may often feel let down when all of the energy and efforts we expend aren't returned. Emotional losses are harder for many women to bear if we lack the consistent, strong sense of self that lasts regardless of the ups and downs of relationships.

A second cause of depression, also especially pertinent to women, is suppressing anger or dissatisfaction. As little girls, most of us were rewarded for building and keeping relationships and being "sweet and nice." The implied message is that expressing anger or standing up for our desires isn't feminine. You can probably recall such messages, whether they were sent to you by parents, relatives, teachers, television, and the like, overtly or covertly. Repressing your true feelings is psychologically unhealthy and further separates you from feeling at one with yourself and from knowing and valuing your feelings.

A third potential contribution to depression is the inhibition of action. Do you frequently find yourself accommodating the wishes and needs of others rather than doing what you want and acting on your own behalf? Finally, low self-esteem (which could fill several volumes of text for women) remains a problem for many of us. Rather than having been brought up to value ourselves or the many of the female elements that are strengths in their own right, we have been taught that to be "good girls"—we must make friends, be passive, quiet, attractive, and polite. While there are benefits to some of these, such as our ability to develop empathy, form friendships, and help others, there are also negative repercussions. We were taught to derive self-esteem from external sources based on external factors such as our beauty, weight, or having a boyfriend or husband. Your ability to feel good about yourself is precarious and risky when it depends on others' approval.

Are You Depressed?

These depression-linked characteristics, like low self-esteem, inhibition of action and denial of one's feelings, also increase the negative stress in your life. We often respond to negative stress with depression. So, we can easily become trapped in a vicious cycle of distress, depression, and trying to be a "real" woman as defined by society. You can informally rate your level of depression by completing the following checklist put out by the National Institute of Mental Health:

- Do you have a depressed mood most of the day, nearly every day, and has it been present for at least two weeks?
- Have you had markedly diminished interest in activities most of the day or nearly every day?
- Have you had significant change in your weight—either loss without dieting or a gain in weight?
- Have you had insomnia or excessive sleepiness?
- Have you felt sped up or slowed down?
- Have you been fatigued or suffered a loss of energy?
- Have you had feelings of guilt or worthlessness?
- Have you had trouble making decisions and trouble concentrating?
- Have you had recurrent thoughts of death or suicide?

If you responded affirmatively to at least five of the nine questions, you could very well be depressed. This survey is an informal one and it would be a good idea for you to contact your physician and/or seek assistance from a therapist. In addition, the techniques you learn in part 2 of this book can help you to alleviate the degree of depression associated with the negative stress in your life and learn how to use prostress to your benefit.

Anxiety

The incidence of various anxiety disorders, such as phobias, panic disorder, and obsessive-compulsive disorder, is also greater in women. Anxiety follows depression as the most frequent reason women seek professional help. Many of the female clients with whom I've worked have wanted help dealing with feelings of generalized, pervasive anxiety or panic attacks.

Panic attacks are particularly troublesome because they seem to come out of the blue. My clients tell me that all of a sudden, for no reason, they become overwhelmingly anxious and fearful, can't breathe, become dizzy, and feel like they're dying or going crazy. Have you ever suddenly experienced a variety of physical symptoms, such as rapid breathing, increased heart rate, sweating, chest pain, and dizziness? Accompanying these physical sensations, did you have thoughts of doom, loss of control, losing your mind, or even death? If so, you may be suffering from panic attacks and the sooner you get help the better (check with a medical doctor first to determine whether there is a physical problem underlying these symptoms). This is definitely a treatable problem.

In addition to panic attacks, women experience agoraphobia and post-traumatic stress disorder (PTSD) more frequently than men. Agoraphobia is a serious problem that has recently received a great deal of public attention. This anxiety disorder often leads to an intense fear of leaving one's home or safe place. Women suffering from agoraphobia try to avoid situations in which they fear being trapped, unable to leave, and open to the scrutiny of others. Post-traumatic stress disorder results from exposure to severe stressors, such as physical or sexual abuse, or exposure to crises. During these crises, the individual experiences a sense of hopelessness, helplessness, and intense fear. Symptoms of PTSD include reexperiencing the traumatic event through intrusive images or thoughts, recurrent distressing dreams, flashbacks or feelings of reliving the event, and distress at exposure to situations or people who are reminders of the traumatic event. The individual can experience irritability, insomnia, and problems concentrating. One of my clients, Angie, was raised in a chaotic household in which her mother had been forced to obtain a restraining order against her abusive, alcoholic husband. The father repeatedly ignored the order and would intermittently appear at the house drunk, enraged, swearing, and trying to break down the doors. He would also make menacing, threatening phone calls late at night, which Angie would sometimes listen to with intense horror. To this day, thirty-one-year-old Angie wakes up with her heart pounding and feelings of intense dread if a telephone rings while she is asleep.

Biology and Anxiety

There may be biological factors underlying the different rates of anxiety in men and women. In Dr. Karen Johnson's 1991 book, *Trusting Ourselves*, she discusses how development of the central nervous system is different in men and women and could account for the varying rates of anxiety. Others biological causes of anxiety in women include problems with thyroid functioning, the hormonal and nervous systems, as well as menstrual changes. Furthermore, many women get hooked on various types of diet pills, recreational drugs, and prescription medications that greatly increase anxiety. Caffeine and refined sugar are also culprits, which will be discussed in chapter 9.

Society and Anxiety

Of course, we can't forget that as women we're prone to particular negative stressors. Spousal abuse, whether verbal, emotional, or physical, is shockingly prevalent. Highly publicized incidents are finally bringing domestic abuse the attention it deserves. Other harmful circumstances we are subject to more than men include incest, violent crimes such as rape, and sexual harassment on and off the job. The fact that we frequently have to occupy multiple, often conflicting roles, together with our assumption that we're to perform excellently in all of these, also contributes to our developing and having prolonged anxiety. Other psychological factors, such as low self-esteem, society's emphasis on our appearance, beliefs about having little control over our lives, and other ways we think about ourselves, others, and the world, are also linked with anxiety. We will get into this in greater detail in later sections. The element of control is central in determining both your experience of stress and your mental health. Many women experience less control in their jobs and over other aspects of their lives than do men. It's quite telling that people defined as psychologically "normal" feel they have a greater sense of control in general than do those with mental disorders. In fact, well-adjusted individuals actually *overestimate* the degree of control they have over situations. They also believe their abilities and talents are greater than they really are.

If you're suffering from some form of anxiety, fortunately, there are both psychological and physiological interventions that you can learn to substantially reduce your distress. In part 2, techniques to deal with anxiety will be explored. I have found these approaches to be very successful with my female clients. If you have a truly serious problem with anxiety, it's important that you check with your medical doctor and psychotherapist.

The Roles We Play

One place we can look to see the different stressors facing men and women is in the roles we enact. As you know, roles are largely determined by social forces. Roles are positions we occupy that come with certain responsibilities, duties, expectations, and rights. You probably occupy several or most of the following roles:

- Employee
- Supervisor
- Wife
- Mother
- Daughter
- Group leader
- Friend
- Lover/Significant other
- Social coordinator
- Coach
- Mentor
- Breadwinner
- Homemaker
- Employer

The shorter lifespan and greater mortality rates of men has often been blamed on men's involvement in the workplace. When women began to work at greater rates than ever before, many concluded that these gender differences in health would wane and that we would suffer the same consequences as men. Sure, we could play (to some extent) on the same playground as men, but we'd have to step up and pay the same costs. In my research, I haven't found this to be the case. In fact, working women are often healthier than their unemployed counterparts. Working women generally have fewer sick days, hospitalizations, acute conditions, and disruptions due to chronic conditions. Although things such as the type of job, a spouse's or significant other's emotional support, and one's expectations make it somewhat difficult to draw a generalized conclusion, overall it does seem that working women report better well-being and health than housewives (LaCroix and Haynes 1987).

Some experts believed that the increased number of roles we occupy these days would lead to increased negative stress. This assumption is based on something called the *scarcity hypothesis* (Barnett and Baruch 1987). According to this theory, your energy is limited and the more roles you occupy, the less energy you have available and the more conflict you will experience. This may sound rational at first, but, as human beings, we don't work this way. In fact, in many cases, the more roles a women enacts, the healthier she is.

Being involved in multiple roles can actually improve your health in several ways. You may gain a greater availability of social support, improved self-esteem, financial benefits from working, and improved access to health services. This is the *expansion hypothesis*—it's based on assumptions opposite to those of the scarcity notion. The expansion view is that rewards such as recognition, prestige, improved self-esteem, and financial compensation more than make up for the costs associated with occupying multiple roles. As I write this, I notice the fit between this theory and my own experience. Staying home several months after having my baby was an enjoyable but tiring and stressful time. I found that when I went back to work my energy level and overall pleasure in my life, both at work with clients and at home with my husband and baby, increased. While the expansion theory is more on target than the scarcity theory, they are both still too simplistic. The real picture is more dynamic and complex. We need to look at whether carrying out multiple roles is better or worse for our health by examining both the *nature of the roles* we're occupying and their *interaction*. I'll be explaining this important discovery in the discussion that follows in this chapter. I hope this will prove enlightening and liberating. The mere fact that you may have to enact several or many roles doesn't mean, in and of itself, that you must suffer from increased negative stress.

Workplace Stress

If asked, you could probably come up fairly easily with characteristics about your job you find distressing and exhausting. Hopefully, you could also come up with aspects that are exciting and challenging. What are some common elements across jobs that can cause distress or prostress for you as working women? In 1979, Robert Karasek presented a model proposing that job strain is determined by the balance between 1) the stressors or physical and psychological demands of a particular job role, and 2) the control one has over the work.

Potential causes of negative stress = demands or costs of a job can be balanced by

Potential causes of positive stress = ability to exert control in one's position; access to resources & ability to meet demands

Think about your job for a moment. If you don't have a lot of job control but do have high job demands, you're more likely to suffer from things like exhaustion, depression, anxiety, difficulty waking up in the morning, and insomnia. You could also be at risk for having more sick days and higher rates of drug usage. On the other hand, people with so-called "active jobs" offering both high job demands and high job control report the greatest satisfaction. So, you may have a very demanding job, but if these demands are balanced by your ability to exert some control, make decisions, and access resources, your work will be less negatively stressful. In fact, if you have these positive attributes in your job, you can actually experience positive stress, or prostress, and personal and professional growth.

How do this model and the findings affect you? As women, our jobs often allow us less of the control and authority that can balance a job's demands. While the situation is slowly changing, men have tended to hold jobs of higher status and greater control than women. This is usually true regardless of whether they are white-collar, blue-collar, or clerical positions (LaCroix and Haynes 1987). In the National Institute of Occupational Safety and Health's ranking of the stressfulness of jobs, it is primarily women who occupy many of the ones most highly associated with heart disease, high blood pressure, nervous disorders, and ulcers. Some of these included: secretary, office manager, waitress, health technologist, licensed practical nurse, nurse's aide, registered nurse, dental assistant, social worker, health aide, and teacher's aide (Padus and the editors of *Prevention* magazine 1986). Most of us would probably think that executives, doctors, and lawyers would head the list. Such was not the case. While these jobs can be quite stressful, they have positive elements which can reduce their levels of negative stress. In particular, these positions generally offer control, responsibility, direct feedback, better financial remuneration, and some personal flexibility in work schedule.

"Female" Job Characteristics

Even today we continue to work in occupations highly segregated by race and gender. The careers we pursue are often more than two-thirds occupied by women. This is one reason men and women face different stressors on the job. The National Institute of Occupational Safety and Health found that women with pink-collar jobs offering less creativity, control, and responsibility have a very high rate of coronary heart disease. Many of these women report frustration and anger at "being kept out of the loop," being forced to follow rigid schedules, receiving minimal feedback from male supervisors, and carrying out repetitive work. Jobs that don't use an employee's talents and abilities are also highly associated with negative stress. What's disturbing to note is that when we occupy the same jobs requiring the same educational preparation as men, we still have less control over other workers and end up doing more support tasks and less decision making and delegating. Jobs with such conditions are associated with feelings of hopelessness and can create a sense of having minimal control in other aspects of life. As you may know, feelings of hopelessness and the absence of control are intimately linked with psychological distress. Do any of these "female" job characteristics sound familiar? In part 2, you'll find a brief questionnaire to help you evaluate negative workplace stress you may have, as well as techniques to help you reduce it.

If different job stressor variables were the whole story, it would be simple to understand negative stress in the workplace due to gender. However, even when the *same* job variable is considered, men's and women's perceptions as to whether it's negatively stressful or not can differ greatly. For example, lack of clear supervision can have an opposite effect on men and women (Miller 1980). In one study, the women perceived the absence of supervision as negatively stressful while this wasn't the case for the men. Here's a reminder that we have to look at the *nature* of men's and women's roles as workers to understand such puzzling differences. Remember, men generally have greater levels of independence and control in their jobs. Accordingly, lack of clear supervision would give them even greater power, autonomy, flexibility in decision making, and greater job satisfaction. On the other hand, for the women who often have the dangerous duo of less control and greater accountability, the lack of clear supervision was of course a negative stressor.

The Gender Gap and Sexual Discrimination

While awareness of the job stressors targeting women has definitely increased, they continue to exist. Women working in careers replete with men have to cope with stressors such as gender-role stereotypes and occupational sex discrimination. One of my clients, Michelle, a thirty-six-year-old woman, was one of a select few women working in a prominent investment banking firm. The regional director consistently assigned the high net worth male clients to male account officers. After working on her assertiveness techniques, she finally approached the director on this matter. In a tone of voice indicating her question was inane, the director told her that male customers *obviously* felt more comfortable working with a man. Michelle never was able to obtain prime assignments in this firm, but did exceedingly well shortly thereafter when she joined a company that was less biased and more realistic. The big loser here was surely not gutsy Michelle.

Although the negative stressors and obstacles we face are often external, they can also be found within ourselves. If you have high career aspirations, you may often have to deal with an internal conflict about achievement and success that directly increases your experience of negative stress. This, coupled with the external negative stress from bias and discrimination, can be overwhelming and paralyzing. A clear example of this dual internal and external negative stress was provided by a cleverly devised study. It involved giving women and men the following leading sentences: "After finals, Ann finds herself at the top of the medical school class . . ." (given to the women to complete). After finals, John finds himself at the top of the medical school class . . ." (given to the men to complete). The participants were asked to finish the story. The results indicated that 65 percent of the women compared to 10 percent of the men completed their respective stories with themes involving fear of success. The women also described their story's character "Ann" as being unhappy, isolated, unfeminine, and rejected by *both* men and women. High striving women can be torn between the drive to achieve and succeed and fearing the consequences of obtaining such success.

The Gender Gap and Your Wages

Most of us know either through personal experience, communicating with other women, or accessing the media or other informational sources that there is a gender wage gap. Men tend to earn more than women in almost all jobs. In addition, those jobs most frequently held by women are the lowest paid of all occupations. It's obviously negatively stressful (and frustrating) for us to work as hard as our equally trained male counterparts and not be compensated equitably. Women's wages as compared to men's range from seventy-two to ninety-five cents on the dollar. While the gender gap in pay is decreasing, certain obstacles still interfere with equalization. Namely, common beliefs about women and their workplace performance are just plain wrong. For example, one of the most harmful beliefs regarding working women is that we don't progress as far or as rapidly in our careers as men largely by our choice because of our commitments to family.

In 1993, M. L. Andersen provided enlightening information: women are behind men in occupational levels and income earnings *regardless* of whether or not we're married or have children!

As I ponder this, my mind immediately jumps to my bright, energetic client, Cathy. She had worked diligently for her competitive, bottom-line oriented company for five years and was well respected and successful. When she became pregnant, however, she experienced a great deal of negative stress. She feared she would now be passed over and labeled "only a 9-to-5er." She tried to hide her pregnancy as long as possible and worried constantly that her male associates would get the prime assignments as soon as the news was out. What a way to feel you have to respond to the news of becoming pregnant! Unfortunately, in the workplace there is this implied message to women that her "female" characteristics make her less valuable.

One reason for the lower overall salaries for women is the disturbing inequity between men and women in upper management. Statistics still show that women have a more difficult time obtaining a certain elevation and status. This has been labeled the "glass ceiling"—although you may not see overt discrimination, you can still experience a definite block when you try to climb the career ladder. An alternative perspective provides a more positive picture. Women are using their creativity and drive to start their own businesses and be less subject to the prejudices and dynamics working against their favor in large corporations.

Sexual Harassment

A politically sensitive issue over the last several years, sexual harassment remains a potent negative stressor faced by women on the job. Sexual harassment has been defined as "unwelcome sexual advances, requests for sexual favors, and other verbal or physical conduct of a sexual nature." Dr. Peter Hanson, in his 1989 book *Stress for Success*, presented figures suggesting that up to 40 percent of women experienced some type of sexual harassment in the workplace.

Aside from the distress arising from the sexual harassment itself is the worry and anxiety felt when women fear losing their jobs or being ridiculed if they decide to report the harassment. Page, a twenty-eight-year-old woman, was a client of mine who was sexually harassed by one of her supervisors. On the one hand she was furious and wanted this man to be punished, yet on the other hand she was terrified that if she told anyone, she would be ostracized and denied any future with the company. She became so negatively stressed that she lost her ability to concentrate or function effectively. Her intense anxiety and conflict eventually led to panic attacks and physical illness. Through attending individual therapy and a women's support group, she mustered up the courage to report the harassment. Page realized that, for her, even having to look for a new job would be much healthier for her sense of self than living with the shame and suppressed truth. Fortunately for all involved, the harasser, already on warning for suspected harassment, was promptly fired because of Page's courageous testimony.

Stress and Your Finances

Now, take a moment to think about one of the greatest sources of negative stress in your life. Without using any powers of ESP, I still feel fairly certain in guessing that a huge number of you thought of money. It's something we seem to endlessly worry about, think about, hope for, pray for, argue about, buy lottery tickets for, get married for, divorce for, and seek freedom by getting it or, for far fewer, giving it away. Money is yet another stressor that is impacting women more strongly today than ever. Financial stressors used to be more important to men than to women. However, a survey in the June 1996 issue of *Money* magazine comparing the financial attitudes of men and women show us this is no longer so. For example, 55 percent of the women as compared to 33 percent of the men surveyed stated that having to pay an unexpected one thousand dollars would pose a great problem. Not unexpectedly, women whose pay for equal work is still not equitable were much more unhappy with their financial remuneration than were men. Almost one-third of the women (29 percent) worried about money frequently, while only 17 percent of men reported the same concerns. Indeed, 60 percent of the women reported thinking more often about money than about sex as compared to only 34 percent of the men. Finally, while only 48 percent of the women expected to live well in retirement, 61 percent of the men expected to do so.

So, as women, we're exposed to a number of different negative stressors as compared to men. We may even perceive events as negative stressors that men see as neutral or even positive stressors. Lower wages, repetitive time-pressured jobs, positions with high demands but low control, gender discrimination, and sexual harassment are just some of the stressors women face more frequently than men. Because we also have to often contend with many stressors away from our jobs, we must learn to balance the conflicting demands of various roles that impact our on-the-job functioning and physical and psychological health and well-being.

Marriage: Boon or Bust?

For years, women faced societal, peer, and family pressures to marry. We were led to believe that, besides having children, marriage was the *pièce de résistance* of a woman's life. For many of you, marriage may well be associated with happiness, security, and social support. A number of studies have shown that married women have a higher degree of well-being than unmarried women. Overall, both marriage and working tend to be associated with less distress in women. Married, employed women generally have less depression, anxiety, and other types of psychiatric distress compared to women who don't work outside of the home.

While marriage is usually associated with less distress and better health for both sexes, men still benefit in these ways more than women. Here's yet another example of how women can undergo the same stressor but be affected by it differently than men. Why would marriage be more of a stress buffer for men? Simply put, women end up having to give a great deal more social support than they receive in such a relationship (Vanfossen 1986). Take a look at your own relationship. Would you say that you give more support and are more emotionally available to your male partner? A number of my female clients have sought individual or couples therapy because they are fed up with this imbalance. I'll be presenting you with more information on the prostress and distress of marriage when we explore how the interaction of a woman's many roles ultimately determines the experience of a stressor as primarily negative or positive.

The Stress of Being "Mom"

Being a mother—probably the toughest job in the world. Motherhood can be associated with psychological distress and low self-esteem, unhappiness, or depression. There is evidence, though, that some mothers do have slight health benefits depending on the number and ages of children, employment status, and marital status. Women with young children suffer from a greater number of physical problems, such as appetite and sleep disturbances. All of us who have gone through this wonderful but taxing experience really don't need to rely on research results to understand this!

As I was editing this book, I looked up to see a mother gazing lovingly into the eyes of her infant. The scene looked so peaceful and natural. I asked a question that moms often ask one another, "Was she going back to work soon, or was she planning on staying at home?" She told me that she planned to stay home for several years. I asked her about this decision and whether she'd felt conflict while making it. She replied that she didn't believe she'd felt as much guilt as had her friends who had been earning more money than she before her baby's arrival. She then talked about the stresses of motherhood and gave me a wonderfully humorous and accurate example. She described how her time is often unstructured (stressful) and at the end of the day there's generally nothing concrete to show for it. A week previously she had seen some old bananas lying around in her kitchen. Out of the blue, she decided to make banana bread. She didn't know why, particularly because she disliked banana bread. However, she spent all day trying to make progress on baking this bread. After finally putting her two-year-old and infant to bed at nine P.M., she'd walked into the kitchen and stared at the bowl of squished, peeled bananas. This was the result of an entire day's effort to complete something while caring for her children. She'd laughed and realized why it had been so important for her to make the bread. It would have given her a feeling of having actually produced something concrete and visible that day and she had desperately wanted a sense of immediate accomplishment. But, as she well knew, the ultimate accomplishment of raising two children in a healthy, loving home would be payback enough. Remember, though, this doesn't negate the fact that mothering can be extremely negatively stressful. Most mothers with whom I've spoken insist that nobody knows how hard it is to mother until they themselves become one.

Certainly, being a parent is a source of stress for both men and women. As with marriage, though, the strains of this role affect women more strongly. Particular elements of being a mother impact how the role affects us. For example, having young children and having several or more children are both related to higher rates of depression. In addition, having young children in the home is more stressful for women of lower income than for others. In 1985, Rosalind Barnett and Grace Baruch reported that among the various roles that women fulfill these days, only that of being a mother (not a wife or employee) was associated with having "role overload" and "role conflict." So, just what is it about the role of mother that's more distressing than wife or worker? One reason is that the main responsibility for the children's welfare and performance still falls largely on our shoulders. Society's expectations for a mother differ than those for a father and our identity is often more closely linked with being a mother than is a man's identity as a father. The result is that the demands of parenting are more stringent and stressful for women. In regards to the balance of control and demands in determining prostress or distress, the maternal role is heavily weighted toward the demand end with little chance of control. As Rosalind Barnett and Grace Baruch have pointed out, even though significant control is lacking, we're still expected to produce perfect, well-behaved children. In addition, our culture expects us to perform this role well naturally. Many of us are too ashamed to admit to distress and difficulties with being Mom. Many women who don't instinctively perform the mother role "ideally and naturally" are judged by themselves and maybe by others as if something were wrong with them. Some women find it almost impossible to stop blaming themselves for their children's physical illnesses or disorders, even when there was absolutely nothing they could have done to prevent them.

Are These Roles Good or Bad for You? (Prostress or Distress?)

The answer to this lies not in the role itself, but in the *interaction* of the roles you fulfill. This has been one of the most important recent discoveries in stress research: to get an accurate understanding of roles and stress, we have to look at the *interaction* of the roles to determine whether you'll be likely to experience prostress or distress. And of course, we have to consider particular psychological aspects of your life.

Not surprisingly, the experience for women who work and mother is greatly affected by their husbands' behavior as fathers. For men, the roles of worker and father typically have overlap in control, power, and prestige. We don't usually see this overlap between the roles of worker and mother. Because of society's view of us as home-makers/caretakers, and because many of our jobs are still lower in income-production and prestige, we have less control over assigning parenting and household responsibilities to our husbands and kids. I can't help but recall a primetime cartoon show that was shown fifteen or so years ago, titled *Wait Till Your Father Gets Home!* The father was the authority figure whose very presence was to magically change the kids from little pests out-of-control to well-behaved little pests. When working women's husbands don't assist in child care, women do not obtain the usual prostress benefits associated with working (Baruch and Barnett 1986). An interesting pattern emerges: the more a wife earns compared to her husband, the greater participation he generally shows in terms of household responsibilities. There's one drawback here. As men contribute more to child care and home chores, they feel more competent but they're also more critical of their wives' per-formance as mothers and how they manage their time (Barnett and Baruch 1987). All in all, women can benefit greatly from working, and the more prestigious and powerful a woman's job, the greater the prostress and physical and mental health benefits.

Mom and Dad—The Parenting Interaction

Women who see their husbands as "liberal and modern" are in for quite a shock when they have children. All of a sudden they may wonder where this man has gone. When children appear in the pic-ture, marital relationships almost inevitably shift to a more traditional mode of gender role-playing. A minimal 20 percent of husbands of working women share the housework and child care equally, and only 7 percent do so if the wife isn't working. We can say that gener-ally the more a husband participates in the housework, the lower the wife's level of distress and depression is.

Nothing is ever clear-cut when it comes to gender and stress. This is where some of us get into a sort of double bind. Those of us who are fortunate enough to have husbands help with child care feel relief. At the same time, we may end up criticizing ourselves for rely-ing on this help. Then we end up expressing even greater concern about how working interferes with our maternal role responsibilities. Our old "guilt button" has been pushed because we feel we're not living up to the familial and/or societal expectations hammered into us over the years. If you find yourself thinking this way, you're definitely interfering with your opportunity to be experiencing significant prostress in your job. You should take a closer look at the accuracy of your thinking. In part 2, we'll explore these types of beliefs and learn how to modify them. In addition, you'll learn assertiveness and communication techniques that are essential in getting you the help you deserve and need.

Working and Mothering Interactions

Let's look at another of the role interaction examples—how negative stress from mothering can be directly affected by a woman's experience working. If you're receiving prostress from your job, this can reduce the amount of negative stress arising from your mother role. For example, if you're a small business owner or a mid-level manager with some degree of control over your work, you can offset much of the potential negative stress from the high-demand, low-control nature of mothering. You must realize that you aren't completely at the mercy of a situation in which you find yourself. The danger is that we may feel we must take on more and more and that we must be able to handle it all by ourselves. When situations are untenable, you have options. You can modify the situation, get assistance, or change your own expectations of how much and how perfectly you "should" be doing everything.

There's another important difference between men and women in terms of the interactions of their roles. For both women and men, satisfaction in the role of spouse compensates for some of the dissatisfaction in the worker role. Interestingly enough, while satisfaction in the role of a father can compensate for dissatisfaction in the role of a husband, the same cannot be said for the role of a mother. This means that if you're not happy in your role as a wife, there isn't too much that your other roles can do to compensate for this. If this is the case, you need to take certain actions to change your life and make every day more enjoyable and healthy.

As more of us are working outside the home and placing greater value on this, the chances for conflicts like those just described are increasing. In general, tensions in the marriage impact women more than men. For the present, at least, a number of women are going to have more increased distress due to these evolving dynamics. However, I believe reading this book is going to provide you with the tools necessary to make the interaction of your various roles more positive. I feel that such differences in strain and negative stress will resolve as some balance and new expectations are established in society.

"Nontraditional" Women: Prostress or Distress?

The "nontraditionalists" among us certainly want to excel in our careers, but we can't always shake socially instilled beliefs that we must also excel as wife, mother, and homemaker. In 1995, Eugenia Proctor Gerdes clarified how those of us who have conflicting roles and aren't necessarily fulfilling society's expectations for what women "should" do are especially susceptible to negative stress. Nontraditional women (that is, females preparing for careers typically held by males) report greater job tension and symptoms than men *in the same field*. They also react more extremely than traditional women to elevated stress levels. Indeed, while these women can still experience prostress from pursuing careers and activities of real interest, they most often still feel the pull to toe the line and do what they've been socialized to do with their lives. In fact, stress from *home events* was a stronger predictor for anxiety for these women with "male" career interests than for the traditional women.

Besides the internal conflict that leads to feelings negatively stressed, if you're a nontraditional woman selecting to break new ground, you're also likely to face different negative stressors than men. You may have to deal with discrimination and stereotypically based judgments. You might be more susceptible to negative stress and suffer more mental and physical problems as a result. For these reasons, it's extremely important for you, if you are struggling to break with the societally dictated female path, to learn how to use your body and mind to relax and gain control over your thoughts. You will think more rationally, learn coping strategies, and face the difficulties as challenges rather than threats. The second section of this book will be a real life-saver, or at least life-optimizer, for you.

Traditional Women

Interestingly, working women with traditional beliefs about marriage and motherhood see potential negative stressors at work as *less* threatening than other women (Long, Kahn, and Schutz 1992).

The importance of marriage and motherhood can help counterbalance the importance of work so they feel less threatened by stressors in the workplace. This certainly isn't to say that highly career-oriented women are doomed to suffer negative stress from working. The tools offered in this book can serve all of us, with all of our differences and similarities, for increasing prostress and decreasing distress.

How Do You View Achievement?

Stop for a moment here and think about depictions on the television or in movies of women as businesspersons. When I did this, I was surprised at how clearly two distinct types of women came to mind. I recalled seeing women who were either, 1) bitchy, coldly attractive, conniving, and aggressive, or 2) silly, emotional, and ditzy (and of course, attractive). Is this reality? Must women in the workplace be either/or? For many women, social interaction, openness, and warmth are important, valued characteristics. However, values and behavioral characteristics such as these aren't necessarily rewarded or desired in the business world. Harriet Braiker in her 1986 book, *The Type E Woman*, writes that high-achieving women have a common dilemma as to how to be successful in arenas emphasizing values stereotypically viewed as male, while at the same time continuing to value their female characteristics. The competitiveness and assertiveness often needed and valued in the business world may lead to a woman being labeled as aggressive and bitchy. (You will find tips on how to be assertive and deal with difficult types of people in part 2 of this book.) Braiker coined the term "Type E stress" to refer to negative stress that affects a woman, regardless of position in life, who's trying to balance multiple roles *and* excel in all of them. Does this description resonate with you? Probably so if you're reading this book.

If you see yourself as a Type E women, there are a variety of reasons for which you may have such intense achievement aspirations. Remember, merely occupying multiple roles isn't inevitably negatively stressful and unhealthy. One thing that affects whether prostress or distress dominates is how you view achievement. Firstly, when excelling is central to your sense of self and secondly when you struggle endlessly because you expect to be excellent in absolutely everything, you place yourself in danger of developing certain problems. This increases your experience of negative stress and decreases opportunities for prostress. When you set unachievable goals, you will never meet them or derive the pleasure and fulfillment of having met a challenge.

Conflict between competing roles is often a source of distress for women. Braiker summed up the situation well: While men can feel satisfied by providing for the families because of their jobs, women often feel they must show that, *in spite* of their careers, they can still be good mothers and wives. Simultaneously, they must show that, *in spite* of their being mothers and wives, they can still be valuable employees who should be considered for advancement and upper-level positions.

Woman as Friend: The Pluses and Minuses

Our relationships with others can be invaluable in getting us through both day-to-day and the unusual, difficult crises. On the other hand, we also probably agree that these relationships can sometimes be more bothersome than beneficial! Research supports these common-sense conclusions by revealing that social interaction can be a source of both distress and prostress. Social support can be extremely helpful in reducing the negative impact of stress. Your friends can help you respond in a healthier way to stress, which directly affects how much negative stress you'll experience. On the other hand, social relationships can also be linked to problems with blood pressure, heart disease, and the immune system. Those of us with troubled or minimal social relationships have a greater chance of developing depression, heart disease, cancer, arthritis, and difficult pregnancies.

Women usually have larger close social networks than men. You might think that this would be a valuable stress reduction resource. Given the importance of social interaction to women, we often do benefit from the distress-reducing and prostress-boosting power of social support. Again, the story isn't so black-and-white. Social support can be a distress buffer if we allow others to help us when we're feeling overwhelmed by demands. Friends or loved ones abate negative stress by helping out with problems, boosting our self-esteem, and easing our adjustment to loss and change. Good relationships can even help us handle distress from work problems, job loss, pregnancy, depression, and other difficulties. Our friendships not only reduce negative stress, but also increase prostress experiences and positive feelings, thus directly improving our well-being and health.

The Drawbacks

Unfortunately, we need to recognize that social relationships are of a dual nature. Their benefits can be counteracted by the drawbacks of betrayal, rejection, dependence, and vicarious pain. The role of helper or peacemaker that so many of us assume without question can be a tremendous source of negative stress and frustration. One reason women experience greater distress in our interpersonal roles is that not only are we impacted by the distress of our own experiences, but we're also deeply affected by the distress of our friends and loved ones. Our socialization as women has trained us to feel obligated to be responsive to others' needs, even at the cost of our own.

It's also been stated that, because of the way we've been socialized, we use less effective stress-coping techniques. This view assumes that women are generally more vulnerable to stressors of all types. This generalization is inaccurate. In fact, women adapt *better* to disruptions in our social support, such as separation, divorce, or the death of a spouse. Underlying this difference is the pattern of relationships and social resources we develop as compared to men. We generally have friends from many areas and time periods of our lives, whereas men tend to have friends or acquaintances currently linked with their jobs, hobbies, or sports' interests. In a marriage or established relationship, it's the woman who usually manages social ties and interaction. As a consequence, when a relationship between a man and woman ends, all of this maintenance work that benefited the man can end as well. Robert Ornstein and David Sobel in their 1987 book, *The Healing Brain*, write that when men are without their wives they have the fewest primary relations in their social networks. The important role played by wives in expanding the social network is echoed by the fact that married men react more strongly to the loss of their wives than vice versa. These two researchers summarized a report showing that for men the effects of divorce on mortality are about the same as smoking more than twenty cigarettes a day!

Stressors for Women Versus Stressors for Men: The Social Interaction

One reason women may experience greater negative stress involves the type of events they perceive as distressors. Two major differences in stressors are that men experience income losses more intensely as a stressor (an *infrequent* event in general), and women experience more network events and deaths of loved ones (*frequent* events in general) (Wethington, McLeod, and Kessler 1987). Network events are events that happen to people that are considered important to the person. For example, a good friend becoming ill or a relative losing her job and being low on financial resources. From personal experience, it probably doesn't surprise you that we respond with greater distress and physical symptoms to negatively stressful network events as compared to men.

Given the frequency of network-type events for women, it's likely that this is one of the major reasons we often experience greater negative stress and its harmful consequences. This alone can account for one-half of the total gender difference in distress levels between men and women (Kessler and McLeod 1984). Even when men and women report a similar incidence of taking care of a relative or close friend, women tend to spend a much greater amount of time doing this caretaking. Social and cultural values emphasizing that we're *supposed* to be more available as caretakers is associated with our greater commitment and emotional involvement. The sheer demand on our energy and time can have a detrimental effect when we're already strapped by participating in a number of other roles.

Helping Others Can Help You

Of course, caretaking and social interaction can also provide many benefits. Caring for and doing things for others can definitely have positive psychological consequences for both men and women. Think of the last time you did something for someone. Did it make you feel better about yourself? I often encourage my clients to do things for others so that they get outside of their heads and their negative thinking. Given the tendency to compare ourselves to others, helping other people often gets us to see that we aren't as useless and as bad off as we might have believed.

So, prostress and stress-buffering effects of social support may be stronger for women than men. Problems in social relations, however, or the absence of sufficient social interaction can cause greater distress for us. Helping others and being there to listen and support is central to the lives of many women. Although this can be gratifying and meaningful for both you and the recipient, when it becomes excessive, it's likely to change from a prostressor to a distressor. It's possible to depend too much on caretaking or helping out to derive a sense of self-worth, or to avoid paying attention to your own needs, conflicts, and feelings.

Balance Equals Stress Management

Therapy can be particularly difficult with women who are workaholics or service-aholics because these patterns are often socially sanctioned. There's nothing so obviously "wrong" with these types of behaviors as there is with the excessive use and dependence on alcohol, drugs, money, or sex. How often have people applauded your endless efforts to help others, smooth situations over, take care of sick friends, volunteer for a task, and so on? As you'll soon be hearing in my "battle cry," stress management is *self management* and *balance*—this is the name of the game. You'll be learning how to say "no" when you're feeling stretched too thin. Most importantly, you'll feel okay with this, because hopefully you'll have a new understanding of what may be an unhealthy need to say "yes," and you'll realize the primary importance of your own needs.

5

Stress and Communication

One of the most frequent reasons I see couples in therapy is because of communication problems. The couples with whom I work are usually unaware of the extent of their troubled communication. If they do realize that they "just never talk anymore," they're often unaware of the pervasive, destructive impact this has on the health of their relationship, their satisfaction, and their well-being. It's important to understand that partners in a troubled relationship *have particular difficulties understanding each other's way of communicating*. Their problems in understanding communication show up only when the messages come from each other and have to do with themselves and their own relationship. When it comes to strangers or people outside the relationship, communication is just fine. We're probably all painfully aware of how much negative stress we can experience when we're having conflict with our partner.

Defensiveness

There are various reasons for problems in communication, but defensiveness is one of the most frequent reasons. To protect ourselves, we often communicate in a vague, confusing manner to avoid triggering what we expect is going to be a negative response from the other. For example, if a woman has forgotten to go shopping again and wants to ask her husband to pick up some take-out dinner, but expects him to be displeased with her forgetfulness and this request, she may say something like this: "Well, we really don't have anything in the house. Maybe we need to get something like the take-out you picked up last week." She may end the conversation at this point, with her husband not realizing that she is actually asking him to pick up dinner. When he comes home without the dinner, both he and his wife will end up blaming the other and feeling angry. She feels frustrated because he didn't understand her message, while he is left confused by the indirect request and the resulting anger. Not to mention, they both missed out on dinner.

Defensiveness also underlies one of the problems I see most frequently in distressed couples. In this case, partners just cannot seem to listen to one another. Rather, they're so intent on protecting themselves and they believe so absolutely that they already know what the other "really means," that they come to their own conclusions about the other's selfish intentions without paying attention to the message the other is trying to send. For example, a man might ask his partner whether she was able to schedule an appointment to meet with their child's teacher. She might immediately jump to the conclusion that what he really means is that she is a poor mother and that if she really cared about the child and about him, she would have made the time, no matter how busy her schedule, to make the appointment. The man might have just been asking for information and might even have been about to volunteer to do the task himself. However, the woman who had leapt to interpet his question in this negative, accusatory way would respond with hostility and the conditions for an argument would be set.

Are You Really Listening?

John Gottman and his colleagues in their 1976 book *A Couple's Guide to Communication* point out certain habits that one or both partners can have that sabotage efforts at true communication and lead to resentment and anger. One of these patterns is known as "yes-butting." One partner attempts to make a point or offer a suggestion to no avail—every effort is met with a "yes, but . . ." The offending partner may be unaware of this habit and may believe he's just trying to clarify a point, but the person subject to this annoying pattern learns that everything she says is met with an objection. The result is that she's likely to give up attempting to communicate.

I often watch as my couples embark upon "cross-complaining" during our therapy sessions. This occurs when one partner issues a complaint that is promptly met with a complaint issued by the other partner. This cycle continues and escalates into an argument. Here's an example:

Partner 1:   You're home late again. The kids really wanted to see you.

Partner 2:   If I hadn't had to do all of the errands yesterday—which you were supposed to do last week—I wouldn't have had to stay late.

Partner 1:   If you weren't so picky about where we have to shop and get the dry cleaning done, I could have finished the errands.

Partner 2:   Just because you have low standards about dining and clothes, doesn't mean that the whole family has to suffer.

Ad infinitum.

Another problem in communication has been coined by Gottman and his colleagues as "kitchen sinking." Many of my clients have really become quite fond of this term and use it to point out to each other in a light, humorous way, when they're beginning to fall into the old pattern. It's fairly self-explanatory. Kitchen sinking happens when a discussion starts about one issue but soon turns to another issue and another issue. . . . Complaints about all types of situations and problems are dragged into the conversation and the original issue is left unresolved. Both partners end up feeling overwhelmed and helpless when faced with all of the many problems they have to tackle.

Indirect Communication

Then there is the belief (held by one or both partners) that the other *should* somehow know what he or she is talking about or really wants without having to spell it out directly. Such an assumption is based on the dangerous, irrational belief that "if he/she really loved me, he/she would understand me perfectly." "Should" appears as the cause of other communication problems. As you'll read in chapter 10 on cognitive techniques, we all have certain deeply held personal beliefs of which we are not consciously aware. Because we're generally unaware of these beliefs even as they affect the conclusions we draw, the assumptions we make, and our behaviors, they've been called "automatic thoughts." Dr. Aaron Beck points out in his 1988 book, *Love Is Never Enough*, that one type of automatic thought and its poisonous impact on communication and entire relationships involves the simple word, "should." We're typically unaware of our own unspoken shoulds that affect how we communicate and react to one another.

Suppose you've had a very difficult day at the office or at home with the kids. You approach your partner ready to unload your story and get some support. He might have also had a particularly strenuous day, or he might be busy when you feel like talking. If he isn't responsive to your trying to talk, you might find yourself blowing up, making accusations, or blaming your partner for your problems. In a calmer, more rational moment, you might be able to see that your partner has nothing to do with your frustration. What went wrong in this scenario of communication? When your partner didn't immediately drop everything to listen to you, your silent self-talk might have gone like this: "If he really cared about me, he *should* be available to me when I need to talk. He *should* want to drop everything to listen to me when I'm obviously upset." Your partner might likewise be thinking that he "should" have the time to relax and "should" not have to be subject to your frequent verbal attacks. The problem here is that you're unaware of how your "shoulds" are warping your perception of the situation and determining your exaggerated, angry responses. With such extreme beliefs and expectations, it's inevitable that you're going to respond in an extreme fashion when your desperate needs aren't satisfied. If instead you think in a less extreme, tolerant manner such as, "it would be nice if my partner were available to listen to me right now," you'll be much less likely to feel immediate anger and rejection if you don't get the exact response you wanted. As a result, your partner won't feel attacked. You also increase your chances of getting the attention and affection you wanted in the first place. In part 2 you'll read about how to get in touch with and modify your extreme, irrational expectations and beliefs. You will find you can communicate more effectively, reduce the negative stress, and increase the prostress in your relationship.

The Talking Game

Men and women have fundamental stylistic differences in communication. This topic has been the subject of a great deal of attention over the last several years. I have, however, seen enough men and women who don't fit into these stereotypes, so I am wary of applying them across the board. At the same time, I have also seen a number of cases in which these differences did fit the men and women in relationships. Making the couple aware of them, at the very least, was very helpful. Here's a brief presentation of some of the most troublesome gender communication differences (Maltz and Borker 1982). When I've discussed these patterns with women who were previously unaware of them, it has allowed them to understand more accurately just what's going on in the talking game. Such understanding can greatly decrease miscommunications and improve the quality of relationships.

A frequent complaint of women is that their male partners never listen to them. We draw this conclusion based on how men behave while we're speaking to them. While men listen, they hardly utter listening signals such as "mm-hmm" or "uh-huh." When they do so, it's to indicate agreement with the speaker. We, on the other hand, use these utterances a lot and do so to show the speaker we're listening. The outcome of this differential pattern is that when we're speaking to a man and don't hear such confirming verbalizations, we assume he's not listening to us. From this assumption, it's a short but dangerous step to concluding that since our partner doesn't care about what we're saying, he doesn't care about or respect us.

Another gender difference that causes problems involves a different use of questioning. We tend to ask more questions during conversations because we feel a greater sense of responsibility for maintaining the conversational flow. Men have a lesser tendency to ask questions, so a man might assume that if his wife has something to tell him, she'll do so without his needing to ask. The woman, on the other hand, might become increasingly angry at her partner who doesn't ask her, "What's wrong?" when she is sending him nonverbal signals that she is disturbed. Women also tend to ask questions as a way to convey caring and intimacy. Unfortunately, her male partner who doesn't understand this might perceive this interest as unnecessarily intrusive and feel resentful or angry. Three other differences often lead women to conclude that their partners don't listen to them or value their opinions:

- Men tend to interrupt conversations more frequently.

- Men often make no response or delayed responses to others' comments.

- Men's communications more often take the form of declarations of fact or opinion.

Most of us have probably heard innumerable jokes about the fact that men are much less likely to talk about feelings. When we speak about problems, we do so to share our experiences, clarify feelings, or to empathize. When a man hears his partner or friend discussing her problems, he assumes she's asking for assistance. This leads him to offer solutions rather than just listening and empathizing, which is often all she really wants. Women can find this infuriating because we don't understand it. How often have you wanted to really get into discussing something, backtracking into the history, enhancing the details and reveling in your feelings, only to have your male partner or friend shut you down by *telling you what you should do about it*? Try to remember this next time your temper begins to flare. Rather than interpreting his advice-giving as an attempt to shut you up or as evidence that he doesn't care about you, it may well be that he thinks this is what you want.

Hopefully having learned about several of these gender communication differences, you may now allow yourself to pause the next time you begin feeling misunderstood and angry and question yourself as to the accuracy of your interpretations. You'll probably find the negative stress and number of arguments between you and your mate "mysteriously" decreasing. Remember, this is not an overnight process, it will take some time to make changes. Also, solving communication issues with your partner isn't just your responsibility—share your new findings with your significant other!

Assessment for You and Your Partner

In Aaron Beck's 1988 *Love Is Never Enough*, he presented two extremely useful and telling questionnaires that can help highlight potential communication hotspots for you and your partner. Understanding is the first step toward making changes that will improve your communication and your relationship, and thereby reduce your level of negative stress. The following is a list of potential problems in communication style.

- In the blank left-hand column, rate the behaviors **your partner uses with you**. Use the following rating to indicate frequency:
  (0) does not apply   (1) rarely   (2) sometimes   (3) frequently   (4) all the time

- In the blank middle column, rate **how bothersome you find the problem**.
  (0) not at all   (1) slightly   (2) moderately   (3) a great deal

- In the blank right-hand column, rate **the behaviors you use with your partner**. Have your partner also complete this questionnaire.

Beck reminds the user with this questionnaire that his/her perception of the partner's behavior may be exaggerated. Of course, the reality is important, but clarifying your perceptions is also essential because that's what determines your reactions to and feelings about your partner.

Communication Style

	Your partner uses with you	This bothers me	You with your partner
• Doesn't listen	_____	_____	_____
• Talks too much	_____	_____	_____
• Doesn't talk enough	_____	_____	_____
• Interrupts	_____	_____	_____
• Too vague	_____	_____	_____
• Never gets to the point	_____	_____	_____
• Doesn't nod or indicate agreement	_____	_____	_____
• Doesn't utter listening signals	_____	_____	_____
• Doesn't give mate chance to talk	_____	_____	_____
• Won't discuss touchy subjects	_____	_____	_____
• Talks too much about touchy subjects	_____	_____	_____
• Asks too many questions	_____	_____	_____
• Doesn't ask enough questions	_____	_____	_____
• Shuts mate up	_____	_____	_____
• Withdraws when upset	_____	_____	_____

After you have each completed the survey, you and your partner can go over all responses together. Discuss the issues and feelings that come up. Remember, it's best to give specific examples when explaining your responses. If you, say, noted that your partner won't discuss touchy subjects, give him an example when and where this last happened, "Last Tuesday night, when I wanted to talk about . . . you changed the subject to . . . You also did the same thing last week when I tried to talk about it then." Decide which areas are most important to each of you and make an agreement, preferably in writing, to take specified steps to make desired changes. Give each other a great deal of positive reinforcement when the requested changes are made and gently remind each other if old undesired behaviors reappear.

Both you and your partner can also complete this second questionnaire to clarify potential psychological problems in communication. After each statement, enter a number from 0–4 that best indicates the frequency of your feelings.

Potential Communication Inhibitors

- I feel inhibited in discussing my problems with my partner. _____

- It's hard for me to express my feelings to my partner. _____

- I'm afraid to ask for what I want. _____

- I don't believe what my partner says. _____

- I'm afraid that what I have to say will make my partner angry. _____

- My partner won't take my concerns seriously. _____

- My partner talks down to me. _____

- My partner doesn't want to hear about my needs and feelings. _____

- I'm afraid that if I begin to express my feelings to my partner, I'll lose control of my emotions. _____

- I'm concerned that if I open up to my partner, he or she will use what I say against me in the future. _____

- If I express my true feelings, I'll regret what I said later. _____

Once you have this information and feel safe to share it with your partner, your chances of improving your communication are much greater. If you still don't feel comfortable, or if there seem to be serious problems revealed by these questionnaires, you might benefit from seeking professional advice or therapy.

You probably now have a better idea of how many ways miscommunication is possible. That is, often the message sent is not the message received. What results is increased tension, distance, and anger. Close relationships are potential sources of great prostress or intense distress. In part 2, you'll learn some valuable techniques to improve communication and to stop the vicious cycle of negative stress arising from communication mess-ups.

6

Women and Unhealthy Coping Skills

"I can't cope with this!" may well be today's mantra for many of us who feel overwhelmed by negative stress in our lives. How do you cope with stress? Your answer to this apparently simple question is the base upon which stress management is built. What's important, aside from much debate and various conclusions from researchers, is that work stress exists for both men and women. Under some circumstances, however, women are hesitant to report this and attempt to deny it. This certainly makes sense when we consider the earlier discussion that distress on the job is more acceptable for men and that because of this it's easier for them to admit and discuss. In fact, when men visit their physician and the subject of negative stress is discussed, the doctors more often collaborate with the men in blaming the stress on work-related concerns. When the same situation rolls around but the patient is a woman, the doctors attribute the stress to relationships and family issues.

Debbie, a client I've been seeing for about one year, tearfully told me how many medical doctors she had visited over the past years and how, almost to the one, they told her all of her physical problems were the result of her husband's personality and her only "cure" for regaining her health was to leave him! While the negative stress of her marriage was probably involved to some extent with her physical suffering, it certainly wasn't the only cause, and their "prescription" was certainly not the only method of helpful intervention. We shouldn't just accept the traditional general assumption that women are more vulnerable to stressors than men. We must consider the *type* of stressor, as well as a number of other internal and external variables. Women can fare better or at least comparably to men under a variety of circumstances.

Emotion-Focused Versus Problem-Focused

Two possible ways to cope with stress are *emotion-focused* or *problem-focused* coping. You're using emotion-focused coping when you focus on controlling your emotions from stress and when you try to stay emotionally balanced. For example, a woman anxious about the stressful process of applying for membership in an exclusive association might focus on trying to alleviate the anxiety by commiserating with a friend who is involved in the same process. On the other hand, with problem-focused coping, efforts are focused on directly or indirectly changing the stressful situation by taking action, changing behavior, or making plans. Here, a woman in the same stressful situation would focus on designing a résumé in a way that would market her for the particular association. She would focus on researching the types of skills and abilities the association was looking for and maybe even take some skill-enhancing workshops. Why should it matter what type you use? The reason is that problem-focused coping often is more effective in resolving the situation and in giving you a sense of control. This may explain why emotion-focused coping has been linked with helplessness and depression (Miller and Kirsch 1987). However, this conclusion isn't absolute. In situations in which control over the stressors is really impossible, the emotion-focused approach can be more acceptable.

In studying coping strategies, it's very difficult to draw any hard and fast conclusions. In 1987, Suzanne Miller and Nicholas Kirsch, examined a variety of studies looking at coping strategies and gender. They found evidence of gender differences with respect to coping. Six out of seven studies reviewed showed that males were more likely to use problem-focused coping than women, especially at work, in situations requiring more information, and in situations offering little control. From their review of many studies, they concluded that men tend to cope with stress by using strategies that directly change the stressors. Women may more often use techniques to change their emotional responses. In addition, they saw evidence that women appraise stressors as more threatening (i.e., a distressor) more so than men.

Obviously, the problems presented to experiment participants impact the type of coping techniques used. Work stressors are often associated with problem-focused coping, while stressors related to illness and marital problems involve more passive, emotion-focused coping. Because women report more stressors involving health and family issues than men, this might be one of the reasons they seem to use different coping strategies.

Your perception of events determines how you choose to manage them. Stressors that appear to be changeable usually elicit problem-focused coping and situations perceived as uncontrollable tend to be handled through emotion-focused coping. This might partially explain the greater depression and sense of helplessness among women as compared to men. Remember that many stressors associated with women really don't offer as much of a chance to be controlled as do those reported by men. (For example, as discussed earlier with respect to the difference in the amount of control men and women have with their jobs.) Some women even perceive that they have less control *in general* over others and their environment. Both of these factors would lead women to use emotion-focused coping more frequently and to experience the emotional and physical distress that can come with this coping strategy.

In 1995, Laura Porter and Arthur Stone reported that men did not necessarily use more active, instrumental coping nor did women use more passive, emotion-focused coping. Their stressors were different—women had more problems involving the self, parenting, and other people, and men experienced more work-related and miscellaneous problems. When men and women had to cope with the same stressors, they apparently coped with them in similar ways! This would support the idea that it might be differences in the *types of stressors* more often facing women than men that underlie the evidence suggesting that men used effective problem-focused coping more often than women. It may be *social roles* and the *types of stressors associated with men and women* and *not necessarily gender differences in choosing coping strategies* that are the most central predictors of distress and illness. So, while there are differing opinions about coping strategies and gender, just to try to be aware of the possibilities.

People use many different ways to cope with stress. Some are better overall than others (for example, drinking or smoking are not good ways of coping) but the situation may dictate which type of coping is superior. The key to good coping is the ability to use a balanced approach and to be flexible enough to apply the coping strategy called for by a particular situation. At times, it's best to directly confront and attack a situation or problem. Other times, the best solution is avoidance. If you have absolutely no chance of controlling or changing a stressful situation, it isn't healthy to expend all of your energy and become increasingly frustrated by using a problem-focused approach. Another stressful situation might be resolved best by increasing your knowledge or resources so that you can meet the demands and grow in the process. This last type of coping can be accomplished through working on your own, asking for help, or using cognitive techniques to view the situation positively and to manage your time and energy. You can also use physical techniques such as relaxation and exercise to maximize your energy and calm your body's stress response.

Substance Abuse

Sometimes we try to deal with negative stress by turning to substances such as alcohol, drugs, and food. These coping efforts are misdirected and only end up increasing our experience of distress. Do we really have to worry about this as women when, for years, statistics have shown a much greater prevalence of alcohol and drug abuse in men? Unfortunately, yes! There are several reasons that the numbers in these surveys weren't completely accurate. It's likely that many women substantially underreport their problems with substance abuse because historically, it's been a much greater stigma for us to report or seek help. Women have often been left to struggle alone with these problems, desperately trying to hide unacceptable "unfeminine" behavior and afraid to seek the help they so need. While such judgmental beliefs are beginning to change, the proportion of women seeking treatment remains below that of men. In fact, women often face resistance from their own friends and family when they do want to obtain treatment. Another realistic reason underlying a woman's fear of entering a treatment program is the risk of losing custody of her children.

It does seem that we're increasingly joining the ranks of those seeking to cope with negative stress through the use of substances. Substance abuse rates among women are increasing and closing in on those of men. The recent National Institute of Mental Health Epidemiological Catchment area study found that substance abuse was the second leading psychiatric disorder among women, and that up to 25 percent of the women asked reported lifetime use of illegal drugs (Anthony and Helzer 1991). What's extremely disturbing is that this increase is coming from use among young women. Although our rates of substance use are still somewhat lower, the economic, physical, social, and psychological effects of abuse are especially destructive to us. Women in treatment programs generally have lower self-esteem than men. And, women who abuse alcohol are more likely to have coexisting psychological disorders: 65 percent of female alcoholics have a secondary diagnosis compared to 44 percent of male alcoholics.

Alcohol Use

Women report that they most often drink to ease the strain of domestic stress. According to Dr. Karen Johnson's 1991 book, *Trusting Ourselves*, women usually have to handle a greater number of different kinds of tasks than do men. Many of us feel guilty about taking the needed time to relax and for some women drinking provides a temporary escape, reducing their guilt about taking time for themselves. Women often believe they must keep doing and performing for others rather than giving themselves permission to be, to relax, and to enjoy. Remember many women become overly involved in the caretaking role because of societal expectations and an inability to set limits. Alcohol can be quite handy because it decreases sensitivity to others and blunts beliefs that they must always be there for everyone. Alcohol also lowers inhibitions and may give some the boost they need to express their feelings and rightful desires. So, drinking can give some women the "courage" to set more rigid boundaries against being the ever-available caretaker, as well as to help them get up the nerve to request and accept attention and care from others.

Self-Assessment

Here are some questions you should ask yourself if you're wondering about your drinking behavior. Go ahead and ask yourself even if you feel okay about your drinking but others have mentioned something about it to you. Of course, this is just an informal measure and cannot be substituted for more formal assessments. But, your honest answers to the following questions could help you detect whether you have, or are developing, a problem with alcohol.

- How difficult would it be for you to stop drinking completely?

- How many nights per week do you have more than two alcoholic beverages?

- Have you ever suffered from a blackout due to drinking (an inability to recall the events for a period of time during which you were intoxicated)?

- Do you find yourself having any difficulty stopping after having one drink?

- When you go out with your friends, do the evening's activities usually involve drinking (more than 1–2 drinks)?

- Do you tend to drink substantially more on the weekends than during the week?

- Are you more interested in attending events at which alcohol will be offered?

- If you go for more than twelve hours without drinking, do you feel ill, weak, or experience tremors?

- Do you have a time in mind (4 P.M., 6 P.M., noon . . .) before which you don't allow yourself to drink?

If you feel you may need further help, please contact organizations such as Alcoholics Anonymous, Al-Anon, or Adult Children of Alcoholics (ACOA).

Prescription and Illegal Drug Use

Prescription drugs tell a different story than alcohol use. Lifetime prescription drug use is greater among women than men. This might not surprise you if you think back to some of the gender-related dynamics already discussed. Remember that women seek help for psychological distress more frequently than men, suffer from greater rates of certain mental disorders, and can be more susceptible to family and work roles (depending on the role interactions). Doctors prescribe psychoactive drugs for women more commonly than they do for men. Also, men often choose alcohol to self-medicate for anxiety and depression, while women more frequently use prescribed medications. For these reasons, it's important that you monitor your use of potentially addictive prescription drugs, especially if they're for anxiety or pain reduction and make you feel relaxed or slightly euphoric. The stress-related gender difference here *isn't* that men or women are more likely to use substances in an attempt to cope with negative stress, but that the poison of choice differs between the two.

The most frequently used illegal drug among women is marijuana, although more men use this particular drug. In terms of cocaine use, the lifetime prevalence rates are approximately equal for women and men. However, females actually begin using cocaine younger and seek treatment sooner than males. Cocaine is also used more by women to self-medicate for depression. While heroin use by women is substantially less than that for men, the impact on women is more severe. Females become addicted to heroin more frequently than men, and female addicts are less frequently employed and more likely to be on welfare. Again, we can see social forces at work as female users are more likely to live with men who are also narcotics addicts and, in fact, are frequently introduced to heroin by men.

Food and Stress: Eating Disorders

An extremely negative stressor for American women is our culture's emphasis on body image and weight. Many blame the media for the excessive pressure placed on women to meet outlandish standards of desirability. I have worked with a number of women and teens suffering distress, depression, and low self-esteem from the pressures to look like an emaciated runway model. However, rarely have I seen such an example of this absurdity as in a case with my client, Alana. A beautiful, very thin young woman, Alana came to my office in tears. She complained of depression and a sense of constant anxiety. Although she had been feeling better about herself for several months, an off-the-cuff comment made by her boyfriend had sent her back into a downward spiral. Having just received the new swimsuit edition of *Sports Illustrated*, her boyfriend told her that if she lost ten pounds, she could be as sexy as the models in the magazine. Alana had earlier confided painfully to this man that she had a problem with her body image and had suffered from anorexia as a teenager. Did this stop him from further discouraging Alana about her body? Unfortunately not.

The majority of women today feel ashamed about their bodies. While this problem used to be seen primarily in women and adolescents, the age of onset is dropping rapidly. The outcome is alarmingly clear—the national reported incidence of both anorexia and bulimia has doubled since 1970 and the patients are younger. Anxiety and obsessions about food and body shape and chronic dieting are now appearing as early as five or six years of age! A recent study by the University of Florida found that 42 percent of six-and seven-year-old girls wanted to be skinnier. By now, you've learned a great deal about the number and types of negative stressors faced primarily by women and stemming from cultural values and socialization. What

stronger evidence can there be for the tremendous power of social influences on us and what a shame that it's directed in such a harmful,
demeaning way. What a gift it would be if we could each, in our own
way, work to harness this power and change social dynamics so they
will challenge, nurture, and support future generations of young girls
and women.

The gender difference with respect to the negative stressors of
body image and weight is clear cut—women are three times as likely
than men to think negatively about their bodies. This isn't surprising
when you consider that the average height and weight of an American woman is five feet four inches and 142 pounds while the average
model is five feet nine inches and 110 pounds. The talk about how
Miss America contests have changed and now focus on inner beauty,
intelligence, and talent notwithstanding, the majority of contestants
are at least *15 percent* below their recommended body weight. This
figure is frightening as it is the *same percentage considered one of the
symptoms in the diagnosis of anorexia nervosa*. There's also hard evidence that this problem impacts women more than it does men. People use judgments based on physical appearance in making
suppositions about desirability, intelligence, and education more so
with respect to women than they do with men (Striegel-Moore, Silberstein, and Rodin 1986). Being overweight, particularly for females,
is negatively stressful and is often linked with self-esteem problems.
The ultimate effect on women from these pressures ranges from causing mild stress to full-blown psychiatric disorders and even death.

If you're like many of us, you don't have to look far to find evidence of this unfortunate reality. Most of us probably believe we
should really lose that extra five, ten, fifteen, or twenty pounds. Underneath this repetitive, even ritualistic thinking is the fantasy that
once we manage to obtain this goal, we'll finally be happier and satisfied and our lives will be exciting and fulfilling. I often ask my female
clients who have issues with food and weight to finish this statement
off the top of their heads: "If I were skinnier . . ." Now it's your turn.
Quickly finish the half-sentence but do this quickly, without allowing
yourself to think too much about your responses. Let it come right
out. The majority of responses I hear have this component of fantasy
to them—I'd be happy, I'd have a wonderful, wealthy husband or
boyfriend, I'd have lots of friends, I'd feel great about myself, or I
wouldn't have any worries. Did any of your responses sound similar
to these? In general, doing this exercise can quickly help you realize
how illogically you're thinking and how these extreme beliefs really
have nothing to do with losing pounds. By taking control over your
thinking and behavior, working on your self-esteem, and including

prostress in your life, you're much more likely to, partly at least, make good headway on these goals. I have yet to talk to more than a handful of women who are satisfied with their bodies no matter how beautiful and sexy they are.

Society teaches and tantalizes. Advertisements use beautiful, thin women to sell their products with the implied promise that we will end up looking like the young beauty or, for ads targeting men, that they might have the chance to end up with one of these beautiful women as a "prize." To make matters worse, today's young, extremely thin models have gained the fame of superstars and are plastered on huge billboards and magazine covers. Women and men are impacted by these images and buy into the desirability of these distortions.

Your Upbringing and Your Eating Habits

Finally, we really do need to take a close look at an area that may be uncomfortable for you. One of the strongest influence on a woman's view of her body and whether or not she develops difficulties with food and weight comes from her own parents. One revealing study showed that when parents had an overweight daughter, they believed it was due to overeating or their emotional patterns and difficulties with peers. However, when their boys were overweight, parents didn't even believe these factors were relevant! The parents were also more controlling about getting their daughters to lose weight (Woody and Costanzo 1981).

Mothers can have a particularly strong impact on the view their daughters develop about their bodies and eating habits. If you're a mother who's dissatisfied with your own body and focus on dieting, you have to be very careful because these messages are easily passed on to your daughters. There is a strong relationship between (1) excessive concern about your body and other eating disorder characteristics, and (2) having had a mother who was dissatisfied with her own body.

Food as a Stress Reliever

Have you ever found yourself preparing for a big presentation at work and being unbearably, repetitively drawn to the kitchen and that big package of chocolate chip cookies? What about cramming for an important exam while you can't stop cramming the potato chips or peanut butter into your mouth? As you probably know all too well, food and eating problems aren't only sources of negative stress, they're also reactions to stress. Food is often used as a source of comfort. The result is compulsive overeating and binging way beyond the point of satiation.

Other women respond to stress by strictly limiting their food intake. Not eating and losing weight is an attempt to gain a sense of control over life when you feel a lack of security. Either way, such behaviors eventually control you and lead to a downward spiral into depression, disgust, self-loathing, and low self-esteem. It's extremely difficult to change this pattern if you don't have an alternative to replace it. Learning the relaxation tools in part 2 will offer some new ways to relieve your stress so that you won't have to use food.

Assessing Your Addictive Behavior

The above review of various addictions shows a number of similarities in personality characteristics and beliefs among women who develop addictions. Addictions can range from alcohol, drugs and food, to shopping, sex, work, exercise, gambling, and so on. There are often underlying commonalties with addiction, which is why programs based on certain principles, such as Alcoholics Anonymous, can be successful. Genetics play a role in the potential for developing alcoholism. However, physical factors aren't sufficient to determine whether a woman will or will not develop alcoholism. What also determines alcoholism, as with other addictions, is the impact of social and familial forces, personal experiences, and a woman's belief about herself and the world. There are many psychological reasons for why we develop addictions: poor self-esteem; feeling incomplete or less than; abuse or incest; shame and anxiety; or an overwhelming need for perfection and approval from others.

Any or all of these factors might be operating. I have worked with female clients suffering from many kinds of addiction. Two women I worked with had actually embezzled from their employers in order to support their shopping addictions. While we may tease each other good-naturedly about being shopping addicts, this can be a real problem. I remember both women describing feeling bewildered and ashamed when they ended up with closets full of clothes and shoes with labels still intact because they had never been worn. Other clients I've worked with have been battling anorexia and bulimia for years, often without their closest loved ones knowing. Others have been addicted to alcohol, cocaine, cigarettes, heroin, or even all of these substances. What's common among these women is an emptiness and painful sense of bewilderment and shame about behavior that initially they thought they could control, but that eventually completely controlled them. Actually, one of my clients, Karen, described this battle in a way I'll never forget. "I feel like an octopus. Every time I think I beat one addiction, another tentacle reaches out and grabs a new one." On the positive note, it's wonderful to see the relief when these women realize there is hope for them. With hard work and honesty with themselves and others, they can regain control over their lives, repair relationships, and become productive, proud individuals. Again, professional help, self-help groups, and stress management tools can be invaluable in helping break out of addictive, unhealthy patterns.

Self-Assessment Test

Ask yourself these questions if you've been worried about having some addictive behaviors like those described. Answer "yes" or "no" to the following statements:

- I tend to think about food and eating many times during the day. _____

- I feel good when I've been able to skip a meal. _____

- If I miss going to the gym for 1–2 days, I feel guilty. _____

- If I overeat, I can't wait to work it off by exercising a lot or not eating. _____

- When I'm feeling anxious, I feel the need to (one of the following):
  - Drink _____
  - Smoke cigarettes _____
  - Get high _____
  - Overexercise _____
  - Eat _____
  - Spend money _____

- I tend to get excited about buying a lot of things that I later return, regret having bought, or never use. _____

Do any of these seem characteristic of you? If so, it's likely to be an area eliciting negative stress in your life. Of course, this is only an informal method and cannot substitute for formal assessment and treatment if you have a serious problem. However, stress management and optimization will definitely prove useful as one method of taking back some control in your life and increasing your well-being.

7

Your Personality: Stress Resistance or Stress Vulnerability?

One of the hottest topics in scientific research has been the relationship between personality, beliefs, stress, and physical and mental health. Much effort has been devoted to studying how your emotions and beliefs, such as humor, empathy, anger, hostility, and optimism can affect your physical health. Your mental state leads to the release of certain neurotransmitters and other physical changes, which can directly affect your immune and other bodily systems. At the same time, changes in your physical functioning can determine your mood or state of mind.

Your Mental State and Your Health—the Connection

Initially, research into personality and illness tried to clarify specific personality types with specific physical illnesses. Cancer was thought to develop in people who reported hopelessness and who were unassertive or suppressed their emotions. Rheumatoid arthritis was thought to be linked with dependence, anxiety, and perfectionism. Such specific personality-illness associations are still the subject of debate. The most consistent evidence, however, shows a connection between heart disease and the psychological characteristics of anger, hostility, and responding negatively to stress. There's also evidence for a general disease-prone personality (Friedman and Booth-Kewley 1987). If you have personality characteristics such as anger, hostility, depression, and anxiety, you have a greater chance of becoming ill in general. What type of illness you could develop depends on things like your family history, individual vulnerabilities, lifestyle habits (smoking, exercise, drinking, and diet), economic status, ethnicity, your environment and medical treatment.

How Effective Do You Feel?

There are some personality traits or styles that impact how you perceive, experience, and are affected by stress, and whether you're likely to experience it as distress or prostress. One personality characteristic playing an important role in the stress process is your sense of efficacy, or effectiveness. If you believe you can be effective in a potentially stressful situation, you're less likely to experience distress than prostress. On the other hand, if you don't have much faith in your power and ability, you'll appraise situations as more negatively stressful. In this case, you might not choose the best coping techniques as you would have had you felt more calm and assured. You'll also experience more anxiety. As a result, you're more likely to experience the harmful consequences of stress, both physically and emotionally. However, a word to the wise—while confidence in your ability to have control can have many positive consequences, it's possible for such beliefs to be too extreme. If you struggle and try against all odds and in situations in which change is highly unlikely, negative stress can result. So, how can you win? You need to be able to appraise the situation realistically and determine whether it's one over which you may have some control.

Get in touch with your sense of effectiveness or personal competence because this can have an odd effect with respect to stress. If you're feeling low in personal competence, the generally stress-reducing impact of social support can backfire! Surprisingly, more support from friends when you're feeling low in personal effectiveness leads to *increased* stress vulnerability (Husaini, Neff, Newbrough, and Moore 1982). You may feel dependent because you're receiving outside help. Let's work through this example together so you can practice the cognitive tools to understand this situation. You can make sense of this reversal vis-à-vis social support by donning the irrational thinking and negative automatic thoughts' cap.

Imagine that you're experiencing a great deal of negative stress in your life at present and you're not feeling very confident about your ability to cope and make the changes you have wanted to for some time. A friend, loved one, or associate offers to help you in some way. Instead of feeling a lessening of negative stress, you feel depressed or angry. By this point in the book, you have hopefully learned to look beyond those triggering, tricky thoughts when you're *puzzled about your feelings or actions*. Think about past experiences and remember that offers of help usually make you feel relaxed and less anxious. This time is different. You're not feeling as confident as usual but you're now aware of the internal talk that made you interpret this generous gesture as a threat to your ego: "They pity me and my incompetence—it's down to them offering to help me out of this. It's obvious they think I can't handle this, or anything important for that matter, on my own." So, by your negative self-talk, which contributed to and is maintaining your feelings of low personal competence, you've taken a stress reducer and turned it into a threat to your ego. If people who care about you volunteer to help while you're feeling low, it's important that you put this into proper perspective and avoid automatically interpreting this negatively as more evidence of your weakness.

Optimism

Belief in your abilities is related to another important stress-related personality characteristic—optimism. There are all sorts of positive consequences linked with having an optimistic view of life and difficult situations. In Bernie Siegel's 1986 book, *Love, Medicine & Miracles*, he presents a study that showed that the ten year survival rate among cancer patients with a "fighting spirit" was 75 percent as opposed to the 22 percent survival rate among patients who expressed passive acceptance, hopelessness, or helplessness.

Being optimistic is related to how you cope with problems. Optimists tend to take a problem-focused approach toward resolving difficult situations and handling stress, while others tend to ignore or avoid resolving problems. The distinction is important because this type of problem-focused coping is often associated with good physical and psychological consequences.

The Placebo Effect

Having an optimistic perspective also has a direct, positive effect on your health. One of the clearest ways to see the psychological impact on physical health is through studying the effects of placebos. Placebos are substances that people believe will help them with a physical or psychological problem but are actually nothing but "sugar pills," or the suggestion of help. Even the mere thought that help is available affects people positively. Placebos with no "real" medical effects have been found to be more effective than "real" medications specifically designed to cure a particular physical problem. For example, sugar pills have been used to successfully relieve everything from headaches and toothaches to asthma and generalized pain. Never underestimate the power of your mind! One of the ways optimism works to improve your health is through boosting your immune system. Robert Ornstein and David Sobel, in their book *Healthy Pleasures*, describe a study of cardiac patients undergoing surgery. Patients defined as optimists had better physical functioning during the surgery and recovered more rapidly than pessimists. Pessimists were actually found to have deficits in immune functioning. Optimism also affects how you perceive, explain, and recall events in your life. Optimists anticipate as well as recall more positive interactions, which means that overall, they're more frequently in a positive state of mind and mood. It isn't surprising then that how optimistic you are also impacts your long-term health and mortality. People who expect to be healthy in the future tend to remain so when compared to those who don't. Even more striking is that people who expect to be in good health and report they are healthy *even when their doctors report that they are unhealthy* survive at higher rates than expected. So, your beliefs and optimism about your health, not necessarily only the "reality" of your current physical state, have much to do with your health down the road.

Hardiness: Commitment, Control, and Challenge

In 1979, Suzanne Kobasa coined the term "hardiness" to describe people who, even when exposed to very negatively stressful situations and conditions, don't suffer the usual negative psychological and physical consequences. Hardiness is composed of three personality characteristics: commitment, control, and challenge.

Commitment

Being committed means you're curious about the environment, interpret situations as meaningful, and are involved in various activities. Whether or not you feel committed and experience both your environment and your self as interesting and satisfying depends largely on your childhood experiences. When parents react with approval and interest to a child's attempts to satisfy her needs and fulfill her abilities, she's more likely to develop a sense of commitment. Unfortunately, there are subtle ways that parents can be unsupportive and interfere with their child's development of commitment to herself and the world. If a particularly physical, active little girl has parents who disapprove of this "unladylike" behavior and reward her only for signs of emotional sensitivity, she may conform to their expectations at the expense of her true nature. Not only is this a waste of true capabilities and interests, but the denial of one's true self leads to problems down the road.

Control

If you generally believe you can impact events through your knowledge, abilities, and decisions, you rate positively on the second hardiness element, control. This is somewhat comparable to the sense of self-efficacy described earlier. As with commitment, one of the most important factors in determining whether you'll grow up with a sense of control over events is how you were raised. Adults who have a sense of control had parents who weren't critical and who both *expected* and *encouraged* them to be independent at a younger age. The responsibilities and tasks that the parents expected weren't overly difficult but were within the bounds of their abilities so they could experience mastery rather than just failure. Parents who are overprotective and only allow their daughters to be involved in simple, easily obtained goals are doing a disservice. These children will often grow up feeling powerless.

Challenge

The last characteristic of hardiness is one that many of my female clients seem to struggle with. This involves having a challenge orientation and seeing change rather than stability as a positive thing. Having this perspective is central to decreasing the distress and increasing the prostress in your life. The degree to which someone sees change as challenging rather than distressing is associated with how much change they experienced as children and whether this change was experienced as exciting or chaotic. Parents play a major role in this process because how they view change, whether as threatening or as exciting or positive, is communicated to the child.

Think back to your own early years. Were the conditions for you to develop commitment, control, and challenge available? If you have your own children, are you providing them with the conditions to help them develop these prostress-building healthy characteristics?

The Locus of Control

People with an *internal locus of control* see themselves as having the power and ability to control many events in their lives. Those with an *external locus of control* have a passive orientation and believe that things happen to them because of uncontrollable external events. As you might expect, having an internal locus of control allows you to better handle negative stress, which, in turn, directly impacts your psychological and physical health. An external locus of control is associated with tendencies toward depression. Studies by the National Cancer Institute show that assertive patients who take control and play a more active role regarding their illnesses (i.e., an internal locus of control) have a greater number of T cells (white cells that destroy cancerous cells) when compared to passive patients who just listen to and accept what doctors tell them.

Sadly, many of us women do have a lesser sense of internal control. This difference is present very early in our lives. For example, when girls fail, they tend to blame it on themselves and long-standing internal factors such as inability. Boys, on the other hand, blame their failure on external factors, such as the teacher, or on internal factors that are only temporary and actually can be under their control, such as lack of effort. These male-associated approaches serve to better protect the old ego. Gender-linked attributional styles have different important consequences. When people are given feedback, those who use external attributions (i.e., more often males) work harder to improve their performance. When feedback is given to internalizers (i.e., more often females), they tend to experience helplessness and decreased performance. These differences continue into adulthood. Women may rate other people's control over a particular task as higher than their own, whereas men don't (Martin, Abramson, and Alloy 1984). Given the different levels of control in the workplace, family, and elsewhere, is it any surprise that many of us have developed a general tendency to believe we have less control over our lives and environment? Hopefully, our society will increasingly encourage young girls to follow their own interests, participate in competitive "male" sports, be assertive, independent, and curious, and plan for so-called "male" careers if they desire. Perhaps then these distress-enhancing and prostress-decreasing perceptions on the part of women will change.

"Type As" and Distress

Media hype together with well-researched and -written articles about Type A individuals have proliferated over the last decade. While I'm not fond of labeling, there do seem to be some real mental and physical differences between "Type As" and others ("Type Bs"). Type As tend to perceive and so experience more negative stress in their lives. They can also develop physical problems, most notably coronary heart disease (CHD). Type As are described as impatient, competitive, ambitious, hostile, and excessively focused on time. Do you feel these characteristics match your personality style? Do you find yourself speaking rapidly and loudly, having tense muscles or body aches, and feeling restless at work and at home? Do you speed through life at a mile a minute, performing everyday activities quickly and doing several things at once? Given the fact that you're reading this book, I suspect I'm not too far off the mark in saying that some, or even all of these characteristics, resonate with you. Type As have also been described as being engaged in a chronic struggle to control their environments. I've written quite a bit about how believing you can control and trying to control situations can be prostress and health-enhancing and now I'm writing that it's unhealthy? The distinction here is very important—remember that prostress involves situations in which the demands and abilities are fairly matched. That is, you get involved in things that you can actually change, produce, or have an effect on. You look at this as a challenge, not a desperate necessity—these are two central elements that make *stress healthy* (prostress). You cannot try endlessly to exert control over uncontrollable situations and perceive the inevitable failure as threatening. This destructive pattern places you on a fast path to excessive negative stress and the resulting negative physical and psychological problems. Type A behavior is seen in people predisposed to respond in this way when faced with triggering stressful situations.

Type As (this refers to "unhealthy" Type As; the distinction will soon be clarified) show particular patterns with respect to stress and this is where we can learn what *not* to do! Type As see situations as more negatively stressful. They also seek out distressful situations and even tend to create more distress. For a clear visual display, you can refer back to chapter 1 for the "You Have a Choice Model" and Type As.

A Type A woman, for example, might take on an ever increasing workload or more responsibilities at home, work, church, or as a volunteer. She thinks, consciously or subconsciously, that this will show others her specialness, strength, and "goodness." This behavior also helps her soothe her own low self-esteem and insecurities. Unfortunately, this also increases the negative stress in her life. She makes it even worse by trying to complete her now excessive workload by herself, resisting others' offers to help. Living at this fast pace, burning the candle at both ends, and experiencing greater distress than a situation realistically warrants takes a toll on psychological and physical health. It isn't surprising that there's a great deal of research showing that Type As suffer from more psychological problems, such as depression and anxiety, as well as physical problems.

The realm of Type A behavior is yet another one in which most of the research has been conducted on men. It's clear, though, that women also exhibit this pattern. We can react just as excessively and with the same unhealthy physical arousal to minor incidents. Although Type A women describe themselves as being more self-confident and achieving high-level occupations, they also report stress symptoms and dissatisfaction with work, life accomplishments, and marriage (Matthews 1982). Traffic lights, boring meetings, arguments with husbands or boyfriends, broken copy machines, long lines—they're truly the enemy, the "charging lions and rhinos" for the Type As of our day.

Type As and the Gender Gap

There are two gender differences we should really take note of with respect to Type A behavior. First, in Cary L. Cooper's 1983 book, *Stress Research: Issues for the Eighties*, he has frightening evidence that Type A working women are twice as likely to develop coronary heart disease as men. He suggests that even in families where the husbands "intellectually" support their wives working, few either truly psychologically or practically (like helping with chores) support them. Another study supports two contentions emphasized throughout this book; namely, that men and women experience different events as distressors (MacDougall, Dembroski, and Krantz 1981). These researchers showed that exposing Type A women to the usual laboratory stressors didn't produce the different cardiovascular arousal effects between Type A and Type B women as it did between Type A and Type B men. Now, when the stressor was switched to involve social interaction and competition, the expected elevated arousal of Type A versus Type B women was seen.

The second type of stressor, involving socializing and competing, was much more important to women. This probably isn't very surprising to you, particularly if you recall the previous discussion about the central importance of interpersonal relationships and social support to women. Furthermore, as women we were often taught to avoid aggression and competition, and enacting such behavior can certainly make us undergo conflict and heightened distress as it did particularly to the highly reactive Type A women.

Self-Assessment

The unhealthy Type A is not really a personality type. Rather, it's a set of behavioral and cognitive patterns. This distinction is important because it implies that you can change these patterns and move away from this harmful negative stress-creating way of being. Take a look at the following list to see how you rate with respect to the Type A behavioral pattern.

Check the following statements that apply to you:

- I feel that if I just try hard and long enough, no problem is beyond my control.   _____

- I often find myself doing more than one thing at a time.   _____

- I feel guilty if I "waste time" doing "nothing" like relaxing, reading, etc.   _____

- I'm always in a race with the clock.   _____

- I always strive for perfection.   _____

- I feel that if I don't complete a task myself, it really won't be done properly.   _____

- I try to do more and more in briefer amounts of time.   _____

- I always say "yes" to projects/requests because this shows other people that I'm special, competent, and superior.   _____

- I often speak rapidly and interrupt others or try to finish their sentences.   _____

- I always want to win when playing a game or sport.   _____

- I think that much of my success and superiority comes from my ability to work faster than others.   _____

- I see others as working too slowly or wasting a lot of time.   _____

- I frequently become very annoyed or irritated over minor frustrations.   _____

- People tell me I'm too impatient.   _____

- I get frustrated when I have to wait in line or stop at a red light.   _____

- I walk, move, and eat rapidly.   _____

Most people usually have at least several of these characteristics. However, the more that are representative of your actions and thoughts, the greater the likelihood that you have a tendency toward Type A thinking and behaving and resulting difficulties dealing with stress.

Balance Is the Key

Most discussions of Type As end here; that is, with a statement concluding that having the Type A behavioral pattern inevitably leads to experiencing great negative stress and harmful consequences on the mind and body. I like to take this, instead, as a starting point. Remember my "battle cry": Stress management is self management and balance is the name of the game. Some of my research and that of others has taken a different look at the Type A phenomenon. The traditional idea of a single unhealthy Type A is inaccurate. There are *subtypes* of Type As: some may be hostile and angry; others mostly time-pressured; some primarily achievement-oriented; and so on. Most importantly, some Type As don't fit the stereotypes and are actually psychologically and physically healthy. Rather than experiencing frustration or depression from a constant pressured drive (these are the "unhealthy" Type As referred to previously), these exceptional people thrive on their fast-paced, challenging lifestyles. You can see healthy Type As differing from unhealthy Type As in their: hostility, anger, irritability, ego strength, and emotional expressiveness. I believe the most crucial difference to be *how you use your mind.* Is it the lock or is it the key? Remember that the meaning you give the potentially stressful event determines how you respond and experience the situation. Typically, Type As are threatened by situations that they view as beyond their control or as a threat to their abilities or self-esteem. However, healthy Type As use healthy self-management and see many situations as challenges and growth opportunities. These people are using their minds as "keys" to free themselves from distress and instead experience prostress and grow in new ways. This difference may well explain why healthy As experience fewer of the psychological and physical problems than the "typical" Type A. In a study I conducted recently, I found that Type As with good ego strength experience events as pleasurable more often and rate events as less negatively stressful than Type As with less ego strength. With greater ego strength, they are probably less likely to be threatened by and insecure about events in their lives and so do not perceive situations so negatively. By giving different meanings to the same events, they can respond to them as challenges and opportunities rather than as threats to be avoided or endured. Not being so frequently angry, irritable, or frustrated allows them to experience more joy and pleasure in their lives. When you feel secure and good about yourself, you'll be more able to enjoy life and tackle opportunities you might otherwise have avoided. The less distress and fear in your life, the more time and energy available to grow and follow your dreams.

Personality and the Physical Link

Physical patterns of arousal show how personality styles and stress are linked. Joel Robertson and Tom Monte, in their 1996 book, *Peak-Performance Living*, point out that certain underlying physical patterns can be seen in people who are exceedingly ambitious and driven to work in an ever increasing spiral of quantity and speed. Certain neurotransmitters, notably dopamine and norepinephrine, have an excitatory influence on the mind and body. Overly ambitious individuals can have high levels of these neurotransmitters. These substances can be beneficial because they assist your creativity, productiveness, and excitability. High levels of neurotransmitters help generate thoughts and ideas at a rapid, seemingly effortless pace. However, there's danger here because if you're someone intent on pushing yourself ever harder and faster, Robertson and Monte warn that you can actually become hooked on the physical and psychological benefits of high neurotransmission speed. If you're one of these individuals, you probably currently or eventually will find it impossible to relax, focus, concentrate, sleep, or deal in a tolerant way with obstacles or other people. You'll crave the hectic stressful lifestyle and feel uncomfortable if forced to move at a slower, relaxed pace. Do these characteristics resonate with you? If so, the techniques in this book are an absolute necessity for you.

While slow neurotransmission can be invaluable in allowing one to concentrate, problem-solve, and focus on details, excessively slow neurotransmission can be as unhealthy as excessively high neurotransmission. As you might expect, people experiencing this imbalance are often depressed, lethargic, passive, and unmotivated. Just another example of the essence of stress management; that is, balance is the key to a healthy state. In this case, the resolution lies in being flexible and obtaining a balance between rapid and slow neurotransmission. Each is essential depending on what type of task or activity you're faced with at a particular time. The good news is that there are measures you can take to modify the speed of neurotransmission to help you obtain your goals and meet situational demands. You'll learn about these techniques, which include diet and exercise, in part 2.

Women and Self-Esteem

Do you find that you feel destroyed or diminished when someone gives you a minor slight, suggests you do something differently, or doesn't give you what you perceive as sufficient praise and acknowledgment? If you overreact to such minor events, it's possible that you are too dependent on validation from others to derive your self-esteem. Self-esteem is another personality variable that is key to how women experience stress. Higher levels of self-esteem increase your confidence in your ability to deal with stress. People with high self-esteem report less negative work stress and fewer unhealthy psychological and physical distress consequences than people with low self-esteem. Having positive rather than negative beliefs about yourself reduces the experience of distressors in marriage, parenting, finances, and work (Pearlin and Schooler 1978). Thus, you can see how utterly essential it is to have good self-esteem. Recall the importance of feeling mastery and control to increase prostress and decrease distress. In this scheme, women frequently rate themselves lower than do men. The same seems true with self-esteem. This is an undesirable situation for us because self-esteem can serve as a powerful distress buffer and prostress booster. So, if you're like the huge number of women in our culture with difficulties in valuing and loving yourself, you'll benefit greatly from learning the self-esteem tactics in part 2.

Development of Self-Esteem: Your Past Experiences

The basis for our self-esteem stems from our early childhood experiences and is further shaped by later experiences of acceptance, rejection, success, or failure. Feeling valued and loved by your family is essential in developing positive self-esteem. If one or both parents are blessed with a baby girl but wanted a baby boy, this message is generally communicated, if not verbally, then at least nonverbally to the child. The child who picks up this message of being less desirable is prone to develop a poor self-image, low self-esteem, and depression. Dr. Karen Johnson, in her thoughtful, enlightening 1991 book, *Trusting Ourselves*, writes of the disturbing fact that recent surveys indicate many parents still prefer male children to female children. Dr. Johnson's book also summarizes the results of a University of Colorado survey that clearly reveals how powerfully and thoroughly societal and family values and norms impact children. Two thousand children in grade three through twelve were asked to describe their feelings about being changed into the opposite gender. Boys described a terrible situation using the words "nightmare" and "disaster." One boy succinctly stated that if he were a girl, then everybody else would be better because boys were better than girls. On the other hand, girls generally stated that their lives would be better if they were boys because they would have greater freedom, status, self-worth, and value in the eyes of their parents. Messages from society, peers, and family impact the growing girl's developing self-esteem. Although patterns in schools are changing, many academic settings still give boys attention for speaking out and being active, while girls are expected to be obedient and quiet. What helps build self-esteem is being given the chance to meet challenges in your life. It's inevitable that sometimes you will succeed and sometimes you will not. However, both experiences are important in developing an accurate view of yourself and in believing in your efforts and strengths. Girls can miss out on this when they're not given as many of these opportunities to struggle and risk failure or garner success.

Adolescence

During adolescence, females receive increasingly intense messages about who they should be and how they should act. There's a great deal of discomfort regarding a girl's sexual development into womanhood. Messages received by young women are frequently restrictive and demeaning and can continue to damage a young girl's self-esteem. A teen sees the media's portrayal of a "real woman" as beautiful, sexy, and thin. Not only are these characteristics superficial, but they're often far out of reach for most girls. How is she to respond to such impossible expectations? All too often these days, she focuses inordinate time and energy on obtaining these superficial goals and blames herself for being weak when unable to do so.

Young women are also sent contradictory messages. While the sexy woman gets admiration and attention in our society, young girls and women are bombarded with rules and judgments about what "good" girls do and do not do. Additionally, many young women continue to lack the support and positive feedback with respect to pursuing activities and interests most highly valued in our society, which just so happen to belong to men and so are off-limits.

Aging

The inequities and messages affecting self-esteem continue as women age. In a society where we're valued for youth and beauty, many of us become extremely distressed when the pounds creep on and we become host to the inevitable wrinkles. I imagine that the face of the marketplace would look quite different if our society's values for women could be changed. What would become of the cosmetics industries, companies researching products to stop or "reverse" aging, doctors competing within the plastic surgery arena to do the best pulling-up, tucking-in, pushing-out, adding, or subtracting? We've all heard elderly men described as distinguished and as having character, while mature women are just described as "old." Studies show that, for many women, their self-esteem is heavily influenced by their perception of physical attractiveness. This is really an area in which we don't have to turn to studies for understanding. Most of us know these pressures, negative stressors, and secrets with an overwhelmingly painful intimacy.

The Danger of Pursuing Superficial Goals

There are a number of problems inherent in deriving self-worth from all of these superficial attributes. First of all, superficial achievements have nothing to do with the internal quality and value of the person herself. Secondly, feedback regarding whether or not you are attractive must come from others. Thus, many of us get caught in a cycle of searching for positive feedback from external sources and, when we don't received such feedback, we feel worthless. One of my female clients, Elizabeth, had a pet phrase to explain her view of women and aging: "After you're fifty, there's just really nothing left." She had been very attractive when young and had successfully competed in beauty pageants beginning at the age of three! Her mother spent a tremendous amount of money and time teaching her how to act like a lady, dress appropriately, exhibit good manners, and so on. As she entered adulthood, she dabbled a bit in modeling and the theater. She had a number of beaus and thrived on the attention from men and women. Not having built any other meaning in her life or having developed any internally generated self-respect for herself as a person, it wasn't surprising that, as she aged, she became depressed. She had no internal motivation or knowledge of how to be an active, interesting, or interested person. It was a rocky road for Elizabeth, but she was eventually able to find meaning and satisfaction from her life. She began involving herself in activities, making new life changes like long- and short-term goals, developing some of her skills into a lucrative business, joining a hiking club, and including other prostress events into her day-to-day activities.

Finally, another danger with getting caught in the beauty race is that there are always other women out there who are more beautiful, more slender, more youthful, more whatever! Continuous comparisons with these "competitors" inevitably causes distress and frustration. We're really derailing our efforts to become more healthy by getting sucked into the superficial external race. Unfortunately, too many women find that relentlessly climbing the corporate ladder, losing ever increasing amounts of weight, perfecting themselves through plastic surgery, or catching the perfect man don't fill the void inside. These outside things simply can't do that. We must struggle to get in touch with the cause of our dissatisfaction and self-doubt. True acceptance and self-love are the only ways out of this vicious cycle.

The second section of this book offers suggestions and techniques for clarifying your values and goals, changing unrealistic beliefs, and building your self-esteem. Self-examination will also help you see how you view yourself, others, and the world. The distress that arises from certain personality styles is largely determined by specific patterns involving how you think and behave. The resolution then is to change thinking patterns and behavior. What the personality patterns discussed in this chapter point out is the importance of obtaining balance in your life. Doing more and getting more is not always more desirable—establishing a sense of excitement, challenge, and satisfaction is. Working on these areas of your life and yourself will prove invaluable in helping you decrease negative stress in your life and let you revel in the excitement and fulfillment available to us all.

Part II

Your Guide to Optimizing Stress

It's now time to move into part 2. Here you'll actively learn techniques and tools to help you optimize stress (i.e., reduce distress and increase prostress). As you've learned, it isn't possible to state across the board that women are more vulnerable to stressors. You must figure into the equation the type of stressor, the nature and interaction of your many roles, your health, lifestyle, and social support; as well as internal characteristics like your expectations, beliefs, and personality traits. The methods in part 2 have proven successful for many people—both men and women—in learning how to manage and optimize stress. Because of the differences in women's experience of stress, I have tailored these techniques and methods to suit women when necessary. The emphasis is on aspects of stress particularly relevant to women. The exercises and examples given are consistent with experiences you and I face each day.

8

How to Be Stress-Wise

You can experience prostress when you're actively involved in a situation you perceive as challenging, interesting, or important, and as offering the opportunity for having some control. Stress-wise means being open to and even actively seeking these potential stressors and that you can interpret these situations as positive and growth-promoting. Such experiences are central to our physical and mental growth. In their 1989 book, *Healthy Pleasures*, Robert Ornstein and David Sobel discuss ways to live with stress that enrich, rather than just maintain or damage, mental and physical health. This can be done through mobilizing positive beliefs, expectations, and emotions. The main idea of their approach, the "Pleasure Principle," is based on the idea that the brain and body have been designed to seek and respond to satisfying sensations—from eating to reproduction to caring for others. Although this wouldn't surprise most people, the idea that pleasure can guide people to better health might. This is the very reason that I have written this book—I want to convey that prostress, a positive, stimulating, and challenging experience, can make you feel better and live better. Perspectives such as these are a far cry from the predominant message these days that "if it feels or tastes good, or is fun or pleasurable, it's got to be bad for you." This isn't true, which is great news for you if you have a sincere desire to improve your well-being and satisfaction with life. Remember, people who are physically and mentally healthiest and the least distressed aren't afraid of:

- Stress

- Expressing their needs

- Experiencing their emotions

- Eating

- Drinking

- Doing nothing

- Being silly

- Showing their vulnerability

- Asking questions or rocking the boat

Obviously, blindly seeking out and creating stress isn't the answer either. The best way to live a full, happy, and healthy life involves the ability to balance your life, be flexible and embrace change, and be stress-wise.

Your health isn't only or, in some case, even primarily determined by your genes, but by your thoughts—which *you can change*. If indeed pleasure and being positive are the keys to good mental and physical health and well-being, what's the problem here? Why don't we all go about naturally pursuing and enjoying, guilt-free, pleasurable events? Our culture is so heavily focused on work, production, and not wasting time, that we feel guilty about taking time for pleasure, enjoyment, or doing things that don't lead directly to productivity. This is especially true for us as women because we have so many conflicting demands, all of which we believe we must satisfy "perfectly," except for our own needs.

Stress-positive people can enjoy small, simple pleasures, such as watching the sun rise or set, enjoying a garden, or playing with your pets. There's an interesting dynamic at work when we look at how people rate and experience pleasure or unhappiness in their lives. There are many people who have prestigious jobs and all of the material goods they have ever wanted—everything they thought would make them finally and completely happy. Why, then, they ask themselves, aren't they? Because, like the majority of us, they judge their status in life on an ever changing scale of unrealistic standards. There are always others who will have more or do more, so it's unlikely we'll ever be able to be "the most" or "the best." For example, you could have a wonderful job and be earning a good salary, but if you compare this salary to that of your friends, you could suddenly feel quite unhappy and distressed. Remember, it's your thoughts that determine your feelings and if you tell yourself that you are less than others, you'll end up feeling depressed, insecure, and worthless. Once you're aware of this human tendency to compare, you can monitor this behavior and put a stop to it. Do you really need to compare yourself to others if you're pleased with what you're doing? Allow yourself to feel satisfaction, peace, and enjoyment. It's the simplest of old truths: The grass always looking greener on the other side.

Optimizing the Stress In Your Life: Day-To-Day Pleasures

It seems that what's most important in determining satisfaction and pleasure aren't the extreme, rare, happy events, but rather everyday prostress activities and pleasurable events. However, in response to today's societal values, most of us feel driven to be very wealthy, powerful, attractive. But, it's actually the day-to-day pleasant events we experience that are most important for our psychological and physical well-being. Take a lesson from lottery winners who are certainly much happier right after learning of their success, but who, only one year later, don't rate themselves as much happier than they were before winning millions of dollars. These people have lost the ability to find pleasure in daily activities and day-to-day life. Here again we see the consequences of expectations shifting upward as a result of comparisons. With their millions, these lucky few expected to be perfectly happy and free. When this didn't happen and buying houses, sports cars, and vacations didn't do the trick, they once again became unsatisfied.

While this news isn't so good for lottery winners and millionaires, it's very good for the rest of us. *Your happiness is determined by how much of the time you spend feeling good* rather than from momentary peaks of extreme pleasure (Diener and Emmons 1984). This is why it's so important that you experience prostress often in your life. Next time you tell yourself that you don't have time to go for a hike, do some painting, work on writing your children's book, or cook a gourmet meal, reconsider this snap judgment that has been dictated by a driven society and that isn't in your best interest. Actually, making certain that you schedule or spontaneously include enough pleasure and excitement in your life doesn't sound all that bad, does it?

What If Everyone Chose Prostress?

Imagine the savings to companies if workers were sent through a stress management seminar or if jobs were designed with stress management in mind. For instance, recall that a great deal of distress is felt in jobs with significant ambiguity or repetitive work with little opportunity for control or inadequate resources to meet demands. Figures from 1993 showed that in terms of absenteeism, reduced productivity, and workers' comp benefits, negative stress costs American industry more than $300 billion annually or $7,500 per worker per year. More recent figures are higher. For example

- 43 percent of all adults suffer negative health effects from stress.

- 75–90 percent of all physician office visits are for stress-related disturbances.

- Stress is linked with the six leading causes of death: heart disease; cancer; lung problems; accidents; cirrhosis of the liver; and suicide.

Remember that stress is a transactional process. This means that stressors in the environment impact you but that you also impact the environment by creating stressful interactions. You're actively involved by how you tend to perceive events—that is, either distressing or challenging. For example, plunging out of an airplane at 5,000 feet would be absolutely terrifying and distressing for most people. However, an experienced skydiver would perceive this as an exciting challenge. Why the different response? Because of different *perception* of the situation—the skydiver has experience, knows how to control the situation to some degree, and feels confident and competent. The little voice in her head tells her she can handle this and so she can see the situation as possibly even fun, and so experiences prostress. Because of this she'll be protected from suffering the harmful consequences of distress and will capitalize on the healthy consequences of prostress.

Distress or Prostress—It's Up to You

So what does this mean for you here and now? It means that depending upon your background, experience, and how you choose to perceive a situation, you can have control over choosing either threatening negative stress or challenging prostress. So, while it's true that stress is inevitable and even necessary, how you manage and perceive it so that it's experienced as positive or negative, healthy or harmful, is largely up to you.

The questions you want to ask when working on managing your stress go beyond merely asking whether stress is good or bad. Instead, you need to pay attention to *how much* and *what types of stress* you're exposed to. Also think about the way you perceive, think about, and react to stress. All of the energy you typically expend on overreacting to situations and on the resulting physical and psychological problems can be freed and made available to you. You can then use this time and energy to learn, grow, and finally make those positive changes in your life you've been putting off for months or years. One pattern I see constantly while hosting workshops and doing therapy is that of women arriving feeling drained, helpless, and hopeless. Gradually, as they begin to understand they can always have some control, if not always over situations, at least over how they choose to react, they begin feeling more optimistic, hopeful, and energetic. Rather than just wanting to withdraw or being chaotically reactive, they choose to confront situations and become proactive with their best interests in mind. The following tools and techniques will help you develop and use this control to maximize your pro-stress, physical and mental health, and enjoyment of life.

Stress-Management Techniques

There are various ways you can intervene in the stress process You can work to change

- The antecedent events (events leading to your behaviors and experiences of distress).
- The consequent events (events following your behaviors).
- The behaviors themselves.

Here is a simple example. Say you feel negatively stressed from the conflict over whether or not to have an ice cream sundae whenever you're in an ice cream parlor. The simplest way to reduce such distress might be to change the antecedent event and stay out of places of temptation. Obviously, this isn't a complex example and, in actuality, changing the antecedent event isn't always possible or even desirable. For example, if you experience distress at social functions, it isn't best that you choose to completely and forever avoid such events. In this case, the third strategy, modifying your behavior and your thinking, could be best. You'd work on developing social skills through visualization, role playing, and modifying any negative thinking. You could then enter social situations feeling relaxed with heightened self-esteem, rather than feeling weaker or negative about yourself as would have been the case had you chosen to forever avoid such situations.

Let's look briefly at an example of the second option, changing consequences of your stress-related behaviors—say, smoking and eating unhealthily. Both of these directly increase your level of distress and can also be behaviors we use to unsuccessfully cope with negative stress. If you give yourself a reward after not performing the behavior (i.e., not smoking a cigarette or not gulping down several desserts), you increase the chances that your desired behavior change will stick. Many of the following stress-management techniques discussed will fall into one or more of these types.

How to Use Part 2

Part 2 is broken down into general categories. They are changing your diet and exercise patterns, physical techniques, cognitive (thought-related) techniques, and behavioral changes such as increasing prostress and modifying coping skills. You'll also learn other stress- and self-management tools essential for women, including communication skills, time management, and assertiveness training. The best way to use this book is to go straight through each subsequent section, doing the suggested exercises and recording your efforts and progress when applicable.

Because stress is a holistic phenomenon, I'm presenting stress management in the same light. Both your mind and body will be used to help you achieve the optimal balance of stress. It's inevitable that you will have strengths and weaknesses in different areas and will find some techniques more useful than others. However, it's best to work through all of the exercises. Some require more practice and time to adopt than others, so make sure to give them an adequate chance in order to derive their full benefits. Eventually, you'll become a stress expert rather than the stress-mess-of-old. You'll find yourself incorporating these tools automatically and effortlessly into your life. The quality of your life and physical and mental health will be far superior to when you began this journey.

Stress Evaluation

Stress management is, in essence, self management. Situations do not by themselves cause you to feel stress, anxiety, frustration, anger, or depression. Contrary to what most of us think, it's what you say to yourself (i.e., your self-talk or thoughts) that lead to your feelings. By learning cognitive techniques to change your way of thinking and physical tools to train your body to respond differently, you can dramatically reduce the negative stress and increase the prostress in your life. Recent research continues to confirm the importance of prostress to your physical and mental health, happiness, growth, and fulfillment. The following questionnaire will show, in a quantifiable way, how this book's stress optimizing tools and techniques have helped you. In addition, you'll be able to see clearly what areas you need to work on.

Below you will find a questionnaire to track your progress in stress manage-ment. Please rate each category: once before you begin the exercises in part 2, and again after you have completed the book and are fairly proficient with these exercises.

0	1 2	3 4	5 6
Not	Mildly	Moderately	Extremely
Bothersome	Bothersome	Bothersome	Bothersome

	Before Stress Management Techniques	After Familiarity and Practice of Stress Manage-ment Techniques
Low self-esteem		
Insomnia		
Excessive sleeping		
Generalized anxiety		
Anxiety around people		
Anxiety in meetings or test-taking		
Anxiety with public speaking		
Lack of pleasure in life		
Procrastination		
Anxiety about socializing		
Unexplainable feelings of dissatisfaction		
Depression		
Loneliness		
Living in the past or future		
Hopelessness		

	Before Stress Management Techniques	After Familiarity and Practice of Stress Management Techniques
Helplessness		
Irritability		
Frustration		
Anger		
Impatience		
Feeling you must do more than one thing at a time		
Difficulty in making decisions		
Poor concentration		
Forgetfulness		
Fears		
Obsessive thoughts		
Overeating		
Undereating		
Excessive alcohol or drug use (including prescription drugs)		
Frequent colds		
Fatigue		
Headaches		
Muscle tension		
High blood pressure		
Arthritis		
Fibromyalgia		
Irritable bowel		
Ulcers		
Shakes/tremors		
Heartburn		

Please rate each category, before and after your self-management training, on the following scale:

0	1	2	3	4	5	6
Unsatisfactory	Mildly Satisfactory		Moderately Satisfactory		Extremely Satisfactory	

	Before Stress Management Techniques	After Familiarity and Practice of Stress Management Techniques
Life satisfaction	_____	_____
Productivity	_____	_____
Mental well-being	_____	_____
Physical well-being	_____	_____

Complete this questionnaire now. When you take the questionnaire for the second time after you've become proficient at minimizing distress and maximizing prostress, I'm sure you'll be very happy and possibly quite surprised at the results.

Please list your most troublesome, frequent hassles. As you learn the stress-management tools, remember to apply them to changing your interpretations of or reducing the frequency of these events. When you get to keeping your Prostress Diary in chapter 13, refer back to this list to make sure you're increasing the prostressors and decreasing the distressors in your life.

Daily Hassles

_____

_____

_____

_____

_____

9

Habits: The Good, the Bad, and the Ugly

Walk into any bookstore and you'll be overwhelmed by the huge number of diet books all promoting the latest panacea guaranteed to make you slender, lower your cholesterol, increase your energy, calm you down, up your sex drive, prolong your life, and, why not, maybe even let you in on the meaning of life. What is so bewildering is that the authors of these books propose differing and even contradictory diets. No protein, all protein, no carbohydrates, primarily carbohydrates, all soup, all fruit, and so on. If you're one of the millions of American women concerned with your weight, you've doubtless tried any number of diets, each time hoping that this one would be the one. It's very difficult for us to know who to trust and which plan to follow. You can take heart in that there are certain basic elements upon which most nutritionists agree. I hope to clearly and simply communicate these to you in this chapter.

Why is this subject important in learning to self-manage stress? Because the physical and mental tools you'll learn can be either improved upon or interfered with by your diet. The relationship between eating and the stress process is a complex one. What you eat can increase your negative stress level both directly and indirectly. On the other hand, smart food choices can increase your body's ability to tolerate stress. When your body is experiencing stress, its nutritional requirements change. When and how you eat can also help or hinder your body's responses to stress. Furthermore, as discussed in chapter 6, food and eating are major distressors for the many women who are excessively concerned about weight and body image. Food can even be used as an unhealthy attempt to cope with stress through eating disorders.

Caffeine and Sugar

Many of us who exhibit the most extreme physical reactions to stress do so because we eat in such a way that our bodies cannot maintain a balanced level of nutrients (McKinney and White 1985). In the United States where there's an abundance of food compared to most other countries, a shocking 60 percent to 70 percent of what we consume doesn't provide us with good nutrition. This is because most of us don't eat enough fresh, natural foods and instead depend on overly processed foods crawling with chemicals and preservatives (this may not sound like your favorite snack but in all probability it could be quite close). Refined sugar and fats devoid of nutrients make up the bulk of our diets.

Certain foods create too much wear and tear on our bodies by propelling it into a negative stress response or by overusing its detoxification system. The two main culprits used excessively in the United States are, not surprisingly, sugar and caffeine. If you feel perpetually wound up, stressed out, jittery, restless, unable to relax or sleep and have a racing heart and don't suffer from a medical condition causing such symptoms, you're probably using a great deal of caffeine and sugar.

Caffeine

Just what's so bad about caffeine, after all, it's legal, isn't it? It may be legal, but it's the quickest road to increased distress. Caffeine is present in many substances, such as colas, some teas, coffee, and our all-time favorite drug of choice—chocolate. Substances containing caffeine are called sympathomimetics because they imitate sympathetic nervous system activity (the nicotine in cigarettes is also a sympathomimetic). Remember from chapter 1 that it's the sympathetic nervous system that activates your body's response to stress. Caffeine revs up the nervous, heart, and respiratory systems and causes the release of adrenaline. Not only does caffeine stimulate the stress response, but it also makes the nervous system more reactive in general. So, by consuming caffeine, you've just directly increased your susceptibility to future stress. This single habit can reverse much of the advances you'll make with the techniques you'll learn in the next few chapters. I hope you're not reading through this book while downing your favorite caffeinated beverages! Another drawback of caffeine is that it acts as a diuretic leading to the loss of a great deal of necessary water and to decreases in vitamins C and B complex. When caffeine and sugar are combined the result is twice as stressful on the liver, pancreas, and other stress-linked systems.

Sugar

Sugars are the central sources of fuel for our body. This doesn't, however, mean in the form of donuts, candy, or desserts. It's actually easy to get enough of this fuel from the natural sugars in fresh fruits, vegetables, grains, potatoes, and other complex carbohydrates. During the stress response, the liver releases glycogen (stored body sugar) into the blood preparing the body for the fight-or-flight stress response. Although sugar is essential in providing the body with energy, refined sugar works in such a way that it dramatically activates the sympathetic nervous system and quickly increases the level of blood sugar. Our bodies interpret this as a sign that we must be in a fight-or-flight situation. The whole body system is thrown out of whack and while we initially feel an energetic "sugar high," we shortly "come down" and feel depressed, weak, and lethargic. Our bodies have no real physiological need for refined sugar.

While you might not think you eat very much refined sugar, you could be unpleasantly surprised at the actual numbers because it's hidden in so many different foods. Would you have suspected that catsup, TV dinners, canned fruits and vegetables, tomato sauce, salad dressing, and mayonnaise are among the worst offenders? Shockingly, the average sugar consumption per person each year in the United States ranges from 100 pounds to 125 pounds! Honey isn't a good substitute because it leads to a similar blood sugar level surge.

Of course, this doesn't mean that you can't occasionally indulge in your favorite chocolate bar, cookie, or your sweet of passion. It isn't abstinence that characterizes the stress positive people but rather balance and flexibility. Enjoy your favorite treat as long as it's in moderation and you're also eating a well-balanced diet with fresh, wholesome foods. There's another hidden danger in the foods we eat these days, namely, the presence of chemicals, such as pesticides, food dyes, flavor enhancers, and spoilage retardants. Even though these substances are removed from our foods once they've been proven harmful, there remain hundreds of chemicals that could have unhealthy effects on our bodies of which we are as yet unaware.

Healthy Alternatives for Caffeine and Sugar

You may well know all about the unhealthy aspects of caffeine and sugar but might be saying to yourself, "Look, when I get up in the morning or have the mid-afternoon slump, I can't function until I have my coffee." Fortunately, there are healthier ways to get an energy boost than simply consuming caffeine or refined sugar. Once you wean yourself off of your usual coffee and sugar boosts, you won't need them the way you feel you do now. An adjusted, healthier lifestyle will give you more overall energy, instead of small superficial jump starts. Try using the relaxation and breathing techniques, exercising, or eating natural, healthy snacks. You don't have to completely eliminate refined sugar from your life at once. Fortunately, new food labeling laws make it much easier to determine how much sugar is in various foods. Pay attention to these labels and work to gradually cut down the amount of refined sugar in your diet. Learn to replace it with sweet, natural, and wholesome foods.

Alcohol

Alcohol, another substance beloved by many, also negatively stresses our bodies. This may sound strange to you because alcohol depresses the nervous system and so you probably think of alcohol as making you feel temporarily relaxed and disinhibited. However, the overall consequence is increased stress on your body and often your mind. Alcohol strains the body's detoxification system, the liver, kidneys, and pancreas. With frequent use, these organs become less able to function. Excessive alcohol use also affects the blood sugar balance and prolonged use has been associated with diabetes or hypoglycemia. Finally, alcohol reduces levels of some vitamins and minerals, including B vitamins and magnesium, most important in combating the negative effects of stress. In part 1, the way in which alcohol use acts as a psychological stressor was discussed. In general, what initially is used as a simple way to relax or as a social behavior can turn into a full-blown addiction with serious mental and physical consequences. Cognitive techniques can help you figure out why you're drinking and how to improve your coping skills so you aren't relying on alcohol to get through tough situations. Physical techniques can help you relax and approach situations in a calm, positive way. The suggestions that follow for changing eating and smoking habits are also helpful in changing your drinking behavior. You may want to seek additional help if drinking is an issue for you.

Food as a Stress Buster

The following foods and eating patterns can provide you with the most energy for the food consumed. You can then accomplish your many daily activities while maintaining a stable, calm demeanor and get enough sleep at night. One thing that most of the diet gurus and nutritionists agree on is the importance of eating sufficient complex carbohydrates, which are replete with vitamins, minerals, and fiber and low in sodium and fat. Complex carbohydrates include pasta, beans, fresh vegetables and fruits, cereals (sorry, not sugar-coated flakes, peanut butter and chocolate grains, or other such "wholesome" cereals), and whole-grain breads.

Proteins

The guidelines for protein are generally 30 to 40 grams of protein per day. Most Americans meet or exceed these recommended guidelines. One fact that is little known but very important is the *timing of your protein consumption*. For most of us, the most important time to consume protein is in the morning. After not having had any food for a period of hours, your blood sugar drops. The best way to *gradually* elevate your blood sugar and thus avoid triggering the stress reaction in your body is to consume protein. Unfortunately, many of us grab a donut, danish, or some such snack as we dash off to work with the excuse that we don't have time for something healthier. Just as bad, many women skip breakfast altogether with the hope of avoiding those dreaded calories. The first strategy isn't a good one because refined carbohydrates and refined sugars immediately flood your system with sugar causing your blood sugar to rise dramatically. Following the balance principle of health, your body's attempt to restore balance will inevitably result in a rapid drop in blood sugar and accompanying feelings of lethargy and irritability. So, if your initial plan was to save time and become more productive, you've just taken great strides toward *not* fulfilling your goals.

This surge and precipitous drop in blood sugar doesn't happen when you consume protein. Instead, protein causes blood sugar to be elevated and sustained at a stable rate. While this has obvious physical benefits, there are also psychological benefits to this healthy way of eating. Eating junk food for breakfast or skipping it altogether are both poor strategies because the brain, unlike other parts of your body, doesn't have the ability to store glucose and use it as needed. Rather, it requires a sustained level of glucose to avoid low blood sugar and the resulting feelings of negative stress, irritability, depression, confusion, and anxiety. To add to feelings of distress, when your blood sugar is low your body releases more adrenaline which is itself part of the stress response. You've probably experienced this response in your own body as a result of having low blood sugar: shakiness, increased pulse rate, difficulty breathing, dry mouth, and moist palms.

In their 1986 book, *The Complete Guide to Your Emotions & Your Health*, Emrika Padus and the editors of *Prevention* magazine suggest that you try to get 15 grams of protein in the morning to derive the physical and psychological benefits. They recommend the following foods to obtain the desired amount of protein. For boosting your protein intake, consider low-fat protein options.

1 cup of skim milk	8 grams of protein
1 large egg	6 grams of protein
8 ounces part skim yogurt	13 grams of protein
1 cup large curd yogurt	31 grams of protein
1 tablespoon brewer's yeast	3 grams of protein

Please note that this and all dietary recommendations presented herein were designed for individuals who are in general good health and are not following special diets as prescribed by their medical doctors. Before following these suggestions, check with your medical doctor if you suffer from or suspect you may be suffering from any physical disorders.

Padus and associates also discuss the importance of protein in dealing with sleep difficulties. Certain proteins contain a substance known as trytophan which relaxes the body and brings sleep on more easily. However, you need to eat carbohydrates because they contain the substances that allow the trytophan in proteins to work effectively. So, for the evening or midnight snack to help you sleep, forget the ice cream and leftover cake and consider a combination of proteins and carbohydrates.

Combine a protein:	cheese, yogurt, milk, eggs, chicken, nuts, cottage cheese
With a carbohydrate:	bread, bran muffin, bananas, apples, watermelon, fruit juice, oatmeal or granola

Recall the discussion in chapter 7 and the section entitled "Personality and the Physical Link." In their 1996 book, *Peak-Performance Living*, Dr. Joel Robertson and Tom Monte look at how personality styles and stress are linked through the physical patterns of arousal. They assert that some people who overwork and place themselves under ever increasing pressure to work harder and faster become addicted to the physiological and psychological rewards associated with high levels of the excitatory neurotransmitters, dopamine and norepinephrine. While it's beneficial for you to be in a "fast neurotransmission" state when brainstorming or working under a deadline, too much time spent in this state is physically and psychologically damaging. They also discuss the benefits of the "slow neurotransmission" state, such as increased concentration, detail orientation, and focus. The message is that an overall balance (the key to stress optimization) of the two states is required to maintain health. Fortunately, through diet and exercise you can exert some control over which state you will be in to suit the demands or requirements of particular situations. Read on!

Up Your Brain's Functioning and Energy Level in under Thirty Minutes

Robertson and Monte suggest that you can boost your energy level and feel increased self-esteem, aggressiveness, and decisiveness by quickly raising your norepinephrine level. This is done by eating protein such as the following:

- Low-fat fish (flounder, cod, halibut, lox)
- Chicken (preferably without steroids or other chemicals)
- Eggs, seeds, and nuts
- Lean red meat (occasionally)
- Bean products, including tofu

Here is an example Robertson and Monte give of an ideal meal to order at an important business lunch where you need to be focused, energetic, and on your toes: 3 ounces of broiled fish (with no butter or dairy-based dressing), followed by a good-sized healthy salad. Avoiding the butter or dairy-based dressing excludes the fat which leads to sluggishness, and the carbohydrates in dairy foods which trigger the relaxation response. You should also avoid any alcohol, breads, pastas, or desserts which will make you feel relaxed and even tired. If you have no trouble sticking to one cup of coffee or tea or one soda, then go ahead and enjoy. Sounds like a boring meal, but remember that the times you need to be so restrictive are infrequent and must be balanced with more exciting and satisfying meals.

Robertson and Monte offer the exciting prospect that over the longer-term, you can actually improve your mental keenness by lowering fat and cholesterol in your diet. Consistent with earlier suggestions, this is accomplished by consuming whole grains, low-fat animal products, fresh fruits and vegetables.

Exercise is another method to increase the flow of oxygen throughout your body, including your brain. So, exercise is another tool to use when you need to briefly rev up your neurotransmission process. We'll go into the exercise factor more later.

Slowing and Relaxing Your Brain and Body

Dairy foods, pastas, breads, and some desserts are recommended when you want to relax. If you're having difficulties with anxiety, you should boost carbohydrates in your diet. Increase your intake of grains, including brown rice, wheat, wheat bread; noodles; popcorn without added fats; some vegetables (particularly squashes and root vegetables such as potatoes, carrots, onions, and celery); and certain fruits like bananas and apples. All of these foods raise serotonin in the brain and boost self-esteem, well-being, and relaxation.

Stress and Food: The Why's and How's

The *way* in which you eat has a big impact on how your body obtains nutrients. If you gobble down your food because you're feeling distress or anxiety, the digestive process cannot be carried out thoroughly and your body won't be able to absorb all of the available nutrients. Another habit many of you may have when under stress is to eat, eat, and eat well beyond the point of being hungry. At this point, you aren't listening to the messages your body is sending you (that is, you have a full stomach), but are behaving instead impulsively and as an unhealthy consequence of negative stress. This is another clear-cut example of the distancing between the mind and body that is characteristic of a "stress-mess." This habit is very troublesome, particularly for women, because it usually leads to weight gain, which then increases the negative stress level and anxiety even further. Now, how do you think women react to experiencing these uncomfortable emotions? That's right, by eating! The vicious cycle is in full swing.

This unhealthy way of "coping" is a serious problem for women. In fact, "overnutrition" (obesity) is one of the top four leading causes of death in the United States. Try to catch yourself next time you become a vacuum cleaner for all of the food around you. You can get extra help by telling your family or friends to gently remind you to slow down when necessary. Many of you will be pleasantly surprised to learn about one of the benefits of eating slowly—when you slow down the pace and savor the food, you eat about one-third less than when you're munching hastily and nervously.

A final word about nutrition and stress. It's important to be aware that when you are under stress, your body's requirements for certain nutrients change. You can boost your body's ability to respond to stress in a healthy way by making sure that you include sufficient levels of these nutrients. For example, your body wants more for B complex vitamins, particularly B6, B12, thiamine, folate, niacin, and pantothenate when responding to stress. Under stress, protein breakdown is increased and so your body uses up more calcium. In addition, various research suggests that the stress response requires greater availability of vitamins A and C, phosphorus, potassium, calcium, magnesium, and zinc. Calcium and magnesium have both been associated with reducing anxiety and arousal in general. Some foods rich in these nutrients include brussel sprouts, potatoes, cauliflower, and broccoli.

Besides assisting your body to respond in a healthy way to stress, certain vitamins and minerals can also help you with a variety of physical and psychological problems. The list below is a modified version of one designed by Emrika Padus and the editors of *Prevention* magazine. Use it as a handy reference guide when you're experiencing negative stress or certain mind and body difficulties. Of course, remember to follow your medical doctor's suggestions or prescriptions first and foremost. If you have any medical problems, consult with her or him before you use the following recommendations. Also, talk to your medical doctor or contact a resource such as the FDA to get information regarding the quantities of the following nutrients that you require.

When you are experiencing:	**You may require more:**
• Emotional stress	B vitamins, vitamin C, calcium
• Illness or injury	Vitamins A, C, and E, iron, zinc, calcium, folate, pantothenate
• Fatigue, irritability nervousness, or insomnia	B6 and B12, thiamine, riboflavin, pantothenate, potassium, magnesium, iron, folate

- Physical activity   B vitamins, vitamins C and E, iron

- Consumption of caffeine   Thiamine, vitamin C, all minerals
- Consumption of alcohol   B12, thiamine, copper, calcium, zinc, potassium, magnesium

- Difficulty concentrating   B12, folate, iron
- Difficulty remembering   Thiamine, iron, choline (lecithin)
- Depression   B6 and B12, thiamine, riboflavin, folate, pantothenate

- PMS   B6, calcium, magnesium
- Pregnancy   B vitamins (especially folate B6), calcium, iron

Changing Your Eating Habits: Stress Management Is Self Management

You have been given some general suggestions for changing your eating habits. By watching out for refined sugar, replacing nonnutritious snacks with wholesome foods, reading content labels, and cutting back on alcohol and caffeine you'll greatly reduce artificially stimulated stress responses in your body. You'll also help your body respond in a more controlled fashion to stressors when they do exist. As you may well know, changing eating habits isn't easy. Below you'll find several other steps to help you change your dietary habits so that food becomes a healthy tool rather than an unhealthy weapon.

One of the most helpful things to do when trying to modify your behavior is self-monitoring. Individuals who track the behaviors they want to change get a much more accurate awareness of what they're actually doing, how often, when, and even why. People often complain that self-monitoring is boring, a hassle, or too disruptive of their busy schedules. The choice to do so is entirely yours and is ultimately based on how serious you are about wanting to learn how to optimize stress and incorporate flexibility and adaptability to be able to maintain *balance* in your life. You have the choice to wholly embrace your experiences and emotions, both negative and positive, and apply the principles you're learning to increase your positive experiences, thus designing and living the best life for you. This is why I equate stress management with self management. This is one area in you're life in which you have control. Think of self-monitoring and other techniques in this book as beginning to "work out" your control muscles using the right equipment (mind and body) and the right kinds of weight (asserting control over situations that you really can control).

Self-Monitoring

Self-monitoring is a first step in being able to change your selected behavior. When clients come to me wanting to lose weight or change their eating patterns, I first instruct them to keep a food diary. They are to write down the situation triggering them to eat, what they eat, when, and their thoughts and feelings before and after the situation. This helps them to realize the many reasons aside from hunger for which they're eating. These can include stress, feelings of emptiness, depression, low self-esteem, boredom, or habit. My clients often tell me that just the mere fact of having to write down what they eat often leads directly to a reduction in how much they're eating.

One of my female clients, Kelly, was drinking quite a bit of caffeine. I suggested this could be associated with her increasing feelings of anxiety and jitteriness. We weren't aware of just how much caffeine she was consuming until she began keeping written track. The results were shocking. Several cups of coffee in the early morning, one or two more in late morning, a number of caffeinated soft drinks throughout the day, coffee in the afternoon and evening—the list was staggering. She was finally able to cut out caffeine and after a few days of withdrawal, including headaches, lethargy, and irritability, she came to a session exclaiming happily that she could not believe the difference. She felt energetic yet calm and relaxed. The jitteriness and tremors in her body disappeared and, just as importantly, she felt pride and a sense of control over her own behavior and life. She brought about the changes using cognitive techniques such as thought stopping (which you'll be learning about in chapter 11), to challenge her "need" for caffeine. Combining this with relaxation and breathing techniques helped her make it safely through the periods of overwhelming urges for caffeine. Another of my caffeine-hooked clients, Robin, reported to me that she'd been very angry at herself for cheating on her plan to quit caffeine. She felt that she just didn't have enough energy at work until she'd downed several cups of coffee. One morning she discovered that this "life-saving, energy-boosting" coffee at her office was actually decaffeinated! This humorous discovery that it was her own mind giving her that happy, energetic feeling gave her the self-confidence to quit for good.

Stimulus Control

A second technique you can incorporate in changing your behavior is called stimulus control. One of the formulas of learning is that a stimulus leads to a response. Many of us have allowed too many stimuli to become associated with the response of eating. For example, watching TV, working on a computer, attending a social event, being bored, angry, happy, or sad have become stimuli for us to eat. To modify your eating patterns, you must separate your eating behavior from other behaviors and situations. To do this, it's helpful to eat only at particular times and at particular locations. Set specific times for your meals and don't allow yourself to snack all day long. (Unless you have more serious low blood sugar problems—discuss this with your doctor. You may need to be eating small snacks all day and avoid the standard three big meals.) Remember that when you eat your digestive system is stimulated to act. Digestion uses a great deal of energy and can sap the energy you need for other daily activities.

Here are some other suggestions. Don't let yourself stand in front of the refrigerator taking a bit of this and a bit of that—it adds up! Don't eat in bed or on the couch. Instead, plan to eat your meals sitting down at a table. Make an event out of it by setting the table, putting flowers in a vase, or doing anything that will make eating a special, structured activity. In addition, go through your refrigerator and get rid of the junk food and replace it with healthy foods and snacks. Remember, though, extremes aren't the way to optimize stress and your health. You certainly don't have to completely exclude the treats you love from your diet. The key is moderation. Have a scoop of ice cream or a few cookies once a week instead of every night. Complete restriction is dangerous because it often triggers a complete loss of control and increased binging. If you've become caught in this cycle, so that one bite of cake leads to eating almost the whole cake, and the episodes are occurring repeatedly, it's best to stay away from those foods and seek professional advice. As you learn what's underlying this behavior, perhaps an inability to handle stress, fear of intimacy, low self-esteem, or feelings of emptiness and loneliness, you'll be better able to work through these issues. You can change your beliefs about food being "forbidden" or you being "bad" for breaking your diet, and learn new behaviors and tools to use.

Social Support

Don't forget to include another important tool in changing your eating behavior—it may be sitting right across from you at the table.

This valuable resource is social support from others in your life. Obviously, if your spouse or partner urges you to sink back into your unhealthy eating patterns or continues to tempt you with your favorite sugary or fatty foods, you're going to have a harder time of it. Tell people about your intention to change to more healthy eating—this lets them respect your wishes and also gives you greater motivation to live up to what you said you wanted to do! Of course, you can benefit from social support in your efforts to change any selected behavior, from improving your communication to becoming more assertive to becoming less of a workaholic. Other people can give you support and play cheerleader, while, as mentioned, you'll also be more likely to stick with your plan because you've shared it with them.

Rewarding Yourself

A final step toward changing your behavior but one we women often forget is to reward yourself for successful changes in behavior. If the behavior change was developing a healthier diet, this doesn't mean to reward yourself with several hot fudge sundaes. Instead, take a relaxing bubble bath, get a massage, buy yourself a book you have wanted to read, or do whatever else feels like a reward to you.

Cigarette Smoking

There has been so much information disseminated about the negative effects of smoking that only a brief discussion is needed here. While overall rates of smoking have declined recently, more women than ever are picking up the habit. This trend underlies the increasing rate of lung cancer seen in women. Various studies have been conducted in order to understand why this is happening. One interesting discovery is that the association between job characteristics and smoking is higher for women than for men. This probably makes sense when you recall that high demand teamed with low control (the equation for negative stress) is much more prevalent in women's jobs than in men's. In an abortive effort to cope with such negative stress, a number of women pick up and continue smoking.

As with alcohol, many women addicted to smoking think it helps them reduce stress. In actuality, smoking interferes with the body's adaptive responses to stress and makes the body vulnerable to a number of diseases and infections. If you're one of those who looks forward to smoking a cigarette at your next break so you can relax, you may be surprised to learn that it isn't nicotine itself that has a calming affect on the body or mind. Instead, once you're addicted to nicotine, the absence of the substance makes you feel irritable and anxious. Because introducing nicotine into your system restores the addictive "balance," you've falsely concluded that it's the cigarettes themselves that are calming. As a woman, you need to be particularly careful of cigarette smoking because evidence suggests that you'll have a harder time quitting than would a man. One reason for this involves another woman's issue, namely, that of body image and weight control. We all know people who have quit or tried to quit smoking only to find that they have put on more than a few pounds. Because body image is so important to many of us, we're more likely to be afraid of trying to quit or we lapse back into the habit if we do notice some extra pounds. In fact, many young girls and women admit to using smoking as a tool to maintain their weight. Exercise and diet are much wiser options for watching your figure.

Rationalizing Your Behavior

Besides the physical and psychological addiction to nicotine, another reason it's so hard to stop smoking or other unhealthy behaviors, is that people use certain mental techniques to make it easier to continue. Studies examining the dynamics of risky behavior have found interesting results. For example, people who drink excessively or smoke tend to overestimate these same behaviors in other people. If we believe that others are doing the same thing, somewhere in our minds this lets us off the hook. Interestingly enough, people engaging in these dangerous behaviors do not deny the riskiness of their actions. What they do is to try to ignore and put the danger out of their minds so they can continue their habits without feeling as much conflict. Do these handy tricks sound familiar to you? If so, you now have the insight to call yourself on it when you catch yourself falling into these patterns.

Modifying Your Behavior

Insight is only the first step in modifying your behaviors. The second, more difficult step is taking action and truly changing what you do. You can use some of the techniques for changing eating habits to quit smoking. It's very helpful to keep a diary or schedule of the situations that trigger your desire to smoke, the feelings before and after smoking, whether or not you did smoke when the urge arose, and, if not, what you did instead. Also, as with changing eating patterns, it helps to elicit social support. When you tell other people that you're going to stop smoking, you have a greater investment in your promise and are more likely to follow through. In line with this are the many groups available to help people interested in smoking cessation. A number of these are based on the principles of Alcoholics Anonymous. These groups provide social support, information, and are often useful in preventing relapse. I have worked with many clients who have talked about their desire to stop smoking and their repeated failed attempts to do so. I have been struck by how many of them talk about cigarettes similarly. On the one hand they realize the danger of cigarettes but on the other hand they describe cigarettes as being their best friends. These are friends you would not wish to inflict on your worst enemies. Social support groups allow you to develop true, real friendships and to realize that your so-called friends are traitors indeed. You are also fortunate these days as there are a number of innovative tools available to help you taper off smoking. There are nicotine patches and nicotine gum. Many people find these make the difference in their ability to quit smoking. Be sure to consult with your physician before choosing one of these means. Smoking cessation can be a very distressful endeavor. Do remember, however, that this distress is relatively short-term and though it may not seem like it, there will be an end to the tortuous experience. In the long-term, quitting smoking is central to your efforts at managing the stress in your life.

Exercise

To any of you who don't believe in the inextricability of the mind and body, I issue a challenge. Next time you're feeling anxious, lethargic, or depressed, set out for a brisk walk or jog (of course, do this only if you are in fairly good health). Almost every time, you'll return feeling more energetic, calm, positive, optimistic, and better able to concentrate. Exercise is definitely one of the most important elements of any stress management program and produces both psychological and physical benefits. As you exercise, hormones are released that make you feel more positive, as well as less stressed, depressed, or anxious. And, aerobic exercise actually rids the body of stress hormones. People who exercise regularly describe having a greater sense of control over their lives. Exercise is even associated with self-esteem. Recall that both having a sense of control and having good self-esteem are characteristics that can reduce or buffer the negative effects of stress. Many studies support these claims. For example, exercisers tend to rate lower on depression scales than non-exercisers.

Exercise has the power to reduce negative emotional states. In one study, mildly depressed women were assigned to three different groups: an aerobic exercise group; a placebo group who practiced relaxation; and a control group who made no changes in their activity level. The last group showed no changes in depression after ten weeks, while the placebo group showed slight reductions in depression. The women who participated in the aerobics group showed great decreases in depression (McCann and Holmes 1984). Exercise also seems to have a positive impact in reducing anxiety.

Another long-term study assigned distressed individuals to one of three groups: an aerobics group; a stress management group; and a control group. The participants were measured in terms of anxiety at different periods following their particular intervention, with the last follow-up occurring fifteen months afterward. Unlike the control group, both the exercise and stress management groups showed reductions in anxiety levels each time they were measured—even at the fifteen month mark (Long 1984, 1985). People who are overwhelmed with problem solving or decision making often say that exercising clears their minds and allows them to reach creative solutions and decisions. Next time you are stumped with a problem or are feeling at a loss creatively, confront that little voice telling you that "Now certainly isn't the time to exercise—you've got a deadline here and people are expecting you to produce!" Go out for a jog, brisk walk, or take an exercise class. Once you aren't actively pressuring yourself for an answer, decision, or plan and your body is experiencing the boost of prostress, your mind is freed to wander new paths, generate new insights, and even produce exciting new ideas.

Boosting Your Self-Esteem and Body Image

Another way in which exercise can be a stress reducer for women is because of its effectiveness in changing body shape and weight. This certainly isn't a prescription for young girls and women who aren't overweight to become compulsive exercisers in pursuit of a perfect body. As you know, weight and appearance are negative stressors for a majority of women today. Women must be extremely careful of getting caught up in an endless, most likely impossible, unhealthy and distressing battle to look like an emaciated supermodel! If you are overweight, exercising burns off calories and boosts your metabolism which can help you lose weight and reduce your distress about your body image. For others of you who just want to tone or lose and keep off that last few pounds, exercise is effective and far more healthy than diet pills or starvation diets. Even with exercise, balance and moderation are key. Be realistic in how you see your body and in realizing that nature has her say here and has created you with only so much latitude in mind. Also, don't throw yourself into advanced exercises if you haven't been active recently. Start and build up slowly. If you haven't exercised for some years you may be initially frustrated with a body that doesn't have as much energy or resilience as you remembered. Take heart and be patient. Start out slowly and try not to have too many expectations. Just doing the activity as a break in your hectic daily routine, you'll naturally increase your regimen and see a difference in your body. There are thousands of women in their fifties, sixties, and seventies who exercise frequently and are in great shape. A word of caution—be careful if you find that you continue to push yourself to exercise even while experiencing pain or if you begin to feel irritable or angry at yourself and others if you have to miss an exercise session. These are warning signs that you could be getting too dependent upon or even addicted to exercise.

Exercise as Prostressor

Exercise is definitely an activity that you can experience as a prostressor. You have probably heard mention of a particular mental and physical state described as a "runner's high." This "high" is described as a feeling that time has slowed; attention and concentration are sharply focused; a sense of unlimited energy and a feeling of unity between their inner and outer worlds are experienced. This wondrous state sounds similar to that described by people who practice meditation. While superficially exercise and meditation might appear so different, they obviously share a similarity in that they can evoke a state of prostress. In both activities, if you focus on the achievement of this state as a goal it will slip away and elude you. As does a Buddhist monk while arranging a floral display or conducting a tea ceremony, you must clear your mind and simply do the activity. You can experience prostress this way but remember that it comes about from releasing yourself from rigidity, narrow-mindedness, and the "musts, shoulds, fears, anxieties, and what ifs." The calm, joy, and peace may then envelop you as you contain it.

There are benefits that are also more easily quantifiable and are also extremely important. For example, Emrika Padus and the editors of *Prevention* magazine in their 1986 book, *The Complete Guide to Your Emotions and Your Health*, discuss studies showing that exercise is associated with improvements in memory and mental sharpness. One study compared the recall abilities of a group of adults who completed a ten-week walking/jogging program to a control group of sedentary adults. The walkers and joggers performed significantly better than the non-exercisers on the memory tasks.

The Physical Benefits: Burning Off Your Stress

So far, you've been reading about the psychological benefits of exercise. You probably know about the numerous positive effects of exercise on your physical health, such as reducing blood pressure and heart rate, increasing endurance, improving lung capacity, digestion and excretion, boosting metabolism, and making your body stronger and more energetic. What's shocking is that estimates suggest that up to four out of five adults in the United States don't exercise enough even to slow the rate of physical decay. Do you fit in the majority or minority category? Congratulations if you're the one of five. If you aren't currently, read on and let's see you make some efforts toward changing this unsatisfactory ratio!

As you recall, one of the biggest problems with negative stress these days is that modern day society doesn't allow for the discharge of tension built up from the fight-or-flight response. Exercise is an ideal way to obtain this much needed discharge and to reestablish the harmony of the parasympathetic and sympathetic nervous systems essential to physical health. Exercise directly benefits the body in terms of its stress response. For instance, one of the body's reactions to the perception of a stressor is an increased heart rate. While the heart rate of an exerciser certainly increases when a stressor is perceived, the *surge* in heartbeat is substantially lower than that of a nonexerciser. Interestingly enough, exercise also seems to boost the efficacy of vitamins in fighting off illness. While vitamins such as C and E help us to ward off sickness, exercise actually increases their effectiveness.

Exercise can indirectly benefit your health as well. People who begin to exercise often feel so good about themselves and their improved physical well-being, that they reduce or eliminate other negative stress-inducing habits, such as smoking, drinking caffeine and/or alcohol, and eating unhealthy sugar-loaded or fatty foods. There's an interesting link between smoking cigarettes and exercising. Cigarette smoking is one of the strongest predictors of whether an individual will commence and stick with an exercise plan. This is an important factor to be aware of so that if you're a smoker you can combat this negative interference. All in all, aerobic exercise is invaluable in making you recover more rapidly from negative stress and experience fewer negative physical and mental consequences.

Now for the Tricky Part—Motivation

In terms of starting or continuing an exercise regimen, there are several points to remember. First, it's important that you check with your medical doctor prior to starting to exercise. Once you have her okay, there are several things you should try to incorporate into your exercise plan. These include, (1) aerobic activity, (2) stretching and flexibility, and (3) developing muscular strength. If you find it very difficult to find the time to exercise, aerobic activity will provide you the maximum benefits. However, it's important to realize that incorporating the other two elements, particularly flexibility, doesn't require much time. The ideal exercise routine includes a variety of activities, thus working on different muscle groups and requiring the development of different motor skills. Aerobic activity is recommended for at least thirty minutes. Work up to the thirty-minute goal. A thirty-minute workout performed three times per week can provide you with the promised rewards of improved mental and physical health and a reduction in negative-stress induced consequences.

Taking Care of Your Needs

You may have exercised in the past or may be attempting to exercise at present and are well aware of many of the benefits of exercise discussed. Since when have what you know and what you do been consistent? While you may know that exercise is a central element of stress and self management and that it improves physical and mental well-being, this doesn't necessarily mean that you're exercising! How many pieces of exercise equipment have you purchased which end up cluttering your house? How many times have you signed up for an exercise class or joined a gym only to watch your attendance slip from frequent to occasional to nil! Why is it so difficult for many of us to stick to our good intentions about exercise? Some excuses certainly seem reasonable. That is, you might tell yourself that after a busy day of work, kids, errands, and crowded freeways you have barely enough energy to stumble to the couch let alone to exercise. On the other hand, you might tell yourself that you just do not have enough time for exercise given all of the deadlines, meetings, social events, and children's demands that you have to meet.

Both of these reasons may well seem realistic; however, there is some faulty reasoning involved.

Firstly, one of exercise's best characteristics is that it's highly effective in boosting energy levels and endurance. While many people may feel exhausted before starting their jog, walk, or exercise class, within minutes, they are feeling incredibly energetic and powerful. This feeling carries over after the exercise has ended. The old lack of energy excuse will really only serve to keep you in a fatigued rut. The second excuse is much more a female than a male one, so let's examine the implicit message. Although you easily accept that you have to meet all of the demands placed on you by others, you too easily forget your own needs and place yourself and your health in a position of lesser importance. As discussed earlier, many of us women pay attention to satisfying everyone but ourselves as a result of overt and hidden messages picked up from social institutions, groups, families, and the media. It's time for you to put yourself first. You deserve to take care of yourself and improve your quality of life. Your increased peace of mind and well-being will likely improve the quality of your interactions with the important people in your life.

Have Fun With Your Exercise Plan

You may have said to yourself while reading all of this, "Yes, exercise is really important and I really should be doing it, but . . ." There is no doubt that sticking with your plan to exercise can be very difficult in your real day-to-day life. Fortunately, there are certain strategies you can follow to increase the likelihood that you will continue to exercise once you start. Obviously, you'll be more likely to stick with activities you find enjoyable. Don't vow to jog four times a week or swim thirty laps several times a week if you can't stand jogging or swimming! Choose something you know you enjoy or try different activities until you find one. You can also maintain your interest as well as obtain the goal of including the three important fitness elements (aerobic activity, strength, flexibility) by varying your routine. If you find yourself getting bored with your routine, expand your activities. Walk briskly two or three times a week, bicycle one or two days, take some exercise classes, or go hiking. Many women these days are becoming involved in previously male-dominated activities, such as boxing, rock climbing, and martial arts.

You don't even need to limit your exercise plan to formal activities. In fact, you can gain many benefits by relabeling yourself an "activity seeker" and then making some minor changes in your daily activities. For example, rather than taking the elevator up and down to your office, use the stairs. Park several blocks away from your destination and walk briskly. In most major cities you usually can't park anywhere near your destination anyway. So, rather than letting the shortage of parking turn into just one of your distressors, look at it positively as a chance to get moving! Rather than sitting around drinking coffee and snacking on junk food during your breaks or lunch, put on some tennis shoes and take a walk around the area where you work.

Motivation also improves when you set your own goals for the number of days to distance walk, jog, lift weights, or whatever activity you've chosen. Again though, it's essential you don't overdo it. This makes exercise more of a chore than an enjoyable event and it also increases the possibility of injury which will put a definite stop to your exercise. Listen to your body and if it's complaining beyond introductory slight muscle stiffness, give it a rest. You may have to choose another type of activity. Swimming or even brisk walking (if it doesn't cause pain or worsen an injury) can be an aerobic activity without being quite so harsh on the body. Again, it's best to consult with your physician if you have physical problems that need to be considered when you exercise. Another helpful tactic is to make a date to exercise with a friend. This increases your commitment to exercise and you can take turns motivating each other when one or both of you want to sit on the couch. You're bound to feel this way every once in a while and if you have really had an exhausting day or week or feel you need some time alone to rest, go ahead. Remember, many of us have the tendency to want to do everything perfectly. The danger of this in terms of exercise lies in becoming obsessed with exercise and feeling angry at yourself if you miss so much as one day of working out. *Balance* is once again the key!

10

The Physical Aspect of Stress Management

Recall from part 1 that you have a natural physical response to stressors or perceived threats called the fight-or-flight response. This involves an elevated heart rate, increased blood pressure, disruption in digestive functions, the release of various hormones, muscular tension, and other bodily changes. If this type of arousal continues for too long or occurs too frequently, many physical disorders can arise. Doctors frequently provide drugs to deal with these problems, but this is generally just a "Band-Aid approach." Too much distress also leads to irritability, frustration, depression, anxiety, and other symptoms of psychological distress. Usually, what needs to be changed to combat this situation can be done only by *you*. You have the power to learn how to change your perceptions and thoughts and to learn relaxation and healthy ways of dealing with stress. These are preventive techniques and get to the root of stress-related problems so that you don't have to keep using a reactive "fix-it" approach.

With physical techniques of stress management, you'll learn to recognize and use your body's reactions to stress as *cues* that your body is experiencing distress. You can then counter the distress with relaxation or an alternative response. This will directly dispel your tension.

Take a Deep Breath

One of the crucial building blocks of stress management is the simple art of breathing. This technique may sound silly, but the majority of us don't breathe properly. When you breathe, energy is brought in while waste is expelled. Furthermore, even though experts remain puzzled as to why, focusing your attention on breathing decreases tension in your body and mind. You'll be amazed at the effectiveness of simply learning better breathing.

Practicing Your Deep Breathing

To tell whether you're breathing in the proper deep, diaphragmatic way, first try this exercise. Place your hand just below your rib cage and just above your stomach. Inhale deeply and pay attention to the movement of your hand—does it move at all? does it move in? does it move out? If you're breathing correctly, your hand should move out as you inhale and in as you exhale. In proper breathing, the abdomen moves outward with your breath flowing upward toward your chest. Try to visualize the air entering your body and moving its way up from the bottom to the top of your lungs. Make sure to take a deep full breath inward, hold it, and then exhale fully, making sure all of the breath leaves your body.

For relaxation, one of the simplest yet most effective methods is deep breathing. When you do the breathing exercises, inhale for the count of five seconds, hold your breath for twenty seconds (or less if you can't manage at first), and then exhale fully for twice as long as your inhalation, or for the count of ten. Imagine that as you exhale, you are getting rid of all of the negative stress and tension built up in your body . . . Let it all just flow out with your breath. Also, as you'll be doing throughout these sessions, pay attention to where you tend to hold your stress. For example, notice if you have tight neck and shoulders, clenched teeth, forehead tension, or whatever happens to be your "zone" of tension.

A brief word on why your exhalation should be twice as long as your inhalation. This pattern stimulates relaxation even more by activating the parasympathetic system rather than the sympathetic system. The parasympathetic system, as you recall, is the part of the autonomic nervous system linked with the relaxation response. (Refer to chapter 1 if you want to review the functioning of your nervous system.)

Breathing Exercise

So, let's try it . . . breathe in deeply again for the count of five and this time pay attention to how you inhale . . . to breathe for relaxation, you need to inhale through your nose . . . feel your abdomen pushing out and imagine the air filling your lungs. Count to twenty. Now exhale for the count of ten through your mouth. Imagine the warm air leaving your body carries with it all of the tension from throughout your body. If you want, you can visualize that stress-loaded breath you're exhaling as a particular color, and watch it flowing from your mouth as you exhale completely. While you might find this type of breathing a bit uncomfortable at first, it will rapidly become more natural with practice. In fact, we all entered the world breathing this way as babies; most of us lost this healthy method somewhere along the way.

Proper Deep Breathing—An Important Building Block

Remember that during the distress response, your breathing becomes shallow and rapid and your heart rate increases. On the other hand, when you're relaxed, your breathing is deeper and your heart rate slows. Because your breathing is the easiest physical system to control and has a great impact on your mind and body, this is the best place to start. If you make yourself breathe the deep, slow breath of relaxation, you trigger the rest of the relaxation response.

Schedule your first exercise—at least thirty-five to forty deep breaths each day. You can break your breathing up into "sessions" of three or more deep breaths. A way to remember to do your exercises is to link a "session" of, say, five or so breaths with an event or stimulus that happens frequently during your daily routine. Joseph, one of my clients who became enamored with deep breathing, chose to link his breathing with his daily turning on and off of his computer at work. He took several deep breaths each time. He linked the other deep breathing sessions with the red lights he hit during his drive to and from work. Joseph was enthused about his "special breathing time" and described it as feeling like he was getting a wonderful massage from the inside out. Now, who of us doesn't love a massage, and at no cost? While you practice the deep breathing, you should also pay attention to any tense muscles in your body, such as your neck, shoulders, or face. Relax these muscles. I find that I need to do this quite often as I drive. I remind myself that I don't need to use my neck or face to drive my car! The main thing is that you find some recurring event in your daily life that you can link with the deep breathing as a reminder. This is a very quick way to begin experiencing the benefits of controlling your responses to stress. The following fill-in section can be used as a "breathing log" to help you get started with your first stress-management technique.

Breathing Log

Goal: Thirty-five to forty deep, diaphragmatic breaths each day

- The following are situations that I will use as cues to practice my deep breathing:

    1. _____

    2. _____

    3. _____

    4. _____

- I met my goal for deep breathing on the following days (yes or no):

    Monday   _____

    Tuesday   _____

    Wednesday   _____

    Thursday   _____

    Friday   _____

    Saturday   _____

    Sunday   _____

Continue to keep track of your practice until it becomes a natural part of your routine.

Progressive Relaxation

The second technique using the physical components of stress arousal is *progressive relaxation*. Progressive relaxation has been extensively studied and found effective in reducing body tension. In 1938, Edmund Jacobson distilled his technique in his book *Progressive Relaxation*. Jacobson identified relaxation as a remedy for individuals suffering from specific disorders. Progressive relaxation is based on the idea that the body responds to anxiety-related thoughts by tensing. This muscular tension then increases your anxiety. In other words, your thoughts lead to bodily tension, which you interpret as meaning you must be experiencing stress; this interpretation then increases your anxiety level. By gaining control over relaxing, you gain control over your feelings of anxiety and stress. Progressive relaxation involves a sequence of tensing and relaxing the muscle groups in your body. During the exercise, your main focus should be on your muscles and on the difference between what they feel like tensed versus what they feel like relaxed. We tend to tense areas completely unrelated to the area we are working on tensing. You're awareness of this pattern is very important to a healthy response to stress. By paying attention to the actual feelings of tensing and holding your muscles tight, you'll notice the tremendous difference when you move on to relax them and to eventually maintain this relaxation for as much of the day as possible.

Being in a state of relaxation is incompatible with being in a state of stress and anxiety. Thus, when you sense the tension and stress arising in your body and mind, you start the relaxation to get rid of your discomfort and inhibit the distress response. Progressive relaxation allows a tensed muscle to automatically become more relaxed. And, as you focus on the difference between muscle tension and relaxation, you'll feel a still greater sense of relaxation. You'll also become an expert on the physical cues (muscle tightness in various parts of your body) that signal distress. These cues will remind you to start the relaxation process. In this way, relaxation actually becomes a coping tool you can use in a variety of situations. You probably have habitual tension in your body of which you're largely unaware. You eventually become unpleasantly familiar with such habitual tension when it makes its presence known in the form of headaches, neck and back pain, anxiety, insomnia, depression, and high blood pressure. By using progressive relaxation, you can reduce many of these problems. Remember that relaxation techniques are not only curative. By learning these tools, you can actually use them as preventive measures to avoid or minimize negative stress.

Practicing Progressive Relaxation

To get the most from this procedure, find a quiet location where you won't be disturbed. That means unplugging the phone, taking off your beeper, telling the kids and husband or boyfriend you're taking time out for yourself. If the place is still somewhat noisy, turn on a fan or an air cleaner to block out the random noise. As you become proficient at progressive relaxation, you'll be able to relax and obtain the benefits even if there are noises or distractions in the environment. Try to wear loose, comfortable clothing and take off your shoes, glasses, or anything confining or constricting. Progressive relaxation can be done either lying down or sitting in a comfortable chair.

To approach this most effectively, tell yourself you truly deserve this time. Taking time out for yourself may be the hardest part of this exercise for you. Learning to give yourself permission and feeling guiltless about it may well be one of the most important aspects of this exercise. You may have to turn off the voice in your head telling you how many other "really important" things you should be doing . . . making phone calls, doing homework, preparing for an office meeting, cleaning the house, and so on. You also may find a little resistance outside of yourself but very close to home. Namely, both kids and your significant other may not see the need for you to take this time for yourself. They might, as they may often do, have other plans for your time in their minds. This is a great time to start constructing limits and showing your loved ones that your needs are just as important as everyone else's. State the "new rules"—that they will give you respect and peace when you ask for it. The good news is that you're likely to be more productive and less stressed out once you have gained the ability to use progressive relaxation.

Enter into this with a calm, detached attitude, don't keep asking yourself, "Am I doing this right or not?" Instead, go through the motions, follow the directions, and let what will happen, happen . . . just let go. It is also strongly recommended that you read through the following directions aloud and record them on tape. You can then play the tape while you work through the entire process and you won't have to concern yourself with recalling the procedure. Use a calm, even voice while you record the directions and you can even add soothing music or sounds of the ocean, rain, and the like to the background to increase your sense of peace and relaxation.

To begin, you can either sit in a chair, preferably one that supports your head, neck, and arms, or lie down on a bed or on the floor. The tension phase will last eight seconds, and then you will abruptly relax the tensed muscle. Continue to relax for ten seconds. Pay attention to how your muscles feel when relaxed compared to when tensed. Remember to incorporate the deep, relaxed breathing you learned in the previous exercise. (Begin recording here:)

Start by taking three deep diaphragmatic breaths. Place your hand on your lower belly and inhale slowly and deeply for five seconds, making sure that your breath is pushing your hand outward. Hold the breath for twenty seconds and then exhale completely for a count of ten. Imagine as you do this that each inward breath brings purifying, nourishing air into your body and each exhalation expels your tension and stress. Second breath . . . in and out. Third breath . . . in and out. Now, take a moment to focus on your body's inner sensations and feelings. Pay attention to the places where your body is touching the floor or chair . . . your head, your shoulders, and back, your buttocks, and your legs. Feel a sense of relaxation flowing smoothly throughout your body.

Now, move your attention to your right hand. Tighten it as hard as you can and hold it tense for the count of eight seconds. Pay attention to the feelings of tension in the muscles of your fist and forearm. Now, quickly and completely relax this wrist and let it relax for ten seconds. Enjoy the relaxation and limpness and notice how it differs from the previous feeling of tension in your hand. Try the same area again. Tighten for the count of eight. Now, fully relax your hand and fist for ten seconds and again notice the difference in the feeling. You may feel some tingling or heaviness in this area. Feel the warmth as the blood flows into your hand and into each finger . . . these are natural relaxation responses and are signs that you're letting go of the tension. Inhale deeply, feel the relaxation and exhale . . . letting all of the tension flow out with your breath.

Now go to the left hand. Repeat the same sequence . . . Tense your hand and fist for the count of eight and then relax your fist completely for ten seconds. Feel the sensations of relaxation and how they differ from those of muscular tension. Don't forget your breathing . . . breathe in deeply and hold it, then exhale completely. Let all tension in your muscles flow out with your breath. Repeat the tensing of your left hand and fist. Tighten the muscles for the count of eight and now relax your hand and fist suddenly and completely for ten seconds. Pay attention to the feelings of warmth and any tingling of relaxation. If you feel yourself becoming distracted and thinking about thoughts other than your inner sensations and feelings of relaxation, don't resist them. Realize them, and then just let those thoughts drift away easily. Imagine them as clouds being blown away by the wind.

Now, move to your biceps. Bend both of your elbows and raise your hands up toward your shoulders, tighten your muscles. Hold this tension for the count of eight. Now, release both

biceps and let your arms fall downward. Feel the soothing comfort of relaxation. Breathe in deeply, and exhale . . . letting all of
your concerns and worries flow outward with your breath. Enjoy
the relaxation of your muscles for ten seconds. Repeat this again
with both arms . . . bend your elbows, raise your hands, and
tense your muscles for eight seconds. Again, let them fall and
notice the relaxation, the tingling, heaviness or warmth, for ten,
nine, eight . . . one.

Now, focus on a different area of the arms—the triceps.
Stretch your right arm out in front of you as far as you can so
that it forms a right angle to your body. Stick out your fingers
and spread them widely. Now tighten your fingers, hands, and
triceps as much as you can. Pay attention to the feeling of the
tension in your triceps muscles. Do this for the usual count of
eight seconds. Let your arm totally relax and drift down to your
side, hanging loose and limp for the count of ten. Remember to
keep taking the slow, deep breaths in and out. Repeat the same
movement with your right arm and triceps again so that you can
really notice the difference between the tension and the relaxation. Tense for eight seconds and then let your arm drift down
and relax for the count of ten. Again, pay attention to any tingling feelings, any warmth, or heaviness. Now, shift the focus to
the same exercise with your left arm. Stretch out your left arm as
far as you can in a right angle to your body. Stick out your fingers and spread them . . . tighten your fingers, hands, and triceps as much as you can. Feel the tension in your triceps muscle
for the count of eight seconds. Now, let your arm totally relax
and drift down to your side, hanging loose and limp for ten seconds. Remember to keep taking slow, deep breaths in and out
throughout this relaxation exercise. Now do the same thing with
your left arm one more time. Stretch out your left arm at a right
angle, spreading your fingers and tightening your muscles, concentrating on the triceps, the muscles in the back of your arm,
for eight seconds and then completely relax for ten seconds. You
may have a strange sensation that your arms feel longer than
before. They really are as your muscles become longer following
the relaxation.

Now, we're going to work on your legs and feet. First take
some time for deep, diaphragmatic breathing . . . breathe slowly
and deeply and imagine letting the tension flow outward as you
exhale. Okay, let's focus on your right foot. Tighten your toes by
bending your foot backward, toes up toward your ankle. Hold the
tension for eight seconds, paying attention to the sensations in

your toes, foot, ankle, and calf. Remember to keep the rest of your body relaxed while you're working on each particular muscle group. You'll learn to keep the tension only in the area of your body that needs to be activated and when the arousal is no longer needed, you'll be able to relax completely. Now, let go of the tension and pay attention to the difference in the sensations. Relax for the count of ten. Repeat the exercise, tensing the right foot . . . feel the tightness for eight seconds and relax for ten seconds. Remember to breathe regularly, slowly and deeply. Now, move on to the left foot and do the same exercise. Bend your foot backward and feel the tension in your toes, foot, ankle, and calf. Hold it for eight seconds and then release for ten seconds. Let's do this one more time. Remembering to breathe slowly and deeply. Tighten for eight . . . and let your foot go limp for ten. Remember that should any distracting thoughts intrude on your serenity, you can easily let them float away like clouds as you return to focusing on the soothing relaxation and peace within your body.

Now, move up a little higher in the legs. Tighten your right thigh and knee area. Hold the tension for eight. You can build the tension in your thigh by pushing your heels down on the ground if you're sitting. Now relax for ten counts and pay attention to the difference in the sensations. Does your leg feel heavy, tingly, and warm? Okay, one more time. Tighten your right thigh and knee and hold it for eight. Now release the tension and relax for ten seconds. Breathe in and out deeply and slowly. Move over to the left leg. Tighten your left thigh and knee area, hold the tension for eight and now relax for ten, nine, all the way down to one. Does this leg feel heavy, tingly, and warm? Okay, one more time . . . tighten your left thigh and knee and hold it for eight. Feel the tightness in your limb. Again, release the tension and relax for ten seconds.

Moving upward, work on your stomach, chest, and shoulders. Beginning with your stomach, tense those muscles . . . try for the sensation you feel when you're doing sit-ups. Hold this for eight, focusing on the tension. Now release the muscles and feel the relaxation for ten seconds. One more time, tighten the stomach muscles, making them taut and firm for eight. Tense only your stomach muscles and make sure you're not tensing any other areas in your body. Now relax for ten, nine, eight, seven, down to one. And remember to keep breathing deeply and slowly . . . in and out . . .

Now move up gradually to the chest, shoulders, and neck where you may hold a lot of tension. Here I want you to build the muscle tension by pushing your shoulders up and back and tightening your neck muscles. Lean a bit forward if you're doing this sitting in a chair. Hold this for eight seconds and feel the entire line of tension from your upper back out to your shoulders and up to your neck. Now release the muscles and feel the relaxation all the way from your upper back, shoulders, chest, and neck. Scan the area, searching for any residual tension and focus on releasing any tightness you find. This is an area of chronic tension for many of us and you may find it difficult to completely relax these muscles at first. As you continue to practice, you'll relax this region as you continue to practice. One more time, push your shoulders up and back and tighten your neck. Feel the discomfort of the tension for eight seconds. Now, completely relax your neck, shoulders, chest, and feel the difference . . . you may feel some tingling or some warmth or heaviness for ten, nine, eight, down to one. Remember to keep breathing in and out, deeply and slowly. Feel the peaceful relaxation in your whole torso and in your limbs.

Try to recall those areas that were particularly tender or sore as you worked through your body. These are the areas that are staying tensed unnecessarily throughout the day and that you will need to work on when you begin to experience negative stress.

Time now to proceed to your face and head. Most of us have no idea how much tension we hold in these areas when we're negatively stressed. First, work on the forehead. To tense the muscles in your forehead, raise and hold your eyebrows up as high as possible. It's generally quite easy to feel the tension you hold in this area. Hold this for eight counts and then completely relax for ten counts. Okay, one more time—raising your eyebrows and tightening the forehead for eight. Now, remembering to breathe deeply and fully, relax the eyebrows and feel the comfortable sensations in your forehead for the count of ten.

The last area which you are going to work on is the face. Here, you'll build the tension by clenching your eyelids shut and opening your mouth as wide as possible. Hold this for eight, seven, six . . . one. Now relax for ten, nine, eight, down to one. Okay, one more time, clench your eyelids shut and open your mouth as wide as possible. Feel the tension for the count of eight. Now, let all of the tension go. Keep your eyes shut and notice the areas around your eyes and mouth feeling loose, smooth, and relaxed. Make sure you aren't clenching your teeth. You may let your mouth remain slightly open and relax your jaw. If you're seated, you may also let your head hang forward if that feels more relaxing for you.

At this point, your entire body should feel completely relaxed. Your legs and arms will feel longer because your muscles have elongated after being tensed and then relaxed. Relax in an enjoyable heaviness and feel the warmth spreading throughout your body. Inhale and exhale several slow, deep releasing breaths. Just relax and enjoy this pleasant, calm feeling and keep your head clear. Should any thoughts come into your mind, just imagine them floating out and away like clouds. Now, gently open your eyes. (Stop recording here.)

If you practice this at least once a day, you'll quickly be able to go through this exercise more easily and rapidly. Practice this exercise until you can do it thoroughly and automatically. As you're learning, record your sessions on the following sheets. If you happen to skip a day of doing PR, make sure to still fill out blanks numbers two and four around the time of day you've been doing the relaxation. Your tension ratings after each session and the decline in tension in general will convince you of the value of this technique. It also feels great!

Relaxation Log

Practiced progressive relaxation today (Yes or No)

1. Date & day   _____

2. Level of tension before practice
   (scale of 1–10 with 10 being very
   stressed and tense and 1 being
   completely relaxed and peaceful).   _____

3. Level of tension after practice   _____

4. Any symptoms of tension (neck pain,
   back pain, headache, etc.) before practice
   on scale of 1 (very minor pain or tension)
   through ten (extreme pain or tension)   _____

5. Rating of tension symptoms after practice _____

Practiced progressive relaxation today (Yes or No)

1. Date & day   _____

2. Level of tension before practice
   (scale of 1–10 with 10 being very
   stressed and tense and 1 being
   completely relaxed and peaceful).   _____

3. Level of tension after practice   _____

4. Any symptoms of tension (neck pain,
   back pain, headache, etc.) before practice
   on scale of 1 (very minor pain or tension)
   through ten (extreme pain or tension)   _____

5. Rating of tension symptoms after practice   _____

Practiced progressive relaxation today (Yes or No)

1. Date & day   _____

2. Level of tension before practice
   (scale of 1–10 with 10 being very
   stressed and tense and 1 being
   completely relaxed and peaceful).   _____

3. Level of tension after practice   _____

4. Any symptoms of tension (neck pain,
   back pain, headache, etc.) before practice
   on scale of 1 (very minor pain or tension)
   through ten (extreme pain or tension)   _____

5. Rating of tension symptoms after practice   _____

Practiced progressive relaxation today (Yes or No)

1. Date & day   _____

2. Level of tension before practice
   (scale of 1–10 with 10 being very
   stressed and tense and 1 being
   completely relaxed and peaceful).   _____

3. Level of tension after practice   _____

4. Any symptoms of tension (neck pain,
   back pain, headache, etc.) before practice
   on scale of 1 (very minor pain or tension)
   through ten (extreme pain or tension)   _____

5. Rating of tension symptoms after practice   _____

Practiced progressive relaxation today (Yes or No)

1. Date & day   _____

2. Level of tension before practice
   (scale of 1–10 with 10 being very
   stressed and tense and 1 being
   completely relaxed and peaceful).   _____

3. Level of tension after practice   _____

4. Any symptoms of tension (neck pain,
   back pain, headache, etc.) before practice
   on scale of 1 (very minor pain or tension)
   through ten (extreme pain or tension)   _____

5. Rating of tension symptoms after practice _____

Practiced progressive relaxation today (Yes or No)

1. Date & day   _____

2. Level of tension before practice
   (scale of 1–10 with 10 being very
   stressed and tense and 1 being
   completely relaxed and peaceful).   _____

3. Level of tension after practice   _____

4. Any symptoms of tension (neck pain,
   back pain, headache, etc.) before practice
   on scale of 1 (very minor pain or tension)
   through ten (extreme pain or tension)   _____

5. Rating of tension symptoms after practice _____

Xerox this sheet and continue to track your practice efforts and the results of progressive relaxation for at least two to three weeks.

Guided Imagery

You can use this method either by itself or as a supplement to progressive relaxation. Guided imagery involves visualization and imagination. It's extremely useful in helping you obtain relief from negative stress, tension, pain, and anxiety. When you don't have the time or appropriate setting for the entire progressive relaxation process, this method is ideal.

One imaging technique I've found very effective is as follows: Close your eyes and take several deep, relaxing breaths. Now, while still inhaling and exhaling deeply and slowly, you imagine yourself descending in an elevator or escalator. You count slowly backward from ten to one for each "floor" that you descend. To increase your sense of peace and serenity, try to decorate your path of descent in a way most pleasing to you. One of my clients, Megan, liked to imagine everything cloaked in white with soft, billowing fabrics, ribbons, and soothing music. Another client, Mara preferred a colorful assemblage and a bright, uplifting atmosphere. Remember to breathe slowly and deeply using the deep diaphragmatic breathing learned in the first exercise. Descend as many "floors" as you feel comfortable, imagining as you descend that all tension, cares, and worries are leaving your body and mind as you go to a calmer, peaceful place deeper within yourself.

Choose Your Peaceful Scene

Here is one of my favorites and many people whom I have taught to use this feel likewise. In this form of guided imagery, you select a scene that's particularly pleasing and relaxing for you. This will be your own temporary escape when pressures or pain become excessive. It will give you time out, a reduction in negative stress, and you'll be able to return to the real world with greater relaxation and well-being. I used this technique while giving birth to my son (which included twenty hours of labor finally ending in a cesarean section) and definitely noticed that it increased my calmness and decreased the pain and anxiety.

When you design your personal escape, make sure to involve all of your senses—smells, sounds, touch, sight, even taste if you choose. I am providing the following example for you to use if you want. However, the technique will work most effectively if you personally choose and design your private place. There is a space provided below if you want to write down and elaborate on the scene.

If you choose to use the imagery included here, it's a good idea to read it aloud on tape so that you can play it back and more easily enter your state of relaxation. Make yourself comfortable by sitting in a chair or lying down. (Begin recording here:)

Close your eyes and take several deep breaths. Pay attention to any areas in your body that feel tense and take a moment to relax those muscles. Visualize areas of tightness as tight knots which are slowly unwinding and releasing. Now, imagine that you're sitting on a towel on a beautiful, tropical beach. You feel the slight balmy breeze caressing your skin, ruffling through your hair. The sun is gently warming your skin, while you listen to the rhythmic, slow crash of the surf followed by the soft sound of the water as it rolls back over pebbles and sand out to the ocean. The water rolls in and out . . . in and out . . . a soothing, even pattern. You have no cares or worries and feel totally at peace and at one with the world around you. You decide to take a stroll down the beach. You rise slowly, stretch luxuriously, and feel the warm grains of sand giving way beneath the soles of your feet and rising up between your toes. The sun continues to gently warm your skin as you slowly stroll along the shore. As you in-hale you detect the musty smell of the sand dunes. A seagull calls from above and soars lazily out of view. You look out to the clear blue sea and notice the silvery diamond flashes of sunlight dancing on the water. The sky is a beautiful light blue and a few white wispy clouds drift easily above. You take slow deep breaths of the clean slightly salty air. As you inhale you feel joyous yet relaxed. You feel at one with nature. A feeling of utter comfort and peacefulness fills your mind and body. You realize this is the truth . . . the here and now. You are simply being. Any negative stressors or problems worrying you earlier now seem unimpor-tant as you stay in the present in this place of beauty and calm. Take a moment to look around you and appreciate the peaceful-ness of nature. Remember that this is your own private place to which you can return whenever you want to regain this feeling of utter relaxation. Now slowly open your eyes and return to your surroundings. Take a moment to calmly adjust. You notice that you still feel the sense of peace and relaxation that you felt in your beach imagery. Minor problems, hassles and deadlines that face you will no longer seem as disturbing as before and you realize you can and will approach them in a calm, organized, and effective fashion. (Stop recording here.)

Now that you're familiar with what's entailed in guided im-agery, please feel free to create your own special place. Think back to places and activities in your life that have made you feel the most re-laxed and peaceful. Write down a script you can easily run through in your mind or play back from a tape recorder. To make your escape most realistic and effective, remember to include all of your senses. What are the sounds you hear, the scents you smell? What is the vis-ual scene? What about your sense of touch? Remind yourself to relax several times throughout the scenario. Tell yourself that you feel the tension leaving your body and that all of your daily concerns and worries float lightly from your mind and away into the sky. Stay in this scene as long as you like and tell yourself that the blissful relaxation and calm will carry over into your daily routine. Believe it or not, it can do so! It may seem counterintuitive that taking time out for techniques such as these actually increase your productivity. The fact is that when you're calm, focused, and have centered your energy, your productivity increases and more than compensates for the "time-outs" when you do relaxation and visualization exercises.

Try to do this exercise at the beginning of each day. It will become easier for you to reach your state of relaxation with practice. Ultimately, you may need only to briefly visualize your scene to feel the distress minimizing and your relaxation and prostress increasing. Describe your place of peace and relaxation here:

_____

_____

_____

_____

_____

_____

_____

_____

_____

Paying Attention to Your Physical Responses

Negative stress, as you know by now, can wreak havoc on your body. Not surprisingly, one of the most important steps we can take is to listen to our own bodies. Unfortunately, we're too often so caught up in rushing from task to task or thinking about the future that we completely ignore the messages our body is trying to send us. We don't feel the build-up of tension until our bodies scream at us through migraine headaches, stiff necks and shoulders, aching backs, or stomachaches. Right now, I want you to take a breath, close your eyes and concentrate on locating any areas of tension in your body. The number of painful or tense areas that you detect, now that you are being quiet and looking inside, may surprise you. Each of us tend to have our own habitual areas of tightness. Common places of tension are the forehead, the neck, the shoulders, and the stomach. Having practiced progressive relaxation and guided imagery, you should be getting a very good idea as to where you habitually hold tension and the areas in your body that become unnecessarily tense when you perceive an event as distressful.

Stress Triggers

The following exercise will help you get an even better idea as to what stressful situations elicit tension and arousal in your body, and where you manifest this tension. Several times each day when you begin to feel irritated, angry, anxious, or physically aroused and tense, note the situation and how your body and mind are reacting. Becoming aware of these patterns is the first step to changing your thoughts and bodily reactions. You can then reduce your experience of negative stress and the resulting negative consequences of distress. As you become aware of your stress triggers, you can use your self-talk and relaxation to modify your perception of the danger or importance of the situation. Your body will no longer be continuously aroused (that is, responding to stress), and so you'll prevent the usual physical damage arising from the incessant, undispersed arousal throughout the day.

The following is an example of a format you can use to realize your dangerous patterns of interpreting events so as to increase negative stress with irrational self-talk (self-talk is what you say to yourself tainted by your irrational thinking). You will also see physical and psychological problems that result. Make certain to include all of the elements in this example. This is one of the clearest ways you can have concrete, objective evidence for the areas you'll want to immediately work on and change. Try to make your entries at least three to four times a day. Xerox this format or write it down in a notebook of assignments and carry it around with you. You don't have to stop reading the book while you practice this technique. Forge ahead while making these entries.

Stress Triggers

Sample

Date _____   Day _____

Time	Stressful Situation	Physical and/or Psychological Symptom
7:30 A.M.	Traffic jam	Neck and shoulders tense Getting very irritated Can't stand this every day
10:30 A.M.	Given a lot of extra paperwork	Stomach tight and achy Anxiety, anger at boss, hopelessness My boss has no respect for me I have no control in this job
6:00 P.M.	All pumps being used at gas station	Headache, neck very tight Irritation, depression Everything is against me

Date _____   Day _____

Time	Stressful Situation	Physical and/or Psychological Symptom

Date _____   Day _____

Time   **Stressful**   **Physical and/or**
                  Situation   **Psychological Symptom**

Date _____   Day _____

Time   **Stressful**   **Physical and/or**
                  Situation   **Psychological Symptom**

Date _____   Day _____

Time	Stressful Situation	Physical and/or Psychological Symptom

As you become proficient with this technique, it will help you to gather many important insights and abilities. You'll realize how you exaggerate everyday events, even minor ones, through extreme, negative self-talk that comes from your absolutistic and catastrophizing thoughts. Also, the particular events that "send you over" will now serve as warnings for you to use your relaxation techniques and balanced, realistic cognitions and appraisals. You'll see that everything isn't against you *personally*, obstacles merely happen sometimes.

Quick Body Relaxers

All of us are subject to waiting periods during the day. Whether this be waiting a few minutes at a red light, waiting in line at the grocery store or bank, or being put on hold on the telephone. These situations are ideal for two reasons. (No, they're not ideal for getting into a screaming match with a rude person in line or talking very loudly about the poor service quality at the local supermarket.) For one thing, these periods give you some available, uninterrupted time to scan your body and detect where you may be holding tension. Two, these are times when many of us become impatient, irritable, and experience distress and physiological arousal. This, then, is the ideal time for you to practicing using your relaxation tools.

After the initial few efforts, you'll be able to proceed rapidly through this exercise and the benefits will astound you. These quick body relaxers help to break your body down into segments:

Focus on your head and face. Scan for tension in the forehead, clenched teeth, or other signs of tightness. Inhale deeply, and then exhale and release this tension.

Move down to your neck, upper back, shoulders, arms and hands. Scan for any tension as you breathe in, and let any tension you might find flow out of your body as you exhale.

Move down to your chest, stomach, and lower back. Scan for any tension as you inhale and release any tension as you exhale.

Finally, focus on your upper and lower legs and feet. Scan for any tension as you inhale, and release it with your exhalation.

Finish up with a few deep, slow diaphragmatic breaths.

Incorporate this routine into your schedule several times a day. With practice and the understanding of your body's typical responses to stress, you'll be able to quickly scan your body or move right to your personal, habitual areas of tension and easily let the tension flow from your body.

Meditation

Although I will not discuss meditation in depth, I do want to briefly introduce it because many people have found it invaluable in increasing relaxation and concentration. I'll give you a few instructions, but the interested reader is urged to seek additional information and training. While meditation has been a tool used in many religious practices, it need not be associated with religion. Rather, you can use meditation as a systematic technique of obtaining balance between your inner and outer worlds. By increasing your acceptance of your true, inner being, you're less likely to be negatively impacted by external events, or to let your mind create needless stress. Meditation differs from hypnosis in that the latter is based upon suggestion (one's own or someone else's), while the former is a state of observation rather than active involvement. Studies have shown that people proficient in meditation have decreased physical indicators of stress and increased psychological stability. Namely, meditation is associated with decreased pulse and blood pressure, a more stable galvanic skin response, and decreased respiratory rate and oxygen consumption. The negative impact of distress on your psyche is also reduced because you are no longer brooding about imagined fears, threats, weaknesses, or disturbing memories. With continued meditation, self-confidence and self-acceptance increase.

There are two things necessary in obtaining a meditative state—relaxation and effortless concentration. Effortless concentration is an essential part of meditation and arises when you aren't actively trying to maintain concentration. When you begin to practice meditation, you'll probably find it very difficult to concentrate on inner objects, thoughts, images, or sounds, and avoid distraction from minor external distractions. Give it a try right now by selecting a word to concentrate on. Allow only that word into your consciousness and see how long you can do this. You'll probably find that your mind starts wandering or that an external noise or sensation distracts you. Don't let this disturb you. Simply let the thoughts or sensations go and return your focus to your selected word. With practice at meditation, these distractions will disappear or decrease dramatically. This type of meditation, in which thoughts or feelings are viewed as distractions and in which focus on a word or one's breath is central, is called "one-pointed meditation." A word of warning: Some people find it difficult to practice meditation at first because they're still driven by "doing" and feel they're wasting time by just sitting not doing anything. Be patient with yourself and tell yourself that what you are *doing* is central to improving your health and well-being. As with the other mind-body techniques, you'll find that you become even more productive in addition to feeling less distress and greater prostress. It's important not to embark upon meditation in a goal-oriented fashion. This destroys your ability to attain a true state of effortless concentration and relaxation. You must give yourself permission to take the time to become calm, focused, and balanced.

For a more in-depth review of the above discussion, you can refer to Phil Nuernberger's 1985 *Freedom from Stress*. The following introduction to meditation is adapted from his book. Meditation should be practiced in a quiet, peaceful room when distractions are unlikely. Your efforts will be more effective if you can practice daily, particularly at a set time. This allows meditation to become habitual and your practice time becomes associated with a sense of peace and relaxation.

Practicing Meditation

Begin by sitting in a comfortable, straight chair, or erect on a pillow with your legs crossed. Start to breathe with the deep, diaphragmatic breaths which you learned in the first exercise. Commence this exercise with the intent that you won't let your mind take you on its usual twists and turns. Attend to the feel of your breath during your inhalations and exhalations. When you inhale focus on either of two areas: the space between your two eyes or the space on your chest between your breasts. Nuernberger suggests that if you are intellectually oriented, focus on your forehead area, or if you're emotionally oriented, focus on your breast space. Don't focus on your skin surface but rather on the space within your body. Let your thoughts start to flow through free association. Stand back and become a voyeur rather than a director of your thoughts and practice this phase for as long as you comfortably can. The period of time will lengthen as you practice. The entrance into meditation lies through inner concentration in which your mind becomes still and calm. The path to developing inner concentration requires that you perform the following daily: sitting quietly with your eyes closed, attending fully to the flow of your breath and then to your selected center, and finally observing the flow of your thoughts and images. An essential part of this process is using a single point, generally called a "mantra," upon which to focus. Select your own mantra, it can be a single word, a sound, or several words. Your mantra is used to soothe your mind and allow access to the deep levels of your mind. This type of meditation will allow you to develop a long-lasting feeling of calm and balance in your life.

Biofeedback

Biofeedback is another mind-body technique useful for stress and pain management. For centuries, it was believed that many of our bodily reactions, particularly those linked with the autonomic nervous system, were "automatic" and beyond our conscious control. Recall our earlier discussion about the two nervous systems that regulate the body: the somatic and the autonomic nervous systems. The former is associated with the functioning of skeletal muscles, those you easily control. For example, you move your arm when you want to pick up a desired object. On the other hand, the autonomic nervous system regulates the stomach, endocrine glands, heart, and other parts of your body that were traditionally considered beyond the realm of conscious control. However, with the help of technological innovation, we've discovered that when individuals are given information about these physical processes, such as heart rate, skin temperature, muscular tension, and brain waves, they can affect these processes with their minds. With the feedback provided through biofeedback, we can learn to control these processes. The principle here is similar to what we've used throughout the stress-management techniques presented herein. Namely, when you tap into cues regarding your body's stress responses, you can then take action to modify these responses to reduce distress. Biofeedback equipment provides information about one or more of the following physical states: skin temperature, brain waves, muscle tension, or heartbeat. The information is presented in auditory or visual form and the recipient uses her mind to change the bodily characteristics or the stress response, such as reducing muscular tension and heart rate, and modifying brain waves. She learns how to make these changes (relaxing) by seeing the effects on her body's systems. Biofeedback has been used for clinical purposes, medical purposes, and even in the world of business. A growing number of progressive companies are including biofeedback in their employee health plans.

Biofeedback has been effectively used with insomnia, anxiety, menstrual pain, muscular tension and pain, cardiac arrhythmia, migraines, Reynaud's disease, high blood pressure, incontinence, nerve damage, and gastrointestinal problems. Although structured relaxation can be as effective for some of these disorders as biofeedback, some are better treated with biofeedback and it's a good idea to consult a professional to learn more. You can find biofeedback organizations in large cities or through contacting your local colleges and universities.

11

Using Your Head:
Cognitive Tools

Your cognitions or thoughts are central to the entire stress process.
Whether an event is stressful for you or not depends on your interpretation of the situation. Your judgments about the importance of
the event and whether or not you think you can meet the situation's
demands determine whether you'll feel stressed out by the situation.
Chapter 10 taught you how to get in touch with your body's
responses to stress. It also gave you tools to change these habitual
responses and avoid the harmful consequences of negative stress. In
this chapter, you'll learn how your thoughts and beliefs can either
create negative stress or prostress and, accordingly, hurt or help your
mental and physical well-being and pleasure with life.

How many times have you made statements like, "He made me
so mad," "My mother-in-law drives me crazy," "He stresses me out,"
or "She makes me feel like an idiot"? Statements like these indicate
that many of us think it's a situation or a person that has the power
to dictate our emotions. The truth is, you dictate how you perceive
and respond to someone or something. It might be easier to blame
something else, but it's what we're telling ourselves about the event
or person that determines our emotional and thus physical reactions.
Let's look at the last statement, "She makes me feel like an idiot." Perhaps you're talking about a co-worker or supervisor who seems to effortlessly zip through her work and is always prepared to spout off
the right answer to anyone's questions. Meanwhile, you're engaged
in one of a woman's favorite ways to put herself down (discussed

earlier) by comparing yourself to her and turning up the sound on your favorite old tune—"Getting Blue with My Bad Self-Talk." Something like this goes around in your head, "She always knows exactly what to say and never makes mistakes. She is much better at this than I am. She always knows what to do and I never do. I probably look like a fool in comparison to her." After talking to yourself this way, why wouldn't you feel like an idiot? You are you're own secret, deadly weapon here. It is *you* who made yourself feel this way by the words you used to talk to yourself. Take another look at the thought process in this example. It's highly unlikely that this person never makes mistakes. She may be better than you at certain things, but is she really a better person than you because she may be more organized, well prepared, or whatever? Describing yourself as a fool in comparison to her is too extreme. Remember, we tend to be much more harsh and judgmental about ourselves than we are about others. Women, especially, are hypercritical and blame themselves for situations more so than men.

For example, let's look at an event like the offer of a job promotion. One woman, Rosita, is ecstatic about the opportunity. She has a number of plans she wants to implement, and believes she can make important changes. She sees this offer as the deserved consequence of her excellent job performance. Rosita feels energized and excited. Another woman, Jackie, feels tense and anxious. She wonders whether her boss's decision was really a well thought-out or wise one. She spends her time thinking about how hard the new position will be and the many ways she might not live up to her superior's expectations. The situation here—an offer of a promotion—is the same for both women. What differs is how each thinks about it. Rosita views it as a challenge and a chance for growth. Accordingly, her healthy feeling of enthusiasm and her productive thought processes (creativity, organization, and planning) and her behavior arise from this positive interpretation. Jackie thinks about the situation in such a way that it becomes a threat. This is because she doesn't believe she has the abilities or resources to meet the unknown demands. Accordingly, Jackie experiences the physical and behavioral drawbacks of negative stress. Because she feels anxious, her thinking process will suffer as distress interferes with the ability to be creative and focused. It's very possible that her negative expectations could lead to a self-fulfilling prophecy of being insecure and ineffective in the new job. What's important to realize is that each woman created her own reality. The way she interpreted the events and the content (negative or positive) of her self-talk determined her reactions and behaviors, which ultimately affect the outcome of the original situation. The idea that our emotions aren't necessarily realistic responses to actual events is certainly not a new one. Two thousand years ago, Epictetus stated that man is not disturbed so much by events themselves but rather by the view he has of them. We must be careful of tendencies toward viewing events and situations in a distorted, negative way because this colors everything we do and feel. The exercises in this chapter will help you discover and change your unhealthy ways of thinking.

Two researchers who contributed much to our understanding of cognitive psychology are Albert Ellis and Aaron Beck. In its most basic format, the content and process of Ellis's rational-emotive therapy (RET) model can be represented by the letters A, B, and C. According to this perspective, emotional and behavioral symptoms, or consequences, C, result from beliefs, B, about particular activating experiences, events, or environments, A. As pointed out in the previous example, it isn't the event but your beliefs about the event that determine your feelings and behaviors. So A doesn't lead directly to C; rather B leads to C (Dryden and Ellis 1986). In the example of a job promotion, the offer of the promotion itself did not cause one woman to be excited and pleased and the other anxious and afraid. Instead, it was each woman's intervening thoughts, B, about the job promotion that led to her particular reactions, C. Before an event can lead to the harmful physical or psychological consequences of stress, it needs to be appraised as a negative stressor.

Stop the Vicious Cycle

Ellis did not believe that this flow was unidirectional. That is, how we behave and feel also can influence our beliefs (C can lead to B). An example of this direction is the self-fulfilling prophecy. For example, if you're anxious and distressed about socializing with others, C, and so tend to avoid social situations, A, it's likely you won't have many friends. This serves to confirm and even make stronger your initial belief, B, that you really are unlikable or socially inept. It's for this reason that I often have clients challenge their depressive and anxiety-inducing beliefs by having them engage in the situations they fear. When the expected catastrophes don't occur, they realize that their distress-producing beliefs aren't accurate. If they don't have any disconfirming evidence (i.e., if they don't see that they *can* socialize and make acquaintances or friends), there's no reason for them to change their negative beliefs about themselves.

Playing Center Stage

There is another technique I use that can be very effective in destroying or weakening your unrealistic, negative views of yourself and the resulting rigid behavior. Write down a paragraph describing the woman you would like to be. You can borrow values and characteristics from a women you know, fictional characters, or whomever you admire, respect, and with whom you'd like to share some aspects. What kinds of activities would you as this woman do? How would you handle social interactions? How would you carry yourself? In what type of work would you be interested? How would you express your feelings and beliefs? When this is complete, your assignment for this particular week will be to have a great deal of fun as you become a temporary actor. In other words, go out and behave as this "ideal, respected" woman. You can talk, walk, eat, and dress the part. You'll change her own routine, attend music or art events, go to movies, research in the library, go to restaurants or dance, attend exercise classes, approach people who you have wanted to speak with, and in so many ways do what you've wanted to do before but have been too afraid or plagued with low self-esteem to do. One of the most important things to remember is to have fun with this and disregard your usual fears and negative stress. The idea that you're playing a role and are thus free to act in a way you typically would not allows you to break free of habitual, limiting, preconceived thoughts and restricted behaviors.

This tool has been incredibly useful for a number of my clients. One of them, Margaret, just couldn't seem to grasp the presence of her automatic negative beliefs and how they were increasing the negative stress and removing prostress from her life. After going out to complete this "fun" project, she came to our next session in an exuberant state. She exclaimed that she'd never realized how much her mind and thinking had been dictating her feelings and behavior. She was delighted with the results as she, typically feeling insecure and inferior, had envisioned herself as the cheerful, assured, and humorous woman she wanted to be. Subsequently, Margaret had been able to much more easily speak to people, share some good jokes with a stranger, and even make two acquaintances in one week. This exercise allowed her to experiment and change her negative preconceived beliefs that she was inferior and would inevitably be rejected by others. Her "predictions" had been disproved and seeing how strongly her thoughts determined her feelings and behavior, she became focused on examining and modifying her unhealthy, distressing thinking. Most importantly, this exercise lets you change the narrative of your life by changing your "script" and the long-standing motivation of your character (that is, fear, insecurity, avoidance of changes, hiding or suppressing your true feelings).

Take advantage of this lighthearted exercise and write down a brief story introducing your desired character. Then, keeping a feeling of fun and excitement involved, take it out to the real world and see how you can have a huge impact on decreasing your typical distress and increasing fun and prostress. You can also put yourself into your role when you're facing some important, traditionally nerve-wracking events such as interviews or examinations. With practice, you'll actually incorporate the desired characteristics and positive orientation into your own persona and thus have much more control over your moods, behaviors, and even success and health in life.

The model upon which cognitive work is based is that thoughts, feelings, and behavior inevitably interact. So, the way you think about an event or situation influences your emotional reactions and behavior. Likewise, your behaviors can impact how you think about something as well as what kind of events you might experience.

Determining Your Distress or Prostress

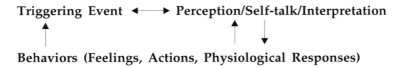

Use this diagram as you read this example that might be familiar. Say you are working on a project when your boss tells you that rather than the month you thought you had to complete the project, you only have two weeks. Let's say this happens to you before you have read this book and learned stress-management techniques. You might have immediately thought, "Oh no, I'll never finish in that time. It's impossible. My presentation won't be very good and then they'll think I'm stupid and unprofessional and I'll never get promoted in this company." As you know, you would then experience many of the usual physiological distress reactions, as well as anxiety and possibly depression. On the other hand, you hear this news from your boss just as you're closing the last pages of this book. You are aware of the choice you can make to interpret this event differently. You have some control over how you are going to respond emotionally. Now you say to yourself, "Well, that's not as much time as I'd like, but it's certainly a challenge. I'll do the best I can and I'll probably impress them with what I was able to produce in such a limited time. Even if it's not the best I could do, they'll be appreciative of my finishing in a timely way." You'll experience the challenge of prostress and will approach the project in a focused, balanced way with greater energy than you ever have before.

Stress-Inducing Thinking

It's fascinating to see that when you dig underneath feelings of negative stress, depression, and anxiety, you'll inevitably find particular irrational ways of thinking that are causing or worsening your emotional and physical state. From the following list, check and see how many types of "stinking thinking" you use. Initially, you might say, "This is too extreme and I certainly don't think like this. It doesn't even make sense!" Many clients I've worked with on this task have responded this way at first. As you go through the list, be rigorously honest as you excavate deeply beneath your superficial thoughts to find your stress-generating mistaken assumptions, perceptions, and beliefs. Once you've had time to really look at these patterns and make a thorough, honest self-analysis, you'll probably identify with several or more types of distorted thinking. Read through this list and circle the numbers of those that characterize your thoughts frequently (McKay, Davis, and Fanning 1981).

Negative Stress-Inducing Thinking

1. **Filtering:** Using tunnel vision to perceive and process only one part of a situation. Generally involves magnifying any negative details and ignoring or minimizing any positive elements. Depressed people focus on aspects suggesting loss; anxious people focus on things that could suggest danger; angry people focus on the issue of injustice. Through filtering, you magnify the bad and lose sight of the good. Incessant thought: "I can't stand it."

2. **Polarized thinking:** Perceiving everything in extremes, in black and white. No ability to perceive moderation. You think that your job, your salary, your significant other, your friends, your life, are either all good or all bad. The stress-inducing element here is applying this erroneous thinking to yourself. "I made a mistake; I am doomed because I forgot where I put something; I'm screwed because I was five minutes late; her presentation was more creative than mine." All

of this self-talk leads to the single horrible conclusion that since you aren't perfect, you're a complete failure and loser.

3. **Overgeneralization:** Taking one or two minor events to draw an irreversible, negative, all-encompassing generalization. One of my clients recently told me, "My Mom and now my friend have let me down—it just goes to show you that you can't depend on anybody. I'll have to be completely responsible and do everything by myself."

4. **Mind reading:** Using guesses, vague feelings, or limited experience to draw arbitrary (ironclad, in your eyes) conclusions about the motivations and intentions of others, particularly with respect to yourself. Mind readers are so certain about their accuracy that they don't test their conclusions and believe everybody else would conclude the same thing.

5. **Catastrophizing:** Believing that every problematic event is momentous and tragic. "I'm a day late with the rent and I know my landlord is going to kick me out." "My boyfriend broke up with me; nobody will ever love me again." Many of my clients suffer from this type of thinking, but they become really involved in catching themselves and one another, and by simply saying, "You're catastrophizing."

6. **Personalization:** Interpreting everything around you (experiences, other people's conversations, other people's feelings) as related you to and ultimately to your self-worth. "My boss chose four people to work on a new task force. They were all from a different division than mine, but he knows I'm interested in that area of technology. He must just think I'm not smart enough."

7. **Control fallacies:** Believing that you're either a helpless victim, with an external locus of control, or you're in control of and responsible for everything and everyone. We've discussed much in this book about how the former view increases your sense of helplessness, depression, and negative stress. It can also be paralyzing to believe something else is in control of your life—why try to change anything? On the other hand, imagine how difficult and worrisome your life would be if you really were responsible for everything and everyone around you. This is an egotistical stance and your energy is better spent focusing on your needs and wants and helping others secondary to these. Women tend to have

these thought patterns and experience the negative stress regarding lack of control over their own lives. We often believe we must help run everybody's else lives, our own work environment, family, and so on.

8. **Fallacy of fairness:** Basing your expectations from others on what you believe is "only fair." This is truly a dangerous mode of thinking because what is "fair" is subjective. You will be easily frustrated and distressed. One of my clients, Laura, had a deeply ingrained belief that things were supposed to be fair. She would become angry or tearful during sessions with the explanation that this situation or that situation simply wasn't fair. It took asking her many times, "Who said life is fair?" and having her explore the reality of this belief before she could begin to let go of it. She was gradually able to understand that, "It would be nice if *xyz* happens, but life isn't always fair. Let's see what I can do about it." By changing her expectations, her level of distress was dramatically reduced and she spent less time resenting others and being passive and more time going after what she wanted.

9. **Emotional reasoning:** Thinking that whatever it is you happen to be feeling is the absolute reality. "If I feel stupid, I am. If I feel bad about myself, I am a bad person." I see many examples of this type of thinking and the damage it causes in adults who grew up in toxic environments. Having had parents who conveyed to them that they were no good, stupid, ugly, and the like, the children began to feel these things were true. As adults who haven't worked through early issues, they still feel bad and stupid (often not knowing why) and so believe that they are bad and stupid. Remember though that it's your negative thoughts that lead to negative feelings and distress; emotions aren't inherently realistic and often stem from illogical or myopic thinking.

10. **Fallacy of change:** Believing that you can change others so that they will perfectly meet your needs, take care of you, make you feel important and good. The problem is you can't really change other people and they will generally end up being angry or resenting you. The underlying trouble here is that you are placing your salvation and your chance to be happy in the hands of another. You are the only person who can finally satisfy yourself and make you happy and assured.

11. **Global labeling:** Going completely overboard and exaggerating (typically in a negative way) in perceiving a situation or another person based on a tiny element of truth. "My so-called friend is late in meeting me for the third time in a row. Obviously she thinks my time isn't as important as hers. She's completely selfish and inconsiderate. She could never be a true friend so I'm going to watch my back and keep my feelings to myself." This type of thinking prohibits you from perceiving or acknowledging any evidence to the contrary.

12. **Blaming:** Attributing problems, you're emotions, failures, disappointments, either completely to others *or* to yourself. The first method is ideal for absolving yourself of any responsibility for changing situations in your life or characteristics in yourself. The second approach is one that has been discussed in this book as frequently typifying women. This can lead to similar results as the first one; namely, since everything is your fault and you're a complete mess, there is really nothing you can do to change the situation or yourself.

13. **Shoulds:** Using your own set of values and beliefs to judge how the world and everybody in it, including yourself, should function. Like blaming, should, or the "s-word," type of thinking can be used against external events and people or against yourself. "I'm feeling completely stressed out and furious and if he really loves me, he should know I'll want to go out to dinner tonight." "If I'm any good at this job, I should finish this whole project by the end of the day." "I should be able to help my kids with their homework, go over the papers I brought home from work, and finish dinner on time." Whenever I catch my clients using the s-word in this extreme, negative stress-inducing way, I point it out to them. Eventually, they're able to catch themselves before or right after they've said it and modify their word choice. Many of them find this simple technique extremely useful at home or at work to help them catch their unrealistic expectations and replace them with realistic ones. This reduces the negative stress they had created for themselves.

14. **Being right:** The need to appear omniscient is the driving force in your life. You have to prove to everybody that you're always right, that you know more than anyone else, and that everything you do is right. Because you ignore any information that doesn't perfectly align with your viewpoint, you

stay stuck in a rigid pattern, cannot relax and enjoy yourself, and cannot have a truly intimate, sharing relationship.

15. **Heaven's reward fallacy:** You do as much as you can for others while ignoring your own needs and feelings. You choose this path because you know that if you just keep working hard enough and sacrifice enough, you'll eventually be rewarded and recognized for the truly special person you are. This is a sure way to miss out on living your own life and being able to enjoy just being or living in the present.

Reading the irrational-thinking patterns can make it easier to notice their judgmental and restrictive nature. The more types of "stinking thinking" you feel that you have, the more distressed you're going to be. When doing cognitive work with my clients, I always include self-monitoring to help increase awareness of such types of thinking. They are always surprised about the results of this exercise in a number of ways. First, it is often difficult to catch these irrational thoughts because they speed like lightning through our minds (of course, many have to first develop the insight as to the existence of erroneous thinking because a lot of times it's still at the subconscious level). This is where people become frustrated and may temporarily give up and state that the technique "doesn't work for them." With a little extra urging and scecific help on my part, they eventually get in touch with these fleeting thoughts and the next time I see them, they're telling me in astonishment how constantly they're being bombarded with them and how they now feel empowered because they have something substantial to target and change. So secondly the relentlessness of these self-damaging, distorted modes of thought is really eye-opening. Third, tracking internal dialogue truly astounds people when they realize how such irrational, unhealthy thinking really does cause so much of their distress, depression, frustration, and anxiety. And finally, when they learn to confront and modify such negative thinking, they're very pleased with the improvement in their mood, energy, and lifestyles. I hope that you too are so thoroughly surprised and then motivated as you continue to learn how to do more such self-monitoring later in this chapter.

In addition to going through the negative stress-inducing thinking, the following Beliefs Inventory from the *Relaxation & Stress Reduction Workbook*, by Martha Davis, Dr. Matthew McKay, and Elizabeth Robbins Eshelman, will further clarify the types of unrealistic thoughts you use in interpreting events in your life that can explain how you often feel and act. By combining your results from this inventory and from the previous list, you'll be well-prepared for the next stage: tracking and changing your unhealthy, distress-increasing thoughts and replacing them with rational, prostress-enhancing beliefs and thoughts.

Directions—Rational Emotive Therapy

Assessment

This Beliefs Inventory is designed to uncover particular irrational ideas which contribute to unhappiness and stress. Take the test now. Score it and note the sections where your scores are highest. Note that it is not necessary to think over any item very long. Mark your answer quickly and go on to the next statement. Be sure to mark how you actually think about the statement, not how you think you should think.

Beliefs Inventory

Agree	Disagree	Score	Belief
• ☐	☐	_____	1. It is important to me that others approve of me.
• ☐	☐	_____	2. I hate to fail at anything.
• ☐	☐	_____	3. People who do wrong deserve what they get.
•• ☐	☐	_____	4. I usually accept what happens philosophically.
•• ☐	☐	_____	5. If a person wants to, he can be happy under almost any circumstances.
• ☐	☐	_____	6. I have a fear of some things that often bothers me.
• ☐	☐	_____	7. I usually put off important decisions.
• ☐	☐	_____	8. Everyone needs someone he can depend on for help and advice.
• ☐	☐	_____	9. "A zebra cannot change his stripes."
• ☐	☐	_____	10. I prefer quiet leisure above all things.
•• ☐	☐	_____	11. I like the respect of others, but I don't have to have it.
• ☐	☐	_____	12. I avoid things I cannot do well.
• ☐	☐	_____	13. Too many evil persons escape the punishment they deserve.
•• ☐	☐	_____	14. Frustrations don't upset me.

Agree	Disagree	Score	Belief
•• □	□	_____	15. People are disturbed not by situations but by the view they take of them.
•• □	□	_____	16. I feel little anxiety over unexpected dangers or future events.
•• □	□	_____	17. I try to go ahead and get irksome tasks behind me when they come up.
• □	□	_____	18. I try to consult an authority on important decisions.
• □	□	_____	19. It is almost impossible to overcome the influences of the past.
•• □	□	_____	20. I like to have a lot of irons in the fire.
• □	□	_____	21. I want everyone to like me.
•• □	□	_____	22. I don't mind competing in activities in which others are better than I.
• □	□	_____	23. Those who do wrong deserve to be blamed.
• □	□	_____	24. Things should be different from the way they are.
•• □	□	_____	25. I cause my own moods.
• □	□	_____	26. I often can't get my mind off some concern.
• □	□	_____	27. I avoid facing my problems.
• □	□	_____	28. People need a source of strength outside themselves.
•• □	□	_____	29. Just because something once affects your life strongly doesn't mean it need do so in the future.
•• □	□	_____	30. I'm most fulfilled when I have lots to do.
•• □	□	_____	31. I can like myself even when many others don't.
•• □	□	_____	32. I like to succeed at something, but I don't feel I have to.
• □	□	_____	33. Immorality should be strongly punished.
• □	□	_____	34. I often get disturbed over situations I don't like.
•• □	□	_____	35. People who are miserable have usually made themselves that way.

Agree	Disagree	Score	Belief
•• □	□	_____	36. If I can't keep something from happening, I don't worry about it.
•• □	□	_____	37. I usually make decisions as promptly as I can.
• □	□	_____	38. There are certain people whom I depend on greatly.
•• □	□	_____	39. People overvalue the influence of the past.
•• □	□	_____	40. I most enjoy throwing myself into a creative project.
•• □	□	_____	41. If others dislike me, that's their problem, not mine.
• □	□	_____	42. It is highly important to me to be successful in everything I do.
•• □	□	_____	43. I seldom blame people for their wrongdoings.
•• □	□	_____	44. I usually accept things the way they are, even if I don't like them.
•• □	□	_____	45. A person won't stay angry or blue long unless he keeps himself that way.
• □	□	_____	46. I can't stand to take chances.
• □	□	_____	47. Life is too short to spend it doing unpleasant tasks.
•• □	□	_____	48. I like to stand on my own two feet.
• □	□	_____	49. If I had had different experiences I could be more like I want to be.
• □	□	_____	50. I'd like to retire and quit working entirely.
• □	□	_____	51. I find it hard to go against what others think.
•• □	□	_____	52. I enjoy activities for their own sake, no matter how good I am at them.
• □	□	_____	53. The fear of punishment helps people be good.
•• □	□	_____	54. If things annoy me, I just ignore them.
• □	□	_____	55. The more problems a person has, the less happy he will be.
•• □	□	_____	56. I am seldom anxious over the future.

Agree	Disagree	Score	Belief
•• ☐	☐	_____	57. I seldom put things off.
•• ☐	☐	_____	58. I am the only one who can really understand and face my problems.
•• ☐	☐	_____	59. I seldom think of past experiences as affecting me now.
•• ☐	☐	_____	60. Too much leisure time is boring.
•• ☐	☐	_____	61. Although I like approval, it's not a real need for me.
• ☐	☐	_____	62. It bothers me when others are better than I am at something.
• ☐	☐	_____	63. Everyone is basically good.
•• ☐	☐	_____	64. I do what I can to get what I want and then don't worry about it.
•• ☐	☐	_____	65. Nothing is upsetting in itself—only in the way you interpret it.
• ☐	☐	_____	66. I worry a lot about certain things in the future.
• ☐	☐	_____	67. It is difficult for me to do unpleasant chores.
•• ☐	☐	_____	68. I dislike having others make my decisions for me.
• ☐	☐	_____	69. We are slaves to our personal histories.
• ☐	☐	_____	70. I sometimes wish I could go to a tropical island and just lie on the beach forever.
• ☐	☐	_____	71. I often worry about how much people approve of and accept me.
• ☐	☐	_____	72. It upsets me to make mistakes.
• ☐	☐	_____	73. It's unfair that "the rain falls on both the just and the unjust."
•• ☐	☐	_____	74. I am fairly easygoing about life.
• ☐	☐	_____	75. More people should face up to the unpleasantness of life.
• ☐	☐	_____	76. Sometimes I can't get a fear off my mind.
•• ☐	☐	_____	77. A life of ease is seldom very rewarding.
• ☐	☐	_____	78. I find it easy to seek advice.
• ☐	☐	_____	79. Once something strongly affects your life, it always will.

Agree	Disagree	Score	Belief
• ☐	☐	_____	80. I love to lie around.
• ☐	☐	_____	81. I have considerable concern with what people are feeling about me.
• ☐	☐	_____	82. I often become quite annoyed over little things.
•• ☐	☐	_____	83. I usually give someone who has wronged me a second chance.
• ☐	☐	_____	84. People are happiest when they have challenges and problems to overcome.
•• ☐	☐	_____	85. There is never any reason to remain sorrowful for very long.
•• ☐	☐	_____	86. I hardly ever think of such things as death or atomic war.
•• ☐	☐	_____	87. I dislike responsibility.
•• ☐	☐	_____	88. I dislike having to depend on others.
• ☐	☐	_____	89. People never change basically.
• ☐	☐	_____	90. Most people work too hard and don't get enough rest.
•• ☐	☐	_____	91. It is annoying but not upsetting to be criticized.
•• ☐	☐	_____	92. I'm not afraid to do things which I cannot do well.
•• ☐	☐	_____	93. No one is evil, even though his deeds may be.
•• ☐	☐	_____	94. I seldom become upset over the mistakes of others.
•• ☐	☐	_____	95. Man makes his own hell within himself.
• ☐	☐	_____	96. I often find myself planning what I would do in different dangerous situations.
•• ☐	☐	_____	97. If something is necessary, I do it even if it is unpleasant.
•• ☐	☐	_____	98. I've learned not to expect someone else to be very concerned about my welfare.
•• ☐	☐	_____	99. I don't look upon the past with any regrets.
• ☐	☐	_____	100. I can't feel really content unless I'm relaxed and doing nothing.

Scoring the Beliefs Inventory

A. Single dot items
If the item has one dot (•) and you checked the "agree" box, give yourself one point in the space provided next to the item.

B. Double dot items
If the item has two dots (••) and you checked the "disagree" box, give yourself a point in the space provided next to the item.

C. Add up your points for items:
1, 11, 21, 31, 41, 51, 61, 71, 81, and 91, and enter the total here: _____.
The higher the total, the greater your agreement with the irrational idea that *it is an absolute necessity for an adult to have love and approval from peers, family, and friends.*

2, 12, 22, 32, 42, 52, 62, 72, 82, and 92, and enter the total here: _____.
The higher the total, the greater your agreement with the irrational idea that *you must be unfailingly competent and almost perfect in all you undertake.*

3, 13, 23, 33, 43, 53, 63, 73, 83, and 93, and enter the total here: _____.
The higher the total, the greater your agreement with the irrational idea that *certain people are evil, wicked, and villainous, and should be punished.*

4, 14, 24, 34, 44, 54, 64, 74, 84, and 94, and enter the total here: _____.
The higher the total, the greater your agreement with the irrational idea that *it is horrible when things are not the way you would like them to be.*

5, 15, 25, 35, 45, 55, 65, 75, 85, and 95, and enter the total here: _____.
The higher the total, the greater your agreement with the irrational idea that *external events cause most human misery—people simply react as events trigger their emotions.*

6, 16, 26, 36, 46, 56, 66, 76, 86, and 96, and enter the total here: _____.
The higher the total, the greater your agreement with the irrational idea that *you should feel fear or anxiety about anything that is unknown, uncertain, or potentially dangerous.*

7, 17, 27, 37, 47, 57, 67, 77, 87, and 97, and enter the total here: _____.
The higher the total, the greater your agreement with the irrational idea that *it is easier to avoid than face life's difficulties and responsibilities.*

8, 18, 28, 38, 48, 58, 68, 78, 88, and 98, and enter the total here: _____.
The higher the total, the greater your agreement with the irrational idea that *you need something other or stronger or greater than yourself to rely on.*

9, 19, 29, 39, 49, 59, 69, 79, 89, and 99, and enter the total here: _____.
The higher the total, the greater your agreement with the irrational idea that *the past has a lot to do with determining the present.*

10, 20, 30, 40, 50, 60, 70, 80, 90, and 100, and enter the total here: ____.
The higher the total, the greater your agreement with the irrational idea that *happiness can be achieved by inaction, passivity, and endless leisure.*

Discovering and Transforming Your Erroneous Thinking Patterns

What can you do about the negative, irrational thought patterns that increase your levels of negative stress, anxiety, and even depression? Aaron Beck designed a technique called the Daily Record of Dysfunctional Thoughts. It is invaluable in allowing you to track this type of thinking, its impact on you, and how to "argue back" against the irrationality of these beliefs. Like Albert Ellis, Aaron Beck addresses the fact that the primary role of our thinking determines our judgments about situations and our resulting emotional and behavioral responses. Beck calls these negative thoughts "automatic thoughts," because they speed through our minds so rapidly and consistently that we're usually unaware of them. However, these automatic thoughts have a major impact on our feelings and behavior. It's actually quite simple. When you tend to have a negative view of yourself, others, and the world and you are faced with a potentially stressful situation, you've programmed yourself to interpret it negatively, and expect a negative outcome. Therefore, accordingly, you experience a great deal of distress.

Beck designed a format to highlight how negative automatic thoughts determine our feelings and how, by substituting rational thoughts, we can experience prostress, positive emotions, or at the very least, be much less distressed. I strongly endorse this exercise because it has been extremely helpful for so many of my clients. Like most of us, you're probably not in touch with your automatic thoughts and will be astonished when you can finally "listen in" to the negative, judgmental, irrational self-talk running endlessly through your mind and determining your moods and physical states.

This is an example in Beck's 1979 Daily Record of Dysfunctional Thoughts, of the work done by my client, Andrea. She was experiencing a great deal of negative stress with her job and was so anxious that she couldn't sleep. This exercise works most effectively if you write down the events, thoughts, and feelings throughout the day as they occur or as soon afterward as possible. Carry a small notepad or several sheets of paper with the following form around with you. Make sure you have at least two entries for each day. At the end of the day, spend some time reviewing what you've written. Pay attention to the types of situations that triggered your negative thoughts and feelings. Also look for repetitive patterns in your negative thinking and how you can argue against and transform these unhealthy and irrational thoughts. With practice, you'll develop a much more flexible, positive way of thinking, thereby avoiding much of the negative stress and unhappiness you've been needlessly experiencing.

The table on page 180 may look confusing at first. Please read these directions several times before and after you've made your entries until you become familiar with the exercise.

1. Under the Event column, briefly describe the actual event associated with the unpleasant emotion.

2. It is this second section, Emotion and Degree, that is actually going to serve as the cue for you to internally "check in" and make an entry in your workbook. Under this column, specify your feelings as well as their degree of intensity—1 percent–100 percent.

3. Under the Automatic Thoughts column, list those fleeting, irrational beliefs—remember, you have to search deeply. When you first list your emotions, as well as when you write them down after having substituted rational thoughts for the automatic thoughts, make sure to reevaluate and rewrite the degree of the feeling. Saying "Angry at boss because I was in a bad mood" is just a superficial explanation and isn't really getting at your underlying automatic thoughts. You need to come to terms with *why* you feel angry at your boss, and this may be because of your own feelings of inadequacy or lack of confidence. It isn't always easy or natural to recognize your automatic thoughts and for some people it can take a great deal of effort at first—effort which definitely pays off.

4. In the Cognitive Distortion column, refer above to the list of fifteen Negative Stress-Inducing Thoughts. Write down the one or two distortions that most typify the incident you're writing about at the time.

5. The next column offers you the chance to confront and challenge the automatic thought while using your new understanding gleaned from the cognitive distortions list. Replace the errors in thinking with some rational, balanced and moderate statements, plans, and explanations.

6. Having replaced your old distressing thoughts with new rational responses, you now check in again with your emotional state to determine the Outcome. How do you rate now (using the same percentage scale) on the emotions you had listed under number two—Emotion and Degree?

It's important to realize that when we're negatively stressed, our beliefs become more rigid than usual. In fact, we'll tend to look for evidence to confirm our unrealistic beliefs while ignoring information that would disprove them. Watch for this as you carry out the above assignment. When you notice that you're feeling tense, stressed, anxious, or depressed, briefly jot down the situation, your feelings, and those destructive, automatic thoughts that are directly causing your negative emotions. The more you practice this exercise, the better you'll become at catching these irrational automatic thoughts early and replacing them with realistic, moderate ways of thinking.

Taking It Off the Page and Into Your Life

Once you become proficient at catching, recording, and modifying your negative thinking with the Daily Record, you'll consciously detect your automatic thoughts just as they start to damage your emotional state. Eventually you will stop keeping the written Daily Record, but for now continue to use it. With or without the record, continue to do the self-monitoring and modifying whenever you detect some distress, anxiety, or discomfort. A little more practice and you'll be able to stop most automatic thoughts from coming into play. Your thoughts will be much healthier, flexible, and realistic. Guess what else happens. You will generally be happier, more energetic, and feeling better about yourself and your life situation. Also, when stressful events do come up, you're much more apt to experience

Daily Record of Dysfunctional Thoughts

Date _____

Event	Emotion & Degree	Automatic Thought(s)	Cognitive Distortion(s)	Rational Response to Replace Automatic Thought	Outcome (Emotion and Degree)
1. Boss gave me additional tasks	Stress 89% Anger 79% Depression 60%	I'll never be able to do this ... I'm too dumb	Polarized Thinking	I can try to do as much as possible; I usually do more than I think I can do and tragedy won't strike if I can't finish this last minute overload	Stress 30% Anger 20% Depression 10%
		He just wants to see me fail	Personalizing Mind Reading	Everyone is getting extra work and he knows I'm efficient	
		If I can't finish this task it will prove I am incompetent, not as talented as they thought	Catastrophizing; Overgeneralization	I'll do what I can and he knows my past work has been good; I know my ability and if the task isn't completed, it is because it was given to me very late	

Date _____

Event	Emotion & Degree	Automatic Thought(s)	Cognitive Distortion(s)	Rational Response to Replace Automatic Thought	Outcome (Emotion and Degree)
1.					
2.					
3.					

them as challenging prostress rather than the threatening distress-of-
old. Here are a few more ways to help you eliminate your irrational,
automatic thinking:

- Use the list of fifteen irrational ways of thinking provided to
  name and understand the type of illogical, automatic thinking
  you're using in any particular situation. Include this in your
  Daily Record Form under the "Cognitive Distortions" section.
  Add several situations to the record each day.

- Ask yourself if rational reasoning underlies your negative
  automatic thoughts. Almost always, your answer will be
  "no." Remember, perceptions of ourselves, others, and the
  world around us are all subjective and based on our expectations, fears, and beliefs. Not performing perfectly on one task
  doesn't mean you're an unlovable failure. The tendency to
  think this way is driven by your unhealthy beliefs that you
  must be perfect if others are to value and accept you. Remember that women can be overly dependent on feedback from
  others to bolster our self-esteem. You'll feel tremendous relief
  and less negative stress when you free yourself from this irrational, demeaning way of thinking.

- When your reasoning is faulty, remember that you'll decrease
  your level of negative stress by accepting the fact that life
  may not always be perfect and fair, but you do have a choice
  about how you interpret reality and respond to it. If you accept the reality of the situation and then take measures to
  control and change what you can and let the rest go, you'll
  feel substantially less mental and physical distress. Just as importantly, you can choose to look at a tough situation as a
  challenge rather than a threat. Then, by taking the actions or
  making the changes you can and want, you'll experience prostress and its benefits, such as increased self-esteem, pride,
  energy, pleasure, and growth.

- Adjust your thinking and your feelings and ask yourself two
  questions:
    1. *What is the worst thing that could happen to me?* I might
       find out that I have an area needing improvement, or,
       someone might think I did not do the best job possible,
       or I might experience some discomfort or inconvenience.
    2. *What positive things might happen to me?* I might boost
       my confidence by meeting an unexpected challenge, or,
       I might become more patient, or, I might learn some

new skills, or, I might boost my self-esteem by being able to make it through a trying time while realizing I don't need to beat myself up or become stressed out. I've turned a distressor into a prostressor!

Along these same lines, use this quick tip to put things into perspective. Do you find yourself obsessing about the possible negative outcomes? "What if this? What if that? But what if . . . ?" By adding the simple word "so" to this chant, you defuse the negative power of such ruminations. Instead of thinking, "What if I don't finish this pile of work on my desk before I go home?" you tell yourself, "*So* what if I don't finish this pile of work on my desk before I go home?" Will you definitely be fired? Will all of your co-workers decide you're lousy, lazy, and just plain bad? Will the world end in a fiery explosion? I think you get the point here.

Put a Stop to Your Negative Thoughts

This technique may seem simple, but it's also a very effective method. Thought stopping deals with those disturbing thoughts you play over and over in your head. This anxiety can be terminated (depending on your location) by saying out loud, or silently, "Stop!" This command disrupts the images and associations in your mind, lets you regain control, and allows you to focus on something else. You then de-catastrophize and replace the negative, disturbing thoughts and images with the rational responses, positive statements, or *so*-what--if's you practiced in the previous exercises. For example, imagine it's the evening before an important business meeting and you find yourself thinking obsessively about your performance. As you keep replaying scenes of all of the mistakes you're certain you will make, you become increasingly distressed and anxious. In fact, by dwelling on all of the negatives and everything that could go wrong, you're intensifying your distress and anxiety to the point that you're actually increasing the likelihood you will perform poorly. The old self-fulfilling prophecy is in action. Even if you do manage to do a good job, you have subjected your mind and body to a great deal of unnecessary negative stress. Of course, some arousal can improve your performance, but too much is destructive and you'll end up sabotaging your best intentions. By using the "stop" technique, you can interrupt this negative, self-sabotaging thought-behavior cycle. It will take some practice for you to be able to completely eliminate the negative thoughts and images with your signal to "stop." Remember to replace them with positive, assertive statements or become involved in some other activity. Some people have found it helpful to let themselves "indulge" in the negative thinking and imagery for a set amount of time, maybe several minutes. Then they interject the "stop" command and replace the extinguished negative thoughts with positive or just more realistic ones. Rather than visualizing all of the mistakes you could make at the business meeting, you could choose instead to envision yourself presenting your material in a calm, professional manner. Imagine that all of the data and information you need will come easily to your mind, uncluttered by anxiety and distress. You can construct a single visualization in which you see yourself performing professionally and calmly. You can also construct various scenes that you can practice visualizing. See yourself behaving assertively, smoothly, and successfully in all of your visualizations.

Organize Your Worries Away

Perhaps you have a tendency to obsess over all of the activities you "must or should" accomplish day-to-day. My client Cindy was obsessed with planning, scheduling, and rescheduling her days, when to start each activity, how long it would take, what to start first, and what might go wrong. By the end of the day, she'd accomplished little and felt hopeless and furious at herself. If this problem sounds familiar to you, you can use the stop technique here as Cindy did to stop obsessing and rationally and calmly plan her day. In the morning, when her confusion and obsessions were most extreme, she learned to write down the day's schedule. If you decide to do this, you'll find it frees you from worrying about everything you need to do. Whenever your ruminations start, simply refer to your schedule and move on to the next activity. It's a good idea to check off those activities you complete so you feel a sense of accomplishment and disprove your beliefs that you never get anything done.

You can also use this as an opportunity to develop some characteristics that actually lessen your chances of experiencing negative stress. You can learn to be flexible—at times, unexpected events will occur that will prevent you from following your schedule "perfectly." Use these incidents as opportunities to develop your flexibility. Tell yourself that change is inevitable and you will find a way to eventually get those things done. Additionally, use this exercise to search out any irrational beliefs, "If I don't finish everything today, I'm a failure," or "I'll get behind and never be able to catch up." This is when you use your new skills to challenge the accuracy of such beliefs and substitute moderate, realistic beliefs that don't make you feel so negatively stressed, hopeless, and inadequate. Scheduling and organization is central to stress management and we'll examine this further in the subsequent time management section.

Letting Go of the Past

Thought stopping is also extremely helpful for those of us who worry obsessively about past events, particularly those for which we blame ourselves. If you're a member of this club, stop here and realize: "What is the benefit of replaying past events over and over? They're in the past and I can't do anything to change them now. What I can do is to learn from the situation and move on." A number of my female clients have come into therapy struggling with letting go of past events or relationships, but wanting to move on. They talk about feeling stuck in their lives and unable to accomplish and grow. A big part of their stagnation comes from this constant obsessing about the past, the self-imposed shame and guilt, and the frequent companion—self-sabotaging behavior. One theme I see women play over and over again involves one or more intimate relationships that turned out to be unhealthy for them and often, if present, for their children. Who among us hasn't made mistakes, great and small, in relationships? We only compound the problem, though, by replaying thoughts like, "If I had only done . . ." or "I should have known . . ." Well, the only answer is "we didn't but I can learn from that and act differently next time." Remember, most of us do the best we can in making decisions with information available at the time. Of course, there are issues of anxiety, low self-esteem, and past trauma that can interfere with coping in the best way possible. If you find yourself repeatedly involved in harmful relationships, professional help can be invaluable. Working through the emotions, gaining feedback from an objective observer, and discovering if your continued grasping onto the past is serving any purpose for you at present will all help in ultimately letting go and moving on.

If you find yourself full of guilt and remorse and are having trouble putting your history into perspective, you should ask yourself a few questions. First of all, were these events over which you could truly have had any control? Remember that we can never truly control most events, situations, and particularly other people. Even if you did have some responsibility for a situation resulting in a less than desirable outcome, ask yourself, "What am I gaining from my continued rumination over my failures?" For one thing, it may be helping you avoid actually moving on. Moving on implies change and as you read about earlier, many women view change as a threat, i.e., as a distressor rather than as a challenge, i.e., a prostressor. You also read about evidence (and may personally have experienced) that many women internalize the derogatory, judgmental voices of family, teachers, or society and believe that they are inadequate and inferior. Thus, when they find themselves in an uncomfortable, unhealthy situation (caught in the past, blaming themselves, not moving on or growing), they find it familiar. This isn't as threatening as becoming assertive, placing responsibility appropriately, and allowing themselves to experience their rage and frustration, and finally going on with their lives. Ask yourself another question: "Is living in the past protecting me from a specific experience in the present?" In particular, is it helping you to avoid intimacy in the present? Having been hurt in the past, you may expect that the same outcome will occur in the future.

Let's try an exercise here. Refer back to the list of the fifteen irrational distressing modes of thinking. Write down the name of the one or more that you think could explain this decision to avoid intimacy because of being hurt in the past. When you're through, turn to the end of this chapter for possible answers. You will find the answers there at the end of this chapter.

Irrational Thinking

For a seemingly simple technique, thought stopping has many uses and can be very effective. In fact, thought stopping has been used effectively in extinguishing phobias, obsessive thoughts, memories over which a person ruminates, and many other troubling patterns like these. It can help decrease your negative stress about day-to-day events, decrease the time you waste obsessing needlessly, put a stop to certain self-sabotaging behaviors, and help you learn from the past, let go and move on as a more intelligent, positive person.

The cognitive techniques you have learned from this chapter will truly change your way of thinking, perceiving, feeling, and behaving. I've little doubt that the change will be a welcome and healthy one. Cognitive techniques allow you to have some control over your thoughts, feelings, and behavior in the here-and-now, as well as over how you plan to think and be in the future. Your new-found awareness and sense of control will reduce your level of negative stress and increase the prostress and positive energy in your life.

Answers: Irrational thinking for the previous example might be, for example, deciding to avoid intimacy due to past hurts because your low self-esteem tells you that if you get into a truly intimate situation, the other person will really see you "warts and all," and will inevitably reject you. Even worse, you would believe you deserve it!

Other possible answers are: filtering (recall that anxious people focus on things suggesting danger); overgeneralization; catastrophizing (I'll always end up being rejected because I'm such a loser, flake, ugly, fat, and so on); control Fallacies (external); or blaming (in this example could be either of the types: others or yourself).

12

Building Your Coping Skills

You are now ready to learn some new tools that are sure to reduce those hair-pulling, nail-biting, teeth-grinding attacks known as "I-can't-cope-itis." To use the coping skills techniques discussed here, it's best that you've become proficient with the relaxation exercises, including deep breathing, progressive relaxation, and visualization.

One way to improve your coping with situations that have traditionally proven distressful and anxiety-producing for you is to "practice" going through them in your mind. Your imagination is a safe place where you won't be at risk of experiencing any dreaded consequences (generally unrealistic) which you've conjured up in your mind. As you may recall, relaxation and anxiety are opposing reactions, so when your body is relaxed, you can't also experience negative stress. You will be using this principle to work through your own stressful events hierarchy. Another thing to keep in mind as you work on improving your coping is that the majority of the negative stress you experience is self-created. It evolves from your *anticipation* that an event is going to be distressing, threatening, or that it will call for resources and abilities you don't think you possess. Once this anticipatory anxiety is generated, it tends to spread in time and place (to other situations). You might become increasingly fearful and avoid more and more situations that you anticipate will be negatively stressful. Obviously, the more you avoid, the less likely you are to learn that all of these horrible, terrifying consequences you've conjured up in your mind are quite unlikely to happen. So, by practicing your very own stressful events in your imagination, and by experiencing and staying with the negative stress and uncomfortable feelings until they pass, you will have the evidence that you can survive both the distress and anxiety. The benefits grow as each time you face and deal with a circumstance you initially feared. Your coping skills become stronger and you'll feel better about yourself. You'll never find out how strong you are unless you stay and fight those battles over which you can make an impact, or stay and accept certain uncomfortable situations that are uncontrollable (as long as they're not harmful to you). These are the challenges that help you realize you're flexible and can cope—such realizations lead to increased self-esteem and pride. The second step that puts you squarely atop the saddle involves your becoming aware of the irrational nature of the feared consequences that you've often made up on your own, with little existing evidence to support them.

Much of our unhealthy behavior and efforts to avoid certain distressors is actually driven by the fear of fear. Because we're afraid of and avoid situations we think will be distressing, we don't get the chance to learn how to cope with these people, places, or things. By using your imagination to work through these situations in advance, you'll be in a safe place because you can control what happens. You can experiment and try behaviors that you would typically shy away from. Gradually, you'll realize that even during the "real" situation, you can also have a great deal of control over how you choose to think and respond to potential stressors.

The technique you'll be using involves the construction of a "stressful events hierarchy" (McKay, Davis, and Fanning 1981). It will take you some time and thought to create your own hierarchy but the investment is well worth the effort. To produce your stressful events hierarchy, list ten to fifteen situations that you encounter with some regularity that you find negatively stressful and anxiety-producing. Write down your list of events starting with the least stressful event (ranked as number 1) and work your way up to the most stressful event. Each event you list should be slightly more stressful than the preceding event. The following example will help to get you started. As you write down each situation, make sure to describe it with enough detail so you can clearly visualize and experience it. As with the previous imagery and visualization exercises, it helps to include sensory details (things you see, hear, smell, etc.) to maximize the realistic nature of the experience and trigger the physical distress that occurs when you are anxious in real life. To rate the degree of negative stress you are experiencing, use the subjective units of distress (SUDS) rating scale, which goes from 0 (no stress) to 5 (moderate stress) to 10 (extreme stress).

Example of a Stressful Events Hierarchy

Least Stressful	Beginning SUDS (A particular trial)	Ending SUDS
• Meeting a friend for lunch. Raining. Don't feel like going out	4	2
• Sitting at my desk writing checks to pay bills	5	3
• Waiting for a friend's call that is already 25 minutes late	5	3
• Driving to work on Monday morning	5	4
• Waiting in my sparsely decorated doctor's office	5	3
• Alarm clock goes off 20 minutes late	6	4
• Argument with significant other about budget	7	5
• Having a deadline for a project shortened	7	5
• Late to an important meeting and there is a lot of traffic	8	4
• Making an oral presentation at work. Many people watching	8	6

Most Stressful

Practicing Visualization

Once you have come up with your list of stressful events, it's time to gradually work your way through it. Just as with the relaxation exercises earlier, make sure that you are in a quiet, comfortable environment where you will not be disturbed. Set aside enough time to work through two or three scenes. An initial important point—sometimes people find it difficult to get into the image fully at the beginning. The more you practice and call into play all of your senses, the more realistic it will feel for you. A very effective technique is to describe each situation in depth, tape them, and play them back as you work through them to help you get a strong image and reaction.

Beginning with the number 1 item or least stressful event, visualize the event in as much detail as you can. Include the surroundings, any sounds or other stimuli, and any people that might typically be involved in the particular situation. Notice any physical signs of tension that arise as you think about the event. These may include a tightness in your stomach, muscular tension, an increase in your heart rate, feeling hot or perspiring, and so on. Rate your feelings on the 1–10 SUDS scale. Scan your body and focus on the physical signs of anxiety. While these often serve to make you more anxious during an actual distressor, they'll be serving a positive purpose for you now. You'll interpret them as helpful cues to begin your deep breathing and relaxation, and as guides helping you to eventually gain control over your reactions to the imagined event. Continue scanning your body for any points of tension or arousal and quickly and efficiently relax and release. Do your deep, diaphragmatic breathing and imagine that you're inhaling healing, calming air. As you exhale, all of the tension and stress is leaving your body. Tell yourself that you are calm and relaxed—calm and relaxed and in control. Any time you detect a sign of tension, tell yourself that it is a helpful cue for you to calmly relax and breathe deeply in and out. You should hold an image in your mind for about thirty seconds while remaining fairly calm and relaxed.

Now you'll include measures to replace the repetitive negative forecasting of failure and anxiety linked with each event. Picture yourself calm and able. For example, making an oral presentation was listed as very stressful in the sample stress hierarchy. What makes it stressful? When you think about it, you probably see yourself as anxious, sweating, mumbling, perhaps forgetting your train of thought. You look around and imagine the stern, judgmental faces of your superiors and co-workers. With such "stinking thinking," you're bound to feel anxious and distressed about this event. Remember, though, that you're in the driver's seat because you're in control of how you imagine, perceive, and interpret the situation. So now, rewrite the story and give yourself a better chance to face the challenge calmly and optimistically. While you are in the relaxed state, visualize yourself getting up and walking to the podium. You look and feel calm. You begin the presentation speaking in a firm voice. You are knowledgeable and well prepared. The presentation goes smoothly. The faces in the audience reflect awareness of your knowledge and professionalism. Now, imagine the question and answer session and people asking you a range of questions. You see yourself easily answering most. There are one or two you aren't familiar with and you calmly tell the person that you will be glad to try to locate the information for them. After imagining this successful scenario, again rate your stress level using the SUDS scale. If it remains at 4 or 5 or above, visualize the situation again. Use the signal of any tension in your body to begin your calming breathing and your bodily relaxation exercises. Play out the successful scenario in your mind. Stick with it until your stress level falls to the 1–3 range. Don't move ahead until you have been able to reach this range for each particular event. Then you can move up to visualizing the next event in your hierarchy and repeat the process. Work through three or fewer events per day so that you're doing a thorough, effective job.

By the time you face these events in real life, you'll be much more comfortable. You may even be experiencing prostress as your negative anticipatory thoughts will have been replaced with positive expectations and beliefs. After learning this technique, your bodily sensations of tension and feelings of distress will no longer be cue for anxiety so much as cue for relaxation and challenge. Remember, you can create new hierarchies as you come across different events that you feel are distressing. Visualizing, physical scanning and relaxing, and modifying negative scenes or scripts to positive ones will become part of your own cognitive and behavioral repertoire. You'll soon be able to rapidly detect when you're falling into creating those catastrophic anticipatory fears. When this happens, you'll be able to write and star in your own successful visualization.

My Own Stressful Events Hierarchy

Least Stressful	Beginning SUDS (A particular trial)	Ending SUDS
• _____	_____	_____
• _____	_____	_____
• _____	_____	_____
• _____	_____	_____
• _____	_____	_____
• _____	_____	_____
• _____	_____	_____
• _____	_____	_____
• _____	_____	_____
• _____	_____	_____

Most Stressful

Reducing Distress by Becoming Your Own Writer and Director

The principle behind the stress hierarchy is also applicable to events other than those that occur regularly in your life. If you're anticipating a one-time event that is causing you significant distress, this technique can prove invaluable. One of my clients, Ava, is a lovely, warm woman who sought therapy prior to attending her son's wedding across the country. As the months dwindled and the time drew near, she became more and more anxious about the event. Ava explained to me that the wedding would also be her first meeting with her ex-husband's new wife. While obviously there are some potentially painful emotional dynamics that could arise, her fearfulness and intimidation were excessive and unhealthy. She was unable to concentrate or make decisions and awoke daily feeling intense anxiety. Any joy that the upcoming event would typically have offered her was unavailable. There was obviously something wrong with the way Ava was thinking about the upcoming meeting. I asked her to describe her thoughts about this meeting, to tell me in detail the horrible story she had written and was replaying over and over in her head. She said, "I am standing face-to-face with her. My heart is pounding and I feel weak. I manage to say hello and then I can't think of anything else to say. I feel ashamed, rejected, and terrible. My ex-husband and sons are watching me make a fool of myself." I challenged this scenario and asked her if it was, maybe, just a little bit exaggerated. She laughed for a moment which gave me some hope that she would be amenable to modifying her rigid expectations.

First, we worked on developing Ava's relaxation, breathing, and visualization skills. Then, I introduced her to the assumptions and techniques of cognitive therapy. The next step was for us to work on creating an alternative scenario (to the terrifying, humiliating one she had created by herself) to practice and visualize after putting herself into a state of relaxation. In her new story, Ava saw herself dressed in the beautiful outfit she had purchased. She walked slowly toward the woman. She extended her hand calmly and said hello. She expressed her pleasure at meeting the woman and carried on a brief conversation about the wedding. At this point, she excused herself and moved on. The exact nature of her revised story was unimportant. What was important was that she was able to see herself smoothly sailing through what she'd originally made into a distressing, demeaning scene. Her anticipatory fear was greatly minimized as she realized how irrational and distorted her forecasting of the meeting had been.

The more she rehearsed this particular revised scenario as well as several related others she created, the less distressed she felt.

We also used some of the cognitive techniques you learned about in chapter 10 to further prepare her for the wedding. For example, we examined her negative, extreme thoughts such as, "I am going to hate her and she'll be rubbing it in my face that she's married to my ex," and "She is intruding on this wedding." Together, we revised them to moderate rational thoughts such as, "I might find out I actually like her," and "I am here for my son's wedding, not to see my ex-husband and his wife. The wonderful marriage is by far the most important part of this event." After this preparation, it turned out that Ava had a wonderful time at her son's wedding. She was minimally nervous upon meeting her ex-husband's new wife and instead was engrossed in enjoying the celebration, her sons, and her relatives and friends. As a result of the work she'd done, Ava had developed her coping skills so that she could easily manage the situation.

You will find this technique very helpful for a variety of situations causing you significant distress. *Remember that what you anticipate will happen is generally much worse than what actually does happen.* Irrational thoughts, such as the cognitive distortions and automatic thoughts, are what cause you to feel the extremes in emotions, such as distress, anxiety, rage, and depression. There will be a blank series of comments and questions for you to complete soon. Refer back to the description of Ava's dilemma if you have difficulty filling out the questionnaire. You can use any event which is coming up within the next three to six months and that is causing you distress and anxiety. The last set of blank lines allows you to symbolically take control by revising what you tell yourself is going to happen. You should then practice your success scenarios while maintaining a relaxed state as you did in the earlier stressful events hierarchy exercises. You'll find your negative stress will be greatly diminished. Your ability to function calmly and effectively and to experience the pleasure and challenge of prostress will be greatly increased. Take control over your reactions to situations you usually perceive as threatening and distressing by using this visualization tool. As a result you'll feel and behave more calmly and may even turn the event into an enjoyable prostressor!

Recreating Upcoming Events

Upcoming stressful event

_____

_____

_____

_____

What is it that I fear will happen? What is the scenario in my mind?

_____

_____

_____

_____

Is my thinking about this event rational? How is it faulty?

_____

_____

_____

_____

My revised scenario in which I am calm and controlled. The outcome is a positive one. (You can create several.)

_____

_____

_____

_____

It's essential to reward yourself once you have made it through the initially feared situation. Things may have gone completely smoothly or there may have been some mishaps and remaining distress. What's important is that you took the steps to develop your coping skills and this is something to celebrate. Reinforce this by re-warding yourself in some way. You deserve it! Remember that the more challenges you allow yourself to meet, the better your self-esteem and the greater the amount of health-inducing prostress in your life will be.

Stress Inoculation Training

Albert Ellis and Aaron Beck focused on identifying and reducing the presence of negative thoughts and irrational beliefs. Now you'll learn a powerful technique created by another leading cognitive therapist, Donald Meichenbaum. Besides looking at the presence and effect of negative beliefs, he also focuses on the *absence of positive thoughts and responses*, and on how to reinforce adaptive coping.

Meichenbaum's focus on cognitions and self-talk stems from his work with hyperactive children who were cognitively impulsive. When children are learning, they go through a three-stage process of verbal control. First, their behavior is controlled externally by the statements of parents, teachers, and others. After this, the child begins talking to himself or herself out loud in directing behavior. Finally, the child's internal, silent self-talk guides his or her behavior. Adults follow a similar pattern in learning a new behavior or response. Mei-chenbaum focuses on the internal speech of the adult in order to im-prove coping with negative stress and learning to change behaviors.

Self-Talk

As you read in the previous chapter, your irrational thinking and negative automatic thoughts will lead you to interpret events as threatening and negatively stressful. As a result, you'll feel distressed, anxious, angry, and the like. Donald Meichenbaum's technique pre-sented in his 1985 book, *Stress Inoculation Training*, attacks this prob-lem by helping you take control and change your self-talk. You learn to say positive self-statements at each of four phases when you're feeling negatively stressed and are facing a negative (according to your interpretation) situation. Meichenbaum's self-instructional ap-proach suggests that people (1) observe their responses to distressors, and (2) use self-talk to select adaptive coping responses.

Having completed the Daily Record of Dysfunctional Thoughts, and familiarized yourself with the types of cognitive distortions and irrational thinking, you've already completed step 1. Now, it's time for step 2. This involves your coming up with positive, more realistic self-statements that you'll say to yourself as you move through the stages of actual stressful events. Meichenbaum has broken the entire process of dealing with a potential stressor into four phases: While I've kept the structure and content of his procedure, I've given my own names to each phase. Each phase begins with "D" to help you remember. What follows is a brief description of these stages and examples of helpful distress-reducing and even prostress-increasing self-talk. There are fill-in lines provided to write down some self-statements in your own words. This often makes it more "user-friendly," and so more effective. To help you generate some of your own ideas, it can help to think about something that is going to happen in the near future and is "making you" feel negatively stressed. Of course, you now know it's not the situation that is making you stressed, but rather your expectations and self-talk. In using this technique, it's best to start with an event that's minimally stressful so that you can slowly practice this method and experience success early on.

The Four "Ds"—Rehearse the Script and You'll Be a Star

Description of upcoming stressful situation:

_____

_____

_____

_____

Deliberating
You are preparing and planning.

1. I'll write down a plan to get organized.

2. Why should I worry? It's a waste of time and doesn't prep me any better.

3. I'm anxious but that's totally natural. I'll use this extra energy to do a good job.

4. I'll write a script and practice beforehand so I'll go in there prepared and more in control.

5. _____

6. _____

7. _____

Doing

While doing the task, you also focus on controlling your stress reactions through relaxation, breathing, using positive thinking, and telling yourself that this is a great chance to challenge yourself and grow (prostress).

1. This tension in my body is my cue to start the relaxation.

2. If I feel negative stress, I'll take a break and focus on breathing and relaxing.

3. Take one step at a time.

4. I'll do whatever I can and then reward myself for that!

5. _____

6. _____

7. _____

Dealing

Stay in the here-and-now and in the situation. Remember that you can have some control even if the worst happens. If you're really becoming distressed, remember to think *realistically*—what is the worst that could happen?

1. I'm just going to slow down for a few minutes.

2. I have completed this much so far—only half more to go.

3. I can ask for help if I need to.

4. I'm feeling more anxious but I know I'll pass through it.

5. I'll keep using my prepared script and it will get me through this hotspot.

6. _____

7. _____

Deserving

Assess how things went, how you coped, what things you might want to change. Reward small steps as much as big steps. Focus on the positives and what you learned.

1. That was easier than I expected.

2. That was worse than I expected but I made it through so it will have to be easier next time!

3. I was able to confront the fear and make it through by relaxing and focusing.

4. The stress I felt from putting this off and worrying about it was worse than just doing it.

5. I learned _____

6. _____

7. _____

Make sure you have a copy of this list of stages and statements readily available as you begin to use this technique. You can carry it around in your purse or wallet or leave it where you'll repeatedly see it, maybe on your desk, bedside table, or car seat. Once you feel comfortable with the process and are more confident about your coping abilities, you can try it with events of greater potential distress. This is similar to the process you followed in visualizing your stressful events hierarchy in terms of working from the least to the most stressful experience. This exposure to gradually increasing levels of stress explains Meichenbaum's name for this technique, "Stress Inoculation Training." When you receive an inoculation or immunization shot to prevent a disease, you're actually given a small amount of the infectious agent. Because it's introduced in a limited amount, your body has a chance to develop antibodies against the disease and thus develop resistance. Similarly, by practicing on situations that are less stressful, you're exposed to limited amounts of the harmful agent (negative stress) and are able to develop antibodies (stress management, coping skills, changing distress into prostress) that boost your resistance to greater levels of stress. Remember, it takes *practice, practice, practice,* but you'll find it pays back *over, over, and over.*

13

Boosting Your
Stress Resistance
and Prostress

As you read through this chapter, you will be able to get an idea as to how you rate on important stress-related characteristics at present and what areas you would do well to develop in yourself. Medical studies have shown that patients who have an active, assertive attitude before surgery or while in the hospital generally fare better than those who are passive. Patients who depend on others for motivation and esteem do more poorly than those with internal motivation and self-esteem. These are just a few examples to supplement what you've read throughout this book. That is, it is essential that you assume responsibility for and control of your life. Ask yourself how you rank in terms of assertiveness. How about your sense of control over your life? Do you feel you are too passive? Stress management equals self management. Take charge of the way you live your life and you'll benefit mentally and physically.

In chapter 7, you were introduced to Suzanne Kobasa's term, "hardiness." Hardy individuals exhibit three characteristics when dealing with stressful situations—challenge, commitment, and control. Although hardy people frequently deal with a great deal of stress in their lives, they tend to have a much lower rate of physical and psychological disturbance than people who are not as hardy. How do you rate on these characteristics? For the reasons discussed in part 1, these are characteristics that benefit you immensely in reducing the negative effects of distress and boosting your healthy prostress.

Stress-Reducing Characteristics

Evidence shows that people who regularly give and receive affection live longer, are healthier, and report a better quality of life than do those who don't. People in loving relationships report less distress, are healthier, and live longer than those without such relationships. Now, this doesn't mean it must be a sexual relationship and it *doesn't even mean your partner has to be a human being!* Widows with pets live longer than those without and single people with pets report being happier, healthier, and living longer than those without.

Humor

Take the advice of old-time folk tales and modern empirical research and introduce humor into your life. Read funny books, watch funny movies, and in general take a lighter view of life. When you're in what you typically view as a distressing situation, evaluate how serious it really is. Is it really the end of the world? Is it truly bad enough to ruin your whole day, week, life? Take a different approach and look at the situation in the most extreme way possible. Isn't there something absurd you can find in the situation? Remember, you do have some control over every situation. Just as your mind makes something seem terrible, horrible, and catastrophic, it can also make it ridiculous, funny, and absurd. Try to add a comedic twist to your interpretations of events. You may even be able to laugh at how seriously you take things that turn out to be truly minor. Being in a positive mind state spreads, that is, it will make you interpret things more positively, remember more positive events, and increase the time you spend in a positive mode. As you may recall from chapter 1, *it's the frequency* of positive events (even minor daily events) and time spent in a positive state, *not the intensity* of a positive event (winning the lottery) that determine your happiness and physical and mental well-being.

Empathy

Your ability to empathize is another great negative stress-reducing characteristic. Maybe the bank clerk, waiter, taxi driver, boss, or police officer who is "rude and obnoxious" is feeling ill or having an awful day. Obviously, they haven't been fortunate enough to learn the tools of stress management! Try to put yourself in this "irritating" person's shoes. Know that you've had days like that yourself. The ability to empathize and give others a break can completely change your view of the situation. You won't be as stressed out—maybe you can even be kind to the offender, making you feel better, rather than worse, about yourself.

Forgiveness

A very important but often difficult characteristic to embrace is the ability to forgive. Forgiveness doesn't require that you forget a wrong someone did to you. It involves placing responsibility where it is due and then *letting go*. After all, when you let somebody's actions continue to affect you negatively, you're essentially letting this person control you. Acknowledge the occurrence of the problem, attribute responsibility appropriately (which isn't on ourselves as so many of us women do), confront the person if this will help resolve the situation or allow you to work through it, and then . . . move on with your life. You will be all the stronger and healthier for this ability. Of course, I realize that some behaviors committed by others are so heinous or traumatic (rape, incest, physical or emotional abuse, to name a few) that letting go and moving on seems impossible. In many cases, tremendous damage has been done to the recipient's psyche and healing and repairing is necessary. If this is the case with you, it is probably best to obtain professional assistance.

Personal Strength

Self-esteem and ego strength are important in buffering negative stress. In addition, having these characteristics helps you experience prostress and its benefits more easily and frequently. These two characteristics can be problem areas for women as was explored in depth earlier. If this is the case for you, you'll find suggestions and techniques to help you improve your self-esteem in the next section.

Victim–Blaming versus Learning–Coping Responses

As you evaluate yourself and work to develop important distress-reducing and prostress-enhancing characteristics, it would be beneficial for you to examine the abilities and habits presented in Dr. Al Siebert's enlightening 1996 version of *The Survivor Personality*. Siebert has detected certain characteristics in people he describes as "life's best survivors." Such people have a learning–coping reaction to difficult situations rather than a victim–blaming reaction. Siebert's concepts are particularly important—recall that women have sometimes been described as having lesser abilities to cope with stressors than men. Recent evidence shows that women may use different coping strategies partly because they tend to face different stressors and more frequent stressors in their lives. Coping is an integral part of reducing the negative consequences of distress and increasing prostress.

Two essential components of coping for women are the ability to learn from past failures and successes in coping, and to be flexible in applying techniques appropriate for the particular stressor they're facing. These issues relate to the health-inducing learning–coping skills that distinguishes Siebert's life survivors from others. As pointed out, women often see themselves as having less control over their lives, homes, and jobs than do men. This can lead to what Siebert defines as victim–blaming reactions. In fact, there is substantial evidence supporting that, in reality, women often do have lesser degrees of control. Accordingly, women may view themselves as helpless or as victims more often than men. Feeling you're the victim and suppressing the expression of your needs causes resentment and can increase the tendency to blame others and to avoid taking responsibility. On the other hand, as a result of socialization, many women have ended up blaming themselves for failures and attributing successes to external factors. So, for these and other reasons, many women in our society have ended up responding to negative stressors with the unhealthy victim–blaming response. Because of the extremely unhealthy nature of living life this way and because there are techniques and tools to help you change this perspective, it's crucial that you keep Siebert's distinctions in mind as you go about your daily life and plan your future. Spend some time now to examine your behavior and thoughts and ask yourself where you lie on the coping continuum (learning–coping reaction versus victim–blaming reaction). You don't have to tell anyone your response so be as honest and open as you can!

Life's Best Survivors

Siebert presented the following aspects as characterizing the survivor personality. Put a check mark next to those you believe you possess.

- The ability to be playful like a happy child and to express the curiosity of a child

- The ability to become completely immersed and involved in an activity of interest so that external factors are temporarily forgotten

- The ability to be both intuitive and logical

- The ability to learn valuable lessons from difficult life experiences

- The ability to be observant and nonjudgmental

- The ability to forge ahead in following your interests despite the risks of making mistakes

- The ability to laugh at yourself and accept criticism from others

- The ability to be creative, imaginative, and immerse yourself in fantasy

- The ability to maintain a positive outlook and a sense of comfort even in difficult, complex situations

First, a congratulations on those abilities you possess. Second, begin working on developing others. It would be very helpful to write this list down and post it somewhere in your house or office as a reminder. Each time you behave according to one of these guidelines, make a note of it (preferably in the stress journal you take everywhere with you!) and be sure to give yourself lots of positive reinforcement. Also, as you write down the specific examples, write down how it made you feel to behave with "survivor characteristics." This will give you a clear understanding of how these abilities improve your feelings, state of mind, behavior, and so on. Track the examples of your progress and work to increase the frequency which with you are able to fulfill these behavioral goals.

Survival Is Balance

Survivors tend to have opposing characteristics within their personality. They are both serious and playful, hardworking and lazy, tough and gentle, introspective and outgoing, and so on. This observation is consistent with one of the most important messages I've tried to convey in this book. Namely, the importance of maintaining an open, balanced, and flexible approach toward living and life. Life is always in flux and it's neither realistic nor adaptive to approach every situation in exactly the same way. The ability to read situations and to respond as required is key to stress management. Taking care of all of your needs, whether they be to work or to play, to laugh or to cry, physical or mental, will keep you in physical and mental health.

Another of Siebert's findings that directly relate to women is that survivors strive not only for improvement in their own lives but also in those of others. From part 1 of this book and from your own experiences, you know that women often expend much of their energy trying to help others. Many of us actually need to increase our focus on learning to value ourselves and our needs. We must take the time and energy to acknowledge and meet our desires and goals for satisfaction and growth. Try to work on improving your own life, satisfying your needs, and taking care of yourself, while balancing this with a healthy amount (as determined by you) of continued interest in helping others. You'll be protecting your well-being, optimizing stress, and thriving on its positive potential.

Developing Your Self-Esteem

Here we are, ready to deal with a real "biggie" for women. Self-esteem is vitally important in maintaining your emotional and physical health. Your self-esteem ultimately determines whether you experience an event as distress or prostress and, accordingly, whether you'll be harming or enhancing your well-being. You aren't born necessarily with good or bad self-esteem. Instead, it stems from your experiences as a child and can be enhanced or further damaged by circumstances throughout your life. As a child, your sense of self-esteem depends upon being supported and valued by others. In healthy adults, external feedback ideally plays a smaller role. However, if you did not get what you needed as a child and if you are still excessively dependent on external attention and acceptance to derive your self-esteem, you are in a vulnerable position, perhaps somewhat comparable to standing on quicksand for support! The techniques that follow are designed to help you move away from relying on others to feel "okay." It's possible to learn to be more accepting of yourself, and to make desired, healthy changes in yourself by yourself. Here are several steps you can take.

Self-Assessment

Take a realistic look at your strengths and areas for improvement (don't forget—the term improvement means there is room for positive change and development). Acknowledge your strengths. Be aware that it is up to you to choose the particular areas for improvement that are most important in obtaining your goals. Many people find it difficult to assess themselves objectively. Women, in particular, seem to have a hard time claiming their good points, especially out loud! A trick I often have my clients use is the out-of-my-body technique. Give this a try—take on the role of one of your good friends or a supportive family member. Describe yourself as you believe your valued friend would. Remember that many women have similar valuable qualities, such as caring for others, having access to one's feelings and being able to express them, working toward creating harmony, building and maintaining social support networks, and bearing and raising children. Don't downplay these!

Assess your strengths and write them down here.

Strengths

_____

_____

_____

_____

_____

Areas for Improvement

_____

_____

_____

_____

_____

The next step is to take some time to write down your areas for improvement. Most of us have an easier time with this task. However, avoid the temptation to immediately judge yourself harshly or to start with the negative self-talk and feelings of unworthiness or hopeless-ness. Instead, take the out-of-my-body technique and turn it around. That is, imagine that it's your friend or relative who has these areas for improvement that you're writing down. It is very important and *very revealing* to ask yourself if you're feeling as condemning or nega-tive about this person's areas of improvement as you do about your own. Keep in mind the research and information discussed earlier about irrational thinking and erroneous assumptions. Beliefs that you need to be perfect, or that any minor weakness you have is terrible and means you're just plain bad, are examples of such illogical thinking.

You can prioritize the areas you want to improve in order of impor-tance to you, toward helping you obtain your goals, or by using some other schedule you define. As you make progress, even if it feels "too slow," reward yourself and rejoice in the fact that you do have con-trol over how you choose to think and behave. You'll find that as you make your desired changes you'll feel better about yourself, improve your self-esteem, and increase your sense of control over your life in general.

Clarifying Your Wants, Needs, and Interests

To improve your self-esteem, you need to get in touch with your feelings, wants, and needs. You deserve to communicate them and have them satisfied. Melissa, a client of mine who when asked to describe her goals and plans, went into a five-minute monologue on how she was helping one friend accomplish A, her father to find B, her sister to acquire C, her best friend to finally begin D, and so on. When she was through, I asked, "And where is Melissa in all of this?" She looked at me, wide-eyed and puzzled, at first as if she didn't un-derstand my question and perhaps wondering if I hadn't listened to her five minute answer to my first question. Her answer never ad-dressed my question about *her* goals, but did reveal much more about her to both of us. After a couple of minutes of silence, tears began to well up in Melissa's eyes and she began crying quietly. "I don't know," she sobbed simply. Oftentimes, women, in their focus on caretaking and helping others, place their own feelings and desires in second place. However, as Melissa and many other women have come to realize, our strivings and emotions don't disappear when they are suppressed. They can only be stuffed for so long before they make their presence known through a variety of unhealthy ways such as feelings of distress, irritability, anxiety, and depression. You must realize that your feelings are valid and are never "wrong" or "right."

Even when they may be unhealthy, you can still accept and express your feelings and decide whether or not they are in your best interest. Remember to use cognitive techniques in evaluating situations and your emotions (given that thoughts are what underlie your feelings). Are you thinking in a rational manner or can you detect the influence of irrational thinking as seen in catastrophizing, either/or thinking, forecasting, or personalizing?

Similarly, it's a good idea to clarify your wants, needs, and interests. Set aside some time to write a list and then prioritize them in the spaces provided here. First, doing this will help you realize what might be underlying your negative stress—namely, situations or people who thwart or ignore those wants and needs you have listed as most important. Of course, you'll not always be able to immediately satisfy your needs so keep in mind two of stress optimization's key words—patience and balance. Second, by clarifying your wants, needs, and interests, you can then plan how to go about satisfying them. If you are uncertain about what you want, you probably won't end up obtaining them. If you're not in touch with your wants and needs, you're likely to walk around feeling angry, depressed, or stressed out. You either won't have any idea why, or will blame it on something or someone else (including yourself, "I'm always depressed. I guess I'm just a loser"). You must believe that your wants and interests are as important as those of anybody else and that you deserve to express and obtain satisfaction of them (as long as they are not harmful to yourself or others). Your needs and interests don't have to be the same as those of your significant others or of your close friends. Go ahead and list your needs, wants, and interests in the spaces provided. Then develop a plan on how to satisfy them. Watch out for getting stuck at this point and spending a huge amount of time getting it "right." If this starts to happen, give yourself a time limit of fifteen minutes. Yes, this is a brief time for making such a plan, but I want you to recognize that this is a rough draft to help you focus and channel your time and energy. You'll be making many changes to this first draft and this is part of learning the negative stress-reducing abilities of being flexible, adaptive, and realizing that change is the name of the game.

In general, it's a good idea to start with the highest priority items first and work your way down the list. Feel free to change the list as you develop new interests and grow and change. Be aware of how you're spending your time only to the extent that, (1) you're leading a balanced life (work, family, joy, rest, relaxing, activity, socializing, learning, etc.), and (2) you do something, even a very small thing, every day indicating some progress toward meeting your list of needs, wants, and interests. Remember that you can pull in goals or objectives you drew from earlier chapters. For example, if you decided earlier that you wanted to work on developing several of Siebert's survivor personality attributes, you write this down in your "wants" category. It's important to continue monitoring and keeping written track of your efforts to obtain your self-selected and defined goals. If you so choose, you can truly remain a wonderful work in progress. Go out and get what it is that you want—you deserve it!

Needs, Wants, and Interests

Needs	Rating of Importance	Steps to Satisfy Needs

Wants	Rating of Importance	Steps to Satisfy Needs

Interests	Rating of Importance	Steps to Satisfy Needs

A final word—you don't need to open up to people who discount your feelings and needs. If you *have* to associate with such people for work or other reasons, then do so but remember that they are just people and are neither omniscient nor inevitably right. Do your business with these people and allow their derogatory statements or selfishness to roll off your back. Surround yourself for intimacy and support with friends and relatives who are secure enough in themselves to be interested in and supportive of you. A friend who listens and accepts you for who you are is certainly one of the best stress-management "tools" around!

Your Prostress Diary

Because your happiness is determined by how *often* you feel good, it's a good idea to take the time to schedule prostress activities into your life. This is a big part of becoming stress-wise, that is, to increase your prostress.

The following instructions will help guide you in increasing the amount of prostress in your life. By this point in the book, you are well-armed with many ways, mental, physical, emotional, and social, to find and develop prostress, as well as being able to move an event from distress to prostress.

Assignment: To complete a certain number of prostress activities.

For this assignment, write down some activities that fit into the category of prostress. They should be challenging, pleasurable, growth-enhancing, get you actively involved, and offer you some degree of control. Your prostressors can range from several moments to several hours. Engage in a minimum of five of these during the week and write down in your journal what it is you did, how you were feeling before the activity, and then how you felt afterward. You can use the following format as a guide.

Prostress Diary

Situation	Feelings Before Activity	Feelings After Activity
Day _____		
1.		
2.		
3.		

Day _____

1.

2.

3.

Day _____

1.

2.

3.

Day _____

1.

2.

3.

Day _____

1.

2.

3.

Day _____

1.

2.

3.

14

Assertiveness Training: Standing Up for Yourself

Your physical and psychological health is linked to your ability to stand up for yourself. Dr. Bernie S. Siegel in his 1986 book, *Love, Medicine & Miracles*, discussed a study conducted by Dr. David Spiegel of Stanford to *disprove* that psychosocial factors were at all related to physical health. Spiegel was astonished to find that a group of women with advanced breast cancer who participated in standard medical treatment *plus* group therapy and autohypnosis lived twice as long as a comparable group of women who received only the standard medical treatment. The improved survival rate of the women who had the additional group therapy and autohypnosis was attributed to their increased assertiveness in dealing with their physicians. The women also learned to experience and express feelings and cope with loss and grief. Women often have difficulty expressing feelings and being assertive, mostly because of socialization. However, you need to do both to reduce your negative stress. You can't afford to miss out on their protective benefits. As a reader of this book, you must honestly appraise your status in these areas and work hard to develop and incorporate them into your daily life!

Throughout this book, you've seen how women have been socialized to put others first, satisfy others' needs before their own, avoid being confrontational, and eschew standing up for themselves. Remember that self-esteem has much to do with whether you feel you have the right to go after what you want and to ensure that those around you consider your desires and needs. Self-esteem, like assertiveness, is an important negative stress reducer and unfortunately, also like assertiveness, is a real battleground for women. Being assertive means communicating your needs, believing that you have the right to be respected, and setting limits. You need to balance your openness to help others with the strength and conviction to say "no" when you're feeling tired, need to reassert some control in your life, or have something on your mind that you want to do. When you cannot be assertive you end up feeling hopeless, unable to exert any control over your situation (you know what that leads to—negative stress), depressed, resentful, and angry at others and yourself.

Assertiveness Versus Aggressiveness

There is a difference between assertiveness and aggressiveness. This is a particularly salient issue for women because many of us believe if we're assertive, we'll be seen as pushy and rude and lose any chance to advance up the career ladder. We might even have a hard time distinguishing between being assertive and aggressive. Why should it matter if women believe their being assertive could be misinterpreted as being aggressive? Men certainly don't sit around wondering if people perceive them as assertive or aggressive. Basically, there are some people who will label women as aggressive because they see us as violating the female stereotype. Hopefully society will eventually catch on that women are changing, our roles and behavior are changing, and thus, society, too, will have to change their expectations and renounce efforts to continue pigeonholing us.

Express Yourself

You have the right to express your wants and needs just as much as anybody else. If you have difficulty with assertiveness, you need to be aware that you have the same basic rights in terms of setting limits, following your own interests, asking for assistance, receiving recognition for your performance, and focusing on your own desires rather than only satisfying those of others. Once you realize you have these rights, you'll feel much less distress in interpersonal relations and relationships. At first it may feel uncomfortable to behave assertively, but in the long run the distress arising from unmet needs, subservience, and frustration will be greatly reduced. Certain other reasons underlying trouble with being assertive include anxiety, irrational cognitive patterns, and deficiencies in behavioral skills. The following exercises address these various causes of difficulty with assertiveness.

Self-Assessment

Section 1

As most of us can be assertive in some situations, the goal is to increase how often you feel comfortable and are able to be assertive in a variety of situations. To get a clear picture of where you stand on assertiveness in terms of particular situations, people, and dynamics, complete the following brief survey.

You'll find that none of these categories is absolute and that for some reason you may have been assertive once or twice when normally you would have been passive. However, the goal is to get an overall picture and move toward eliciting specific examples to provide you with material you can use to build your assertiveness skills. When you rate the degree of discomfort, use a scale from 1–10 with 1 being slightly disturbed about not being assertive and 10 being extremely disturbed about not being assertive.

1. When friends ask me for help, I can say no or not right now if I need some time out or have something else I have to do.

    Y   N   Rate degree of discomfort _____

2. When supervisors or authority figures ask me for help, I can say no or not right now if I need some time out or have something else I have to do.

    Y   N   Rate degree of discomfort _____

3. When relatives ask me for help, I can say no or not right now if I need some time out or have something else I have to do.

    Y   N   Rate degree of discomfort _____

4. When colleagues ask me for help, I can say no or not right now if I need some time out or have something else I have to do.

    Y   N   Rate degree of discomfort _____

5. When strangers ask me for help, I can say no or not right now if I need some time out or have something else I have to do.

    Y   N   Rate degree of discomfort _____

6. When people who work for me ask me for help, I can say no or not right now if I need some time out or have something else I have to do.

   Y   N   Rate degree of discomfort _____

7. I can set limits and state my needs and rights with friends.

   Y   N   Rate degree of discomfort _____

8. I can set limits and state my needs and rights with supervisors or authority figures.

   Y   N   Rate degree of discomfort _____

9. I can set limits and state my needs and rights with relatives.

   Y   N   Rate degree of discomfort _____

10. I can set limits and state my needs and rights with colleagues.

    Y   N   Rate degree of discomfort _____

11. I can set limits and state my needs and rights with strangers.

    Y   N   Rate degree of discomfort _____

12. I can set limits and state my needs and rights with people who work for me.

    Y   N   Rate degree of discomfort _____

13. I can express negative feelings or give negative feedback to friends.

    Y   N   Rate degree of discomfort _____

14. I can express negative feelings or give negative feedback to supervisors or authority figures.

    Y   N   Rate degree of discomfort _____

15. I can express negative feelings or give negative feedback to relatives.

    Y   N   Rate degree of discomfort _____

16. I can express negative feelings or give negative feedback to colleagues.

    Y   N   Rate degree of discomfort _____

17. I can express negative feelings or give negative feedback to strangers.

    Y   N   Rate degree of discomfort _____

18. I can express negative feelings or give negative feedback to people who work for me.

   Y   N   Rate degree of discomfort _____

19. I can express negative feelings or give negative feedback to salespeople or servicepeople.

   Y   N   Rate degree of discomfort _____

20. I can ask for assistance or for a favor from friends.

   Y   N   Rate degree of discomfort _____

21. I can ask for assistance or for a favor from supervisors or authority figures.

   Y   N   Rate degree of discomfort _____

22. I can ask for assistance or for a favor from relatives.

   Y   N   Rate degree of discomfort _____

23. I can ask for assistance or for a favor from colleagues.

   Y   N   Rate degree of discomfort _____

24. I can ask for assistance or for a favor from strangers.

   Y   N   Rate degree of discomfort _____

25. I can ask for assistance or for a favor from people who work for me.

   Y   N   Rate degree of discomfort _____

26. I can ask for assistance or for a favor from salespeople or servicepeople.

   Y   N   Rate degree of discomfort _____

27. I can accept criticism or negative feelings from friends.

   Y   N   Rate degree of discomfort _____

28. I can accept criticism or negative feelings from supervisors or authority figures.

   Y   N   Rate degree of discomfort _____

29. I can accept criticism or negative feelings from relatives.

   Y   N   Rate degree of discomfort _____

30. I can accept criticism or negative feelings from colleagues.

   Y   N   Rate degree of discomfort _____

31. I can accept criticism or negative feelings from strangers.

    Y   N   Rate degree of discomfort _____

32. I can accept criticism or negative feelings from people who work for me.

    Y   N   Rate degree of discomfort _____

33. I can accept criticism or negative feelings from salespeople or servicepeople.

    Y   N   Rate degree of discomfort _____

34. I can express positive feelings or positive feedback to friends.

    Y   N   Rate degree of discomfort _____

35. I can express positive feelings or positive feedback to supervisors or authority figures.

    Y   N   Rate degree of discomfort _____

36. I can express positive feelings or positive feedback to relatives.

    Y   N   Rate degree of discomfort _____

37. I can express positive feelings or positive feedback to colleagues.

    Y   N   Rate degree of discomfort _____

38. I can express positive feelings or positive feedback to strangers.

    Y   N   Rate degree of discomfort _____

39. I can express positive feelings or positive feedback to people who work for me.

    Y   N   Rate degree of discomfort _____

40. I can express positive feelings or positive feedback to salespeople or servicepeople.

    Y   N   Rate degree of discomfort _____

41. I can express my opinion even if it differs from that of friends.

    Y   N   Rate degree of discomfort _____

42. I can express my opinion even if it differs from that of supervisors or authority figures.

    Y   N   Rate degree of discomfort _____

43. I can express my opinion even if it differs from that of relatives.

    Y   N   Rate degree of discomfort _____

44. I can express my opinion even if it differs from that of colleagues.

    Y   N   Rate degree of discomfort _____

45. I can express my opinion even if it differs from that of strangers.

    Y   N   Rate degree of discomfort _____

46. I can express my opinion even if it differs from that of people who work for me.

    Y   N   Rate degree of discomfort _____

47. I can express my opinion even if it differs from that of salespeople or servicepeople.

    Y   N   Rate degree of discomfort _____

Goals

Section 2

Before you do anything with the numerical results of this survey, complete the following twelve questions. The intent is to get a clear picture of what your goals are and what you hope to change by changing passive behavior to assertive behavior. Use a similar rating scale as above to rate the importance of the following goals. The scale ranges from 1–10 with 1 being slightly important or desirable to 10 being extremely important or desirable.

Goal	Rating
1. Have more time for myself even when it involves turning down some requests from others	_____

Goal	Rating
2. Accept positive feedback and compliments from others	_____
3. Have others listen to me more attentively	_____
4. Get recognition for performance at work	_____
5. Get recognition for performance at home	_____
6. Have more time with spouse, significant other, or friend	_____
7. Get help from others when I need it	_____
8. Express my true feelings or needs	_____

9. Feel greater control over my interactions with others   _____

10. Feel more self-respect after difficult confrontations   _____

11. Have fewer physical symptoms in difficult situations (sweaty palms, pounding heart, tight stomach, tense muscles, etc.)   _____

12. Feel more comfortable around strangers or in new situations   _____

Keep these goals in mind as you complete section 3 below and as you rehearse being assertive in your various personal scenarios. Being assertive will help you accomplish the goals you endorse as important above. You also need to be aware of those goals most important to you so you can track your progress in obtaining them over time. After you practice your visualizations in the following section, and actually engage in assertive behavior in "real life," check back to see where you stand on the particular goals rated as most important. You'll be pleasantly surprised and pleased to note that you have made substantial strides in achieving these outcomes.

Retraining Yourself

Section 3

Now return to section 1, scan the results, and divide up the elements by the degree of discomfort the inability to be assertive causes you. Tackle the situations that aren't the hardest for you first. Go through the events that you rated 4 or less and write down some real life examples of those you want to work on. Start with those that occur regularly. Remember, the frequency of your daily negative stressors or hassles is highly related to your physical and psychological problems.

Using the following format, write down a script of the scenarios of the events so you can work through each of them. Remember to make them realistic by including details, such as your surroundings, people who are generally involved, how you usually react behaviorally, physically, and cognitively (what are your thoughts?). On the next form, "Rewrite Your Way to Assertiveness," you'll see a separate section on desired changes in response. This is where you include how you would like to react differently in terms of behavior, physical responses, and thinking. Use this format for the minor distressing events over which you first choose to take control. After this, you can move on and do the same for those events you wish to work on that are ranked as moderately distressing (5–7 on the scale). Finally, address those that are greatly distressing (8–10 on the scale). To get the information on your "usual" physical and psychological responses, play through the scene in your mind and pay attention to the bodily changes and the thoughts and feelings you experience. Better yet, if you're actually experiencing one of the situations you have written about, pay attention to your feelings and thoughts. Write these down.

After you complete the original experience section, move to the second part and rewrite the situation the way you would like to handle it and with the goals (from section 2 above) you wish to obtain. Follow the following example given. Include a summary of how you plan to actively change your thoughts so that they are more rational and adaptive, as well as how your bodily reactions will change as a result of different self-talk, behavior, and relaxation techniques. Rehearse the revised situation in your mind over and over as you did in the guided imagery exercises. Pay attention as your body and mind begin to respond differently.

Make sure that you begin with the mildly distressing situations so that you have a greater chance of being successful and gaining an initial sense of mastery. Don't immediately set out to try to conquer the most stressful events because your chance of having difficulty and not being quite successful will be greater until you have built your abilities in this area. Having a "failure" experience at the beginning is often a sure road to giving up on these exercises or on even trying to change yourself at all, "I can't even do this, I'm no good so why try to change anything—I'll only fail and feel like the complete loser I really am." Don't fall into this trap! Work on developing your skills so that you're ready to tackle the greater challenges as you move on to moderately and then extremely distressing situations. In addition to using your visualization techniques to practice your list of situations, you can also use actual role play with willing partners. This is a helpful technique because it's more realistic and you can get a better sense of how your body language may indicate passivity. It will also give you practice in how to handle the unexpected twists and turns that occur in human interactions. You can even construct various dynamics and outcomes to your scenes and have your partner change his or her behavior so that you get a wider range of practice.

Overpractice your responses to these situations because it's easy to slip back into old patterns when you are confronted abruptly with the stressful situations in the real world. Also, if you find that you reacted in your old, passive way to an event, don't be angry at yourself and begin the old negative self-talk. Use this as a sign that you need more practice and that you need to be more aware of what types of situations trigger your habitual passive response. Reward yourself for any gradual changes that you do make and continue working until you have gained mastery over typical situations. Eventually, you'll integrate assertiveness into your behavioral repertoire and it will become a much more automatic response.

Rewriting Your Way to Assertiveness

1.

- **Original experience—passive response/mildly disturbing**

Description of event:

My supervisor, Ms. Jones, came over to my desk at 5:30 P.M., and asked if I could just stay a little late again to finish a last minute project. I was feeling so tired and was really looking forward to going home and getting some sleep. I thought I'd better stay late again—I had to tell my family I'd be later than I'd promised.

Cognitive and physical responses:

* I become angry at her and at myself and anxious because I know that it's always more than a "little late." I'm also getting very tired of her pulling this trick on me last minute. Why can't I stand up for myself?
* My neck and shoulders get tight, I clench my teeth and I know a headache is just around the corner.

- Altered experience—assertive response

Altered description of event:

My supervisor, Ms. Jones, came over to my desk at 5:30 P.M., and asked if I could stay a little late again to finish a last minute project. I realized that it was the third time she has asked me to do this this week. I told her that I had other plans for the evening and would get to it as soon as possible the next morning.

Altered cognitive and physical responses:

* I feel pleased and proud of myself that I was able to set limits and that I'll have more time for myself. Everybody has the right to say "no" to requests from others. Ms. Jones may be surprised at first but will probably treat me with more consideration as she does her other employees from now on.

* I feel a little rush of excitement at my ability to change my behavior and take over more control of my life. I breathe in deeply several times to relax further.

Now Write Your Own Examples Using This Format:

1.

- **Original experience—passive response/mildly disturbing**

  Description of event:

  Cognitive and physical responses:

- **Altered experience—assertive response**

  Altered description of event:

  Altered cognitive and physical responses:

2.

- **Original experience—passive response/mildly disturbing**

  Description of event:

Cognitive and physical responses:

- **Altered experience—assertive response**

  Altered description of event:

  Altered cognitive and physical responses:

3.

- **Original experience—passive response/mildly disturbing**

  Description of event:

  Cognitive and physical responses:

- **Altered experience—assertive response**

  Altered description of event:

  Altered cognitive and physical responses:

Assertiveness in Difficult Situations

It would be wonderful if after you'd worked through these assertiveness exercises and developed your self-esteem and ability to be assertive, you were prepared for the rest of your life. But, this is a fantasy because there will inevitably be times when your efforts to be assertive will be met with resistance. There are, however, several tricks you can use to handle these situations and to increase your being successfully assertive while avoiding negative reactions on the part of other people.

One difficulty arises when the other party is completely unaware that he or she is infringing upon your rights or causing you distress. People like this have a problem with understanding the effects of their behavior. In such cases, you must clearly communicate your feelings, the difficulties or problems their behavior is causing you, and what specific changes you want. A key to alleviating a negative response on the part of the other is to clarify the consequences (for your partner, boss, employee, friend, etc.) if the situation is changed in the manner you request. Notice that these four elements—your feelings, the problems the situation is causing you, what you want, the consequences for the other to agreeing to your suggestions or requests—are found in the following example.

Let's assume that your partner frequently makes plans to spend time with you only to back out at the last minute because of a project at work, a sports game on TV, or any of a number of familiar excuses. Assume you typically take a passive approach and accept this type of behavior without saying what is really on your mind about such treatment.

Partner: Sorry, I can't make it tonight after all. I really want to get a head start on some work at the office.

You: Fine. I'll just stay in and watch TV.

On the other hand, assume you take an aggressive approach and lash out at your partner by yelling and making all sorts of accusations.

Partner: Sorry, I can't make it tonight after all. I really want to get a head start on some work at the office.

You: I can't believe you're doing this again! You always do this to me. You are so incredibly selfish. I wouldn't want to see you anyway.

Neither of these approaches is going to resolve the situation, nor are they going to reduce your distress about the problem. Imagine instead that you followed the four assertiveness guidelines and came up with the following scenario.

You: It seems to me that we don't usually end up going out even when we schedule it because you want to do something on your own. For the past few weekends, you've canceled three of our dates at the last minute and this is really interfering with my being able to make my own plans. I feel unimportant and rejected when you do this. I certainly want you to have time for yourself and your own activities but I would like you to stick with our plans once they are made. This will avoid a lot of the tension that comes up when you break the appointments and will let us enjoy the time that we do spend together.

Nonverbal Messages

The impact of making your desires and needs known and setting guidelines for the other person is greatly increased if you present your case in a calm, rational manner. This means communicating in a modulated, clear voice rather than a pressured, high-pitched voice, yelling or becoming tearful. Obviously, this takes some practice and should be included in your imagery practice, role rehearsal with a friend, or in taping some practice episodes so that you can listen to yourself objectively. When you're in the situation, remember to take a few deep breaths and relax any muscular tension you pinpoint in your body. Look directly at your listener and make eye contact. The listener is less able to dismiss your requests and statements as irrational or emotional demands when you present them in such a calm, rational manner. If you notice the listener sending some nonverbals conveying irritability or not paying attention, you can state that maybe now isn't the best time to talk and set a fixed time with the other to return to the discussion. Remember, all of these changes take time, but you have control over how you choose to behave and interact with others.

15

Time Is More
Than Money

One of the comments I hear most frequently from "stress-messes" is that there just aren't enough hours in the day to do everything they have to do. Are you one of the many women suffering from the hurry sickness? First off, you need to reexamine your beliefs about time. Do you really *have* to accomplish everything that you think you do? Take a minute to consider your typical day before you leap to the conclusion "of course!" Do you detect the presence of any irrational beliefs you learned about earlier, such as either/or thinking, "I have to finish everything or else I'm incompetent," or catastrophizing, "If I don't finish everything today, it'll be terrible and I'll never catch up!" Remember the old "what if's" and their ability to greatly increase your experience of distress? "What if I don't finish this financial analysis in time? There's no way my boss will ever think I could handle a promotion." "I told the chairman of the volunteer committee that I'd finish this by tonight, but I also promised the kids and my husband we'd go out for an early pizza. What if I can't give the chairman all of the invitations and menus tonight?" When these distressing thoughts start dancing through your head, remember the "So, what if?" technique. "So what if everything isn't ready for the chairman tonight. I'll explain it's going to take longer than I thought, what's he going to do, fire me from a volunteer agency?" In general, when you find yourself feeling negative stress from trying to beat the clock, ask yourself questions and look for those unhealthy, irrational thoughts and assumptions underlying your self-imposed pressure to complete everything now! Recall that many women believe we must or should perform everything we have to do perfectly. If you're one of these many women, distressing about time is a typical symptom.

Time Management

A word of warning about the term and techniques of time management. Obviously, there are only twenty-four hours in the day and you cannot expand the absolute limit of time. The term "time management" may give some people the illusion that if they can just become organized, cut out the fun but "unnecessary" parts of their lives, and prioritize all of their tasks, they'll finally be able to accomplish everything they *must* do. These are not the goals of the following time-management techniques. Rather, the techniques I discuss here will help you differentiate among tasks and responsibilities so that you can spend your time *efficiently* on those that are most important, while at the same time allowing you time for essential prostress activities, spontaneity, and relaxation. You will hopefully come to realize that not all of your tasks need to be accomplished right away. Just as important as anything else on your schedule is your inclusion of your own special, personal "downtime." "Downtime" means having some leisure time, getting into some prostress, pursuing activities and interests you enjoy, or doing absolutely nothing. If your reaction to this suggestion is, "I don't even have enough time to do what I am supposed to, let alone what I want to," a personal examination of your deeper, underlying beliefs and assumptions is in order.

By now, you've hopefully grasped the fact that prostress not only improves mental and physical health, but that it's also a necessary component in your life if you desire to obtain the healthy, optimal balance of stress. Check out your resistance to this concept. Do you feel having leisure or personal time is frivolous and that other people and other things are more important than your own needs, or that others don't take time off (you may well be quite wrong here), so why should you? Also explore potential fears you may have that if you don't do everything you're supposed to, others will see the real you, the you that is far from perfect. None of us is perfect and striving to maintain this illusion will ultimately be more destructive than if someone "finds you out." You have the right to pursue your own interests and to take care of yourself. By doing so you'll actually be able to perform better in the other spheres of your life.

Prioritizing

The techniques of time management are designed to assist you in using your time most effectively and efficiently. Time management involves prioritizing your activities, duties, and interests and setting aside the bulk of your time for those that are most important. It may be more difficult than you think to clarify your priorities. Many of us cannot distinguish differences in importance and tend to globally conclude that everything we need to do is of equal import!

You need to take some time now to relax and think objectively about your various commitments and tasks and how each contributes to your goals. Consider also how to take care of the central parts of your life, whether they be work, family, relationship, and so on. It helps to talk with others in these spheres of your life. Ask your boss for input in establishing priorities. This is particularly helpful with those supervisors who continuously come to your desk with last minute projects and requests that are "extremely important and can't wait." Joanne, a woman in one of my stress-management seminars, was experiencing overwhelming negative stress because her boss would habitually do this. Finally, she was able to compile a list of all of her daily maintenance tasks together and all of the last minute requests her boss had brought to her that day. She took this list into her boss's office at the end of the day to provide him with some enlightening, objective evidence about the daily routine. He was shocked at the length of the list and admitted that he hadn't realized the consequences of what he had been doing. He assisted her in prioritizing what really needed to be done and worked more closely with her in scheduling future tasks and maintaining realistic goals.

You too should have your boss clarify what she or he thinks are the tasks and duties most essential and which are less vital to the success of the business. Most likely your boss will view this as conscientiousness, not incompetence. If you're the boss, assist your employees by helping them or conjointly establishing priorities with them. Do the same with your family by asking your children and your partner about what areas they perceive as most important. Your children might value ten minutes of playtime and your partner some relaxation time with you more than your cooking meals from scratch or making sure the house is spotless. Of course, remember that your input in terms of what you value and want for yourself is a central consideration.

Instructions

The prioritizing of most time-management systems is based on assigning labels to differentiate among the importance of items. Frequently used is a scale such as: "A" items are the highest priority, "B" items are of moderate priority, and "C" items are of low priority. The A items are those to be addressed first followed by B items. C items are of lesser importance and if they cannot be completed, it's pretty much okay. One of the difficulties people experience in completing their A items is that these tasks are often more complex and detailed than are the one-step C items. Naturally, people are drawn to do the C items because they look so simple and offer the gratification of being able to complete a task in its entirety. The way around this tendency is to break down the A and B items so that you can work on them in segments or steps. Just break them down into manageable steps and after several endeavors you'll be very surprised and pleased about how much progress you've made. Procrastinators thrive when it comes to A and B items. They procrastinate marvelously with the excuse that they simply don't have enough time to complete the entire project and so keep waiting for a huge amount of "empty time" to magically appear so that they can complete the entire project. If you're a procrastinator and find yourself doing this, think about the likelihood that this will happen. In the meantime, as you wait for this ghostly apparition and keep putting off doing the tasks or projects, you become increasingly distressed. The answer lies in realizing that you cannot complete the whole thing at once. Then, you take it step by step, using self-talk and behavioral techniques to reward yourself for completing the various phases.

Your Time-Management Plan

Step 1:

The first step to take in designing a time-management plan is to clarify your goals. This step is a must so you can then move on to prioritize those tasks and duties that are helping you to obtain those goals. Take some time now to write down a list of your short-term (within one year) goals and your longer-term goals. Your short-term goals are likely to be more concrete and specific while your long-term goals will probably be more general. Spend five minutes at the most in writing down these goals. This time limit will not allow you to censor yourself. In other words, write down those things that you really want to accomplish and don't get sidetracked by considering all of the roadblocks and excuses you typically say to yourself and others.

Short-term goals (one year or less):

_____

_____

_____

_____

_____

_____

_____

_____

Long-term goals (five years or more):

_____

_____

_____

_____

_____

_____

_____

_____

Step 2:

After you've completed this exercise, you're ready to begin prioritizing your tasks and activities. This exercise is most effective in organizing and prioritizing your responsibilities and activities if you do it daily. Although this might seem a time-consuming task at the beginning, with practice you'll become much quicker. It will even save you time during the day because you'll know to focus on the A and B tasks. Alan Lakein, a time-management consultant to major corporations who uses his own techniques himself, offers the following tips from his 1973 book, *How to Get Control of Your Time and Your Life.*

- Create a daily list of things to do.

- Realize that 80 percent of what you list is not essential but rather 80 percent of the importance lies in 20 percent of the items listed. (This is consistent with the instructions given to categorize your tasks into A, B, and C categories.)

- Focus on accomplishing the task of high priorities (i.e., the A and then B items).

- Establish the time of the day in which you are most productive and assign the A items to that time. Set aside your less demanding, more routine tasks for the time of the day or night when you are not at your peak in energy and efficiency.

- Try to schedule certain activities into the same daily time slots so that you do not have to spend time or energy making repetitive decisions about such events.

- Schedule at least one hour of open time each day to allow for inevitable surprises, crises, and the like.

To this list, another element must be added to give you the opportunity to boost your well-being and design an optimally balanced lifestyle. While it is last on this list, it is first in importance to your growth, happiness, health, and pleasure.

- Schedule a minimum of thirty minutes daily for relaxation, meditation, jogging, reading, writing, skydiving, etc. Include such health-enhancing prostress activities each day to reduce the negative stress and increase the positive stress in your life. Remember that the very absence of prostress and pleasurable events in your life actually increases your negative stress!

Procrastination: The "I'll Do It Later" Trap

If you think you might be a procrastinator, settle down and read this section *now, not later.* One of the reasons people procrastinate is that they're afraid what they produce will not good enough. Now, if you're one of those who defines "good enough" as being perfect or the best, it's not surprising that you would want to put off the inevitable. After all, with such unrealistic standards, you're bound to let yourself down (not to mention that such extreme, irrational beliefs will make you believe you'll be letting others down as well). Putting a task or situation off might seem to reduce negative stress; however, it almost always backfires. Procrastinators spend so much time and energy making excuses for themselves and then trying to catch up and finish things at the last minute that they actually submit themselves to greater distress.

If you're a procrastinator, it's essential to once again examine your beliefs and self-talk. What are you saying to yourself to rationalize not getting started on a particular task. It may be difficult to get at the actual underlying beliefs and assumptions and not be derailed by excuses such as "I just don't feel like it right now," or "I'll do it tomorrow." Underneath these two and other well-worn excuses are usually fears about performance and not being able to live up to your own or others' expectations. When you put such great pressure on yourself about having to produce excellently, your anxiety level is bound to increase dramatically. The misguided way to escape this anxiety and stress is to avoid doing the task.

Procrastinators have the tendency to perceive a task as a huge, complex entity that must be completed within one attempt or in one sitting. By perceiving a task or event in such a looming, threatening way, it's natural to want to evade the resulting tension and anxiety by avoidance. This is definitely no way to decrease your distress. You will only increase it. What you need to change if you want to reduce the negative stress is your unrealistic thinking so that you can break the task into manageable steps.

Tracking Your Procrastination Perpetrators

Keep a list for several days of excuses you use for procrastinating or irrational thoughts that make it unlikely you'll embark on doing things or making changes that you have told yourself or others you're going to do. When you become familiar with the habitual self-talk you use to get out of doing what you need to, when you need to, such excuses lose their power and are amenable to challenge and change:

Example:

- This is a really important assignment and I have to do it perfectly. I better wait until I'm feeling my best.

- This is such a time-consuming task that I need to find a large block of time so that I can complete the whole thing.

- I have to do this entire thing by myself. *(This conclusion can result from two unhealthy, distress-inducing ways of thinking: (a) I can't trust anybody else to do this right so I have to do the whole thing by myself; (b) I don't want anyone else involved because then they'll try to take the credit and I should have it all to myself.)* I'm really not looking forward to getting started.

Write down you own perpetrating thoughts.

- _____

- _____

- _____

Performance Anxiety

There are several ways to combat procrastination. One is to examine your beliefs that create anxiety about beginning a task. If you believe that you have to perform flawlessly or that any deviation from excellence will be catastrophic, you're bound to be hesitant about starting a project. Try to put the project or task into perspective. Ask yourself about the worst case scenario and what would occur if you failed completely. The chances are slim that the consequences will be as life threatening as your automatic thoughts would have you believe. Then, consider the fact that you will probably not *completely* fail on the task. You may perform some parts better than others, you may perform quite well on the entire task, you may not do so well this time, or you may not be the superstar you'd hoped to be this time (see chapter 11, Using Your Head—Cognitive Tools). Recall the dangers of black and white thinking and the detrimental impact it has on your mental and physical health.

The Self-Handicapping Strategy

Imagine that you have a deadline for a work project or for an exam which you put off doing as long as possible. The result is that you have only a limited time to complete the task. If you do not perform as well as you *should*, you have a handy excuse to salve your ego and explain your less than ideal performance to others—thus the self-handicapping strategy. "Well, I just started on this last night so I'm not surprised at the outcome." Beware of this hidden attempt to fool yourself and others as ultimately it only undermines your self-confidence and never allows you to see how well you can truly perform.

Managing Your A Item Tasks

The second trick to beating procrastination is to break down tasks that are complex and time-consuming (those A item tasks discussed in the prioritizing section) into manageable portions. You will rarely have a single block of time available to start and finish a big job. In fact, thinking that you have to do it as a one-shot deal is a procrastinator's favorite line and a great excuse for not doing anything at all. Instead, divide the task into smaller steps and start with one at a time. Schedule one step a day or whatever is manageable. Make sure you write down specific, concrete goals rather than vague objectives so that your behavior is targeted and chances of succeeding are better. Remember that the process is important and each step completed is an accomplishment. Reward yourself for finishing each step rather than seeing only the completion of the entire task as worthwhile. Going out for dinner, a warm bubble bath, time with a friend, or even a pat on your own back and a silent congratulations will go far to keeping you motivated and feeling good about your progress.

Use the following format to gain experience in breaking down a time-consuming or complex task into smaller, specifically detailed steps.

Description of project and ultimate product:

_____

_____

_____

_____

Step 1: _____ Reward: _____

Step 2: _____ Reward: _____

Step 3: _____ Reward: _____

Step 4: _____ Reward: _____

Step 5: _____ Reward: _____

Tackling Job Stress

As you learned in part 1, the nature of women's work roles and the interaction with outside roles can be directly linked with negative stress. Paul Goldbert, in his 1978 book, *Executive Health: How to Recognize Health Danger Signals and Manage Stress Successfully*, points out specific dynamics of your job which can be associated with the experience of distress. For example, how well your personality type fits your job. While job prestige, salary, and corner offices are all important, remember that you spend a huge part of your life carrying out the duties of your job. If you feel irritated, bored, or threatened, chances are you'll experience negative stress. Do you enjoy variety, a quick pace, and competition? Or do you prefer quiet, a relatively set routine, and a solitary work environment? Many supervisors and managers do not take into account such psychological factors when promoting or changing the positions of their employees. It's up to you to be in touch with the factors you desire in a position so you can tell whether you're in such a mismatch at present or so you can detect whether this promotion or job change might make you unhappy. Negative stress on the job is tricky because it includes so many different facets: the duties of your job; control and feedback availability; the type of organization and industry; bias or discrimination; gender stereotypes; the characteristics of your supervisor; relationships with peers; compensation decisions; and many more.

The Social Factor

Just as with your personal life, social support in your work environment can be both a great negative stress reducer and a source of enjoyment and pleasure. Having a sense of teamwork and sharing as you prepare and handle moderated challenges can set up the conditions for prostress on-the-job. Of course, it's important to be professional about your friendships with co-workers. There are, however, many benefits to having friendships on the job. Not only can they increase your pleasure and humor at work, but they can also be a way to hook up with the informal but important information network, help you deal with specific distressors that others may even share, and give you ideas and enlist their creativity to help out on a specific project. The friendships you make at work can bolster your self-esteem in areas relatively untouched by your "outside" friends and family. This is because they share they environment, often the same distressors, and understand just what it is that you accomplish and contribute within the organization. Little comments like, "great job," or "you aced that one," can go far to catch and negate any potential negative self-talk, give us a boost, and really enhance the potential for prostress at work.

Assessing the Stress of Your Job

Here is an informal survey to give you an idea of whether your job is a potential negative stressor in your life. Put a "Yes" or "No" in the blank following each statement. A "Yes" indicates the statement accurately reflects your job or work situation while a "No" indicates that the statement is not characteristic of your job or workplace.

1. My company has an open communication network. All employees can readily access information about the company's current state of health in the market- place, job openings, operational changes being consid- ered by upper management, how to send in complaints or praise to upper management and receive a response, short-term and long-term plans, etc. _____

2. My company has a sense of teamwork and offers things like internal sports competitions, picnics, or discounts on movie tickets. _____

3. Part of the company culture is the expectation that we will all stay late or take work home to make sure we finish what we have to do. _____

4. I find myself often having to bring work home at night or go into the office on the weekends just to keep up with all of the work I have. _____

5. Company policy is that supervisors set goals for their subordinates by themselves with no input from the employees. We are expected to somehow meet these goals no matter what. _____

6. When upper management tells us that they are going to increase wages, give us more holidays, buy more computers or copy machines and so on, they live up to their promises. _____

7. My job is the type that, at the end of the day or week, I don't really have anything concrete to look at or show that I have produced. _____

8. I get as much feedback as I want and need about my work and how well I'm doing from my supervisor and others. _____

9. My job is very demanding and I usually don't have the resources (special computer software, secretarial help, training, or knowledge) that I need to meet the demands. _____

10. It's pretty clear that men make more money and/ or get more promotions in my company than women. _____

11. I have a clear understanding of what my job includes; I feel comfortable with how well my supervisors have defined the areas, duties, and responsibilities my job entails. _____

12. I feel like I'm always getting bombarded with assignments and tasks that seem to have nothing to do with my job description. My bosses don't ask if I can handle this or want to do this, they just tell me to do it. _____

13. I really feel that my talents and abilities are being fully used and that my interests are well satisfied. _____

14. I find that I'm usually excited and challenged at work. _____

15. I think that I've gotten as far as I'll ever be able to go with this company; my job pays the rent but is a real dead-ender. _____

16. My company offers some reimbursement if we want to take outside classes from a broad range of offerings. _____

Scoring:
PROSTRESS: The following statements indicate that the conditions for prostress are available in your job and workplace: 1, 2, 6, 8, 11, 13, 14, 16
DISTRESS: The following statements indicate that the conditions for distress are probably available in your job and workplace: 3, 4, 5, 7, 9, 10, 12, 15
The more prostress statements you endorsed, the more likely it is that you have a fulfilling, challenging job that can improve your mental and physical health. This prostress can help balance any negative stress you may be experiencing from other areas in your life. The

more distress statements typifying your job and workplace, the more likely it is that your worker role is a distressor. This may greatly increase your negative stress when combined with the other roles (distressors) you have. Your mental and physical health can certainly be suffering from a negatively stressful job and the techniques in this book for reducing distress and increasing prostress are a real necessity for you.

Changing Careers

Most of us today will pursue many different types of careers throughout our lifetime. Gone are the days of staying with one company for the majority of your working life. Job, company, or industry-hopping is often the only way you can obtain more responsible or interesting positions. There are several things you can do to prepare yourself for career changes and to minimize a great deal of potential negative stress. One approach for you is to find a mentor working in the position or industry that you're interested in. Establish contacts and learn as much as possible about the job and what you'll be expected to know or learn to achieve a desirable position. It can be difficult for a woman to find a female role model occupying a position that she's interested in. This has often been touted as one of the most difficult barriers facing women in the workplace. While a role model doesn't have to be female, if you can find a female mentor, try to cultivate and take advantage of the relationship. A woman can give you crucial insight about the barriers she has had to face and the strategies that have worked best for her.

A second step in exploring other career options is to get vocational guidance. There are myriad psychological testing services to assist you in clarifying your abilities and interests. Design a self-development plan that includes your goals, objectives, and rough time frames for accomplishing them. This should also include other areas or skills you need to develop to make yourself marketable and able to succeed in your chosen field. You can take classes to update or improve upon skills you already have. And finally, as you design your plan, include strengths that you may not think of as skills, but a career counselor might find valuable.

Women-Specific Job Stressors

Remember the discussion in part 1 that illustrated how women experience different job stressors than men depending upon both the type of work and their personality characteristics? You can gain a sense of control over a distressing work environment by practicing the stress-optimizing techniques of relaxation and cognitive modification. These techniques also will help you view situations that previously seemed threatening as providing challenge and opportunities for growth. Also, remember to communicate with your supervisor or peers about your perceptions, their input can be invaluable. Because so many women have been taught since day one to avoid conflict, we may act kindly to a person treating us poorly and then turn around and tell everyone else in the workplace about the "insensitive, irritable, selfish . . ." boss, associate, etc. This stems from our desire to have the offending person learn of our displeasure without our having to confront him or her directly. You may have been told as a child, like so many of us women, to be nice and get along with others. Now, though, you are an adult and need to stand up for your rights and set limits and boundaries. Men have much less difficulty with this because as little boys they grew up playing competitive team sports where the goal was to win. They didn't have to hold back and be nice during the game. When the game was over, it was over and they could socialize with the opponent. As women, we have a hard time limiting conflict to one period of time or one situation and then easily moving on after being confronted. Here are several steps you can take to try to improve your communication in the workplace:

- **Take the initiative**—don't let suspicions or misunderstandings put a stop to communication. Open lines of communication should be maintained even if you have to be the one to "bite the bullet." You might want to practice or rehearse alternate scenarios that might come up in your conversation. Remember to include the use of breathing and relaxation techniques when you sense increasing tension. Pay attention to any negative self-talk that might come to your mind as you rehearse, confront, and challenge it immediately. Choose the right time and place to take up an issue with your boss or co-worker. Don't start a conversation when the other person is clearly in a bad mood or trying to meet a deadline. Also, if the issue is just between you and one other person, keep it that way by meeting in private.

- **Ask for feedback**—simply ask the other person for her or his perception of your behavior.

- **Ask for clarification**—when dealing with your supervisor, ask for a clear, specific description of your job and the measures used to judge your job performance. Ideally, managers and employees can work together as much as possible in creating such standards.

- **Be quiet and listen**—this means really listening and hearing, not just being silent and staying in your own thoughts while someone else is speaking.

While some people may be amenable to modifying their behavior and to working to create a more productive environment, it's a fact of life that others will be unwilling to change or even be hostile. If you've applied all of the techniques you've learned and still have excessive distress on the job, it's in your best interest (for your self-esteem, self-confidence, assertiveness, and mental and physical health) to seriously consider leaving the situation.

The Glass-Ceiling Dilemma: Standing Up for Yourself

Another subject involving women and stress in the workplace also discussed in part 1 was the continued presence of the limiting glass ceiling. Although women are entering the many typically male-dominated fields in ever increasing numbers, the statistics show a continued deficit of women in top positions and with significant authority. This situation, in which progress and promotions are not forthcoming, is what leads to burnout. Dr. Peter G. Hanson in his 1989 book, *Stress for Success*, suggests that women experience the negative stress, frustration, and helplessness of such blockages about ten years earlier than do men. What can be done about it? Continuing to lobby for the equality of women in the workplace is a step you can take and one which can have far-reaching consequences. Make sure you communicate your interest in progressing within the organization and, very importantly, take whatever additional courses or training that can help you become the best candidate for promotion. Unfortunately, you might have to work harder than a male candidate who has equivalent or lesser experience, education, abilities, and intelligence. Many of us might catch the automatic thought, "It isn't fair," running through our minds. Remember, life is often unfair and this is one of the irrational thoughts that make us feel distressed, depressed, hopeless, and so on. You might have to work harder than a male under certain circumstances, but if it's something you really want, moping about it not being fair won't get you where you want to go. We can also work for and hope that changes in society's values and people's beliefs will someday make this pervasive bias and discrimination a mere memory.

What else can you do to position yourself for advancement and growth? Consider expanding your range of responsibilities and skills by becoming involved in some type of cross-training. Make yourself marketable so that if options are not forthcoming within your company, you can seek and find elsewhere. Another strategy increasingly selected by energetic, motivated women is the exodus from the big world of corporate business into the world of small business. Women are opening small businesses in ever increasing numbers and while such ventures can be risky, many women are making huge successes. Estimates suggest that at least half of all small businesses will be owned by women within several years. Personal businesses offer women the chance to excel without the political forces and blockades of corporate America. Here we have a chance to use our creativity and energy in ways which might otherwise be constrained. If you decide to pursue such a path, be sure to perform extensive research before getting too far into the process. Take advantage of the fact that many women are already in such positions and join networking groups or arrange appointments to obtain advice and tips from them. Recall a lot of negative stress on the job is associated with a combination of high demands and low control and variety. This is a combination that you're less likely to experience if you're a female business owner.

Balancing Your Roles

Just because you have a job and family doesn't mean you have to experience negative stress. As you know, it is the demands of your conflicting roles and the interaction of such roles that leads to psychological and/or physical distress. You must work to establish a balance between the demands you experience. Recall the difficulties arising for the Type E woman who strives to excel in every sphere of her life. Certainly try to do your best and be proud about this but also be willing to make compromises. There are only so many pieces to the pie of your life and energy. Also, establish priorities to help yourself make decisions about how to spend your time and energy when demands from work and home conflict. Clarify your position in terms of what, in the final analysis, is your priority. If your family is your number one priority this fact would help you decide how to resolve situations seemingly pulling you in different directions. A recent survey reported in the September 22, 1996 issue of the *Los Angeles Times* revealed that two-thirds of working women would turn down an offer to become company president to spend more personal and family time and to experience less negative stress. It's necessary that you work with your partner to attain some type of balance between home and family responsibilities. You can't be solely in charge of these duties if you're also holding down a job. Set a time to meet with your partner and decide on how to assign tasks and obtain as equal a balance in home and personal responsibilities as possible. Include your older children by giving them tasks to accomplish as well. Finally, a further word about balance. You have to schedule some time for yourself—this might seem an impossible task given demands from work and family. By now, I hope you're convinced by all of the evidence of the tremendous physical and mental benefits of the following: prostress; being involved in prostress activities; and developing prostress interests. Not only will they energize and refresh you, they'll also allow you to release a great deal of the tension that builds up from work and family demands. Then you can return to your home, job, or whichever role with a balanced, more positive and flexible attitude that will greatly improve your ability to cope with stressors from these different areas of your life.

16

The Art of Skillful Communication

Relationships are a double-edged sword for women. When all is not well in a relationship, it can be a tremendous source of negative stress in your life. On the other hand, relationships and social support can be tools for managing stress. The distressed couples I see in therapy come for help with any number of troubles and complaints. What frequently impresses me is how often poor communication greatly exacerbates these problems. By itself, it can be the reason for stress and dysfunction in a marriage. On the other hand, a couple may be having difficulties for other reasons but if poor communication is also present, it only intensifies the distressfulness and pain. Often, as my couples work through the process of learning how to communicate and listen, the relationship improves dramatically and they develop a level of intimacy previously unknown and unexpected. After reading chapter 5, you have an understanding of the many ways communication can go awry. While it does take dedication to practice certain exercises, improvements in communication can be rapid and extremely effective in deterring stress and in improving your relationship overall.

Improving Your Communication Skills

There are several rules to incorporate in working on improved communication. At a very basic level, most problems in communication arise because the message sent by the speaker isn't the one picked up by the receiver. Many factors interfere such as defensiveness, errone-ous beliefs, assumptions, personal conclusions, differences in commu-nication style, and poor speaking habits, such as speaking in vague generalities. One of the strongest ways to increase the chance that the message sent will equal the message received is for the listener to re-peat her interpretation of what was said to her. For example, if your partner says, "I had a tough day and can't wait to hit the couch," you might conclude and say, "So you're saying you want to stay in again on a weekend night." You might be angry and disappointed because you've come to the conclusion that your partner is more focused on work than on your relationship and that he or she is, yet again, back-ing out of plans for a night on the town. The second step is to com-municate such feelings to your partner. By using an "I feel" format, you're less likely to come across as aggressive or condemning. This approach doesn't put your partner on the defense. You might say, "I feel I'm less important to you than your work and it seems that you use up all of your energy at work so you can't ever do anything fun or exciting with me anymore." It's important that you give such feed-back to the speaker so that he or she will know just what it is that you have actually "heard." You must then give your partner a chance to respond and, most importantly, *listen* while suspending preconcep-tions and judgments. Give him or her a fair chance to explain the situation. You may have constructed a whole storyline about your partner's being bored with you and so avoiding going out on week-ends. If so, you're going to be looking for any evidence, or even "cre-ating" evidence, to substantiate your plot. If your beliefs are inaccurate, and you don't communicate them to your partner, he or she will be confused and probably frustrated by your "erratic" or "il-logical" behavior.

Validating

Another technique that takes some practice but is highly effec-tive in defusing tension and improving communication is called vali-dating. This requires you to empathize or try to take the speaker's perspective to see that what they said and feel is reasonable *from their point of view* (Gottman, Notarius, Gonso, and Markman 1976). This can be very tricky as you have to suspend your tendencies to be de-fensive or judgmental. You may not agree in the slightest with what the speaker has said but you can admit that, from his or her perspec-tive, the conclusion or point of view might be understandable. Vali-dating the speaker's perspective can have an immediate impact on defusing tension in an encounter. Most of us just want to hear that what we think is important. The result of your telling your partner you understand her or his point of view is that she or he will be more willing to come to some type of mutual agreement than when confronted with the usual expected attack.

Challenging Your Automatic Thoughts

The problem of how our automatic thoughts interfere with communication was also discussed in chapter 5. In particular, the danger of the "shoulds" deserves further comment here. Recall that accusations and blame can arise when your partner doesn't satisfy your absolutistic demands or shoulds (of which you might not even be aware). For example, without being aware of it, you may believe that your partner *should* always be ready and waiting to listen to your problems or that your partner *should* realize when you want to be alone or want some personal space. Then, if your partner doesn't behave in accordance with how you think he or she *should*, you feel slighted, angry, and upset. You might say to yourself that if your partner really cared about you or was really right for you, he or she would automatically know these things.

When you sense your anger increasing during a conversation or after an argument, try to replay the scenario to see if any of your destructive shoulds played a role. A hint to the presence of shoulds is a conversation about some minor or largely unimportant topic that ends with you or your partner making wild accusations and issuing blame. For example, suppose you have worked hard to prepare a fine meal and spend some time alone with your partner. Your partner thanks you but you decide that the response he or she gave you was not as appreciative as it *should* have been. This triggers your automatic thoughts, "He/she is always ungrateful; nothing I do seems to matters; he/she takes what I do for granted." If you check your thinking you might find the troublesome shoulds that are leading to your extreme, negative responses and high levels of distress. The following thought might be present, "He/she should know how hard I worked on this and thank me profusely." With such extreme expectations, your responses and feelings will probably be extreme as well. Instead, suppose you countered the automatic thinking, "It would be nice if he/she acknowledged my efforts and thanked me." Your reactions would likely be much less extreme and you would be more apt to obtain the gratitude and satisfaction from your partner than if you began the usual attack, withdraw, or sulk. You could even say in a calm, assertive fashion, "You know, I enjoy making you happy with a great meal and it really makes me feel good when you acknowledge the time and effort I've spent on cooking for you." Your partner will get the clear message rather than feeling subject to a seemingly irrational, random attack on your part. With some familiarity, you'll be able to quickly recognize your extreme and judgmental comments before they leave your lips and determine whether there are any implied shoulds which need to be recognized and transformed.

Rules for the Speaker and Listener

The following rules will help to improve communication and reduce the negative stress in your interactions. As the *active speaker*, these suggestions are important for you to follow:

- Communicate your feelings using "I" statements. Don't get into the trap of blaming your partner. This will immediately cause him or her to be defensive and will terminate any chance of his or her listening to you. Blaming also leads to increased tension and arguments.

- Use specific examples—"Yesterday when you ... " or, "Do you remember when you ... "

- Avoid speaking in vague generalities or sweeping statements—"You never help me," or, "You always do that and obviously don't love me."

- Avoid making assumptions about your partner's behavior. Try to give him or her the benefit of the doubt.

- Avoid using the "should" mentality in talking to your partner.

- Avoid telling the listener what he or she does wrong, try to instead phrase your statements in positive terms—replace, "You never clean up properly," with, "I appreciate your helping me. Could you also do x, y, and z?"

- Reinforce your partner or listener when he or she makes desired changes in communication and behavior in general. Look for the positives rather than the negatives in the other's behavior.

- Use time-outs if you sense the listener is becoming agitated, angry, and so on. Suggest that you both come back to the conversation later.

- Don't use extreme, loaded words such as "never" and "always." Statements with these words put the listener on the defensive and are easily disproved. "You never give me any support," might lead to the retort, "Who sat and listened to you complain about your old job and helped you rewrite your résumé last week?"

As the *active listener*, the following suggestions are important for you to follow:

- Repeat what you heard your partner say—your rendition may or may not be accurate.

- Ask for feedback regarding whether you heard the message correctly.

- Give your partner validation for his or her point of view.

- Ask for specific examples when your partner speaks in vague generalities.

- Try to actually listen rather than jumping to conclusions about what the speaker "really" means based on your own assumptions, fears, etc.

- Reinforce your partner's efforts to communicate clearly.

- Avoid the tendency to respond defensively—try to really consider what the person is telling you.

- Look for and communicate points made by the speaker with which you may agree.

- Ask for a time-out if you begin to lose control and set a time to return to the discussion.

Take a moment now to recall a recent conversation with your partner, boss, or friend that ended in an argument or a feeling of tension. Try to see how you may have played a part in getting the conversation to end negatively. Write in the following communication log a summary of how the conversation went, including both your comments and those of the other. Then rewrite the scenario using the above rules to change what you said and how you spoke or listened. Do this several times for troublesome exchanges. After you begin practicing the rules for improved communication and obtain less stressful and even positive exchanges, also write several of these down. This will reinforce the rules in your mind reminding you of how effective they can be.

Communication Log

Negative exchange:

Me: _____

He/She: _____

Me: _____
He/She: _____

Me: _____
He/She: _____

How I could have responded using the rules for improved communication:

_____

_____

_____

Negative exchange:
Me: _____
He/She: _____

Me: _____
He/She: _____

Me: _____
He/She: _____

How I could have responded using the rules for improved communication:

_____

_____

_____

Negative exchange:

Me: _____

He/She: _____

Me: _____

He/She: _____

Me: _____

He/She: _____

How I could have responded using the rules for improved communication:

_____

_____

_____

Positive exchange:

Me: _____

He/She: _____

Me: _____

He/She: _____

Me: _____

He/She: _____

Rules I used for improved communication:

_____

_____

_____

Positive exchange:

Me: _____

He/She: _____

Me: _____

He/She: _____

Me: _____

He/She: _____

Rules I used for improved communication:

_____

_____

_____

Positive exchange:

Me: _____

He/She: _____

Me: _____

He/She: _____

Me: _____

He/She: _____

Rules I used for improved communication:

_____

_____

_____

17

Optimizing Your Stress: An Overview

Hopefully you've become more stress-wise and are working on turning your unhealthy stressful habits into healthy distress-reducing, prostress-boosting ones. It's not always easy to change our behavior or our tendencies to think in certain ways. It takes a great deal of dedication, effort, faith, and motivation. Stress-management techniques initially take time and may not be consistent with the modern-day attitude of, "I want it now; I've got to have it now." Much more important than immediate satisfaction and payback is your ability to tolerate delays, to be flexible adapting to changing situations and to take disruptions in your life less seriously. Try to enjoy both small pleasures and challenges in the here-and-now rather than waiting for infrequent, major life events. It necessarily takes some time for you to learn how to

- Work with your body to relax

- Challenge and modify your negative thoughts about yourself, others, and the world

- Change your unhealthy personality characteristics and behaviors (drinking, smoking, not exercising, or racing the clock

- Develop a balanced lifestyle

- Search out and include the healing, challenging, growth-promoting prostress in your life

Letting Go of Your Unhealthy Patterns

Besides the inherent difficulty in changing ourselves, there might be reasons for not wanting to give up our unhealthy patterns. Some of us crave the arousal generated by arguments and procrastinating until the last minute. This craving might actually come from having grown up in a chaotic environment and still feeling comfortable in this unhealthy but familiar dramatic and erratic situation. If this rings a bell, you need to realize that this type of arousal is negative, harmful stress. Instead, try to attain arousal through healthier means, such as exercise or challenging yourself to learn new skills and develop talents.

Others of us hold on to symptoms of stress, such as exhaustion or illness, in order to get attention and care from other people or to avoid situations in which we do not feel comfortable. Again, think of the boost in self-esteem you'll have when you no longer need to depend on others for validation and caretaking or when you master situations previously distressing to you.

You might use the excuse that you just don't have the time to practice the techniques, do the written self-monitoring, start the exercise, or change your unhealthy lifestyle. Remember, burning the candle at both ends means the candle burns out more quickly. First of all, you do deserve the time to do the things that you want to do and that are good for you. Secondly, the suggestions and techniques offered in this book will actually give you increased energy and productivity so that you can get the more taxing things accomplished. The healthiest principle to follow in your life is one of balance. You cannot keep on doing and doing for others or working at a faster and faster pace. Eventually, you'll burn out mentally and physically. Spice up and balance your life by making sure you have enough prostress in it. We all have things in our life that we must do and that aren't always pleasant or interesting. However, nobody is meant to live a life limited to these activities. By balancing your experiences you'll find you can be physically and mentally healthy and enjoy a full, challenging, joyous, loving, and happy life—the way it was meant to be!

In Closing

Although our society is becoming more accepting of women choosing to occupy traditionally male dominated fields and expressing ambition and assertiveness, we still face many barriers. These range on a continuum from being overt to covert. For example, the existence of schools that forbid female applicants is an obvious, overt barrier. The emphasis on a woman's appearance as portrayed in the media is a more subtle way of devaluing women and sending the message that we aren't desirable unless we meet certain physical criteria. The techniques presented in this book provide you with tools to use as you choose to gain control over areas in your life that may be causing you distress. This is not to say you should adopt male patterns of cognition or behavior. Hold onto and value your feminine characteristics and develop your strengths and assets. Many of the reasons why women perceive particular events as distressful are because of messages we pick up through socialization, as well as actual situations in the environment. Socialization sends messages that girls aren't as strong or smart as boys, or that girls aren't acceptable unless they look and act a certain way. Situations we undergo include jobs that offer less control, power, and financial remuneration. Meanwhile, society bombards us with messages that we must be the family caretaker and ignore our own needs and desires. These characteristics play into the likelihood of experiencing increased negative stress at home, with friends, and on the job. I hope that you'll take the information you have learned, together with the tools presented, to build your awareness about forces influencing you, your tendencies to act, perceive, and respond in certain ways, and how you can choose to respond in a more affirming, healthy way. Next time you say you have too much stress in your life, I hope you're smiling happily and speaking of prostress! Remember that stress management is a balancing game of self management and I hope this book gives you invaluable knowledge to use on your journey.

Here's a final, easy trick to help you remember the essential techniques of stress optimization. Use the following acronym:
B reathing, **R** elaxation, **A** utomatic **T** houghts **S** topping—**BRATS!**

Best wishes and good luck!

References

Allen, R. J. 1983. *Human Stress: Its Nature and Control*. Minneapolis: Burgess Publishing Company.

Andersen, M. L. 1993. *Thinking About Women: Sociological Perspectives on Sex and Gender*. New York: Macmillan Publishing Company.

Anthony, J. C., and J. E. Helzer. 1991. "Syndromes of Drug Abuse and Dependence." In *Psychiatric Disorders in America: The Epidemiologic Catchment Area Study*, edited by L. N. Robins and D. A. Reiger. New York: The Free Press.

Baruch, G. K., and R. C. Barnett. 1986. "Role Quality, Multiple Role Involvement, and Psychological Well Being in Midlife Women." *Journal of Personality and Social Psychology* 51:578–585.

Barnett, R. C., and G. K. Baruch. 1985. "Women's Involvement in Multiple Roles and Psychological Distress." *Journal of Personality and Social Psychology*. 49:135–145.

———. 1987. "Social Roles, Gender, and Psychological Distress." In *Gender & Stress*, edited by R. Barnett, L. Biener, and G. Baruch. New York: The Free Press.

Beck, A. T. 1988. *Love Is Never Enough*. New York: HarperPerennial.

Braiker, H. B. 1986. *The Type E Woman: How to Overcome the Stress of Being Everything to Everybody*. New York: Dodd, Mead & Company.

Chopra, D. 1987. *Creating Health: Beyond Prevention, Toward Perfection*. Boston: Houghton Mifflin Company.

Cleary, P. D. 1987. "Gender Differences in Stress-Related Disorders." In *Gender & Stress*, edited by R. Barnett, L. Biener and G. Baruch. New York: The Free Press.

Cooper, C. L. 1983. "Problem Areas for Future Stress Research: Cancer and Working Women." In *Stress Research: Issues for the Eighties*, New York: John Wiley and Sons.

Csikszentmihalyi, M. 1990. *Flow: The Psychology of Optimal Experience*. New York: Harper & Row, Publishers.

Davis, M., M. McKay, and E. R. Eshelman. 1980. *The Relaxation & Stress Reduction Workbook*. Oakland, CA: New Harbinger Publications.

Diener, E., and R. S. Emmons. 1984. "The Independence of Positive and Negative Affect." *Journal of Personality and Social Psychology* 47:1105–1117.

Dryden, W., and A. Ellis. 1986. "Rational-Emotive Therapy." In *Handbook of Cognitive-Behavioral Therapies*, edited by K. Dobson. New York: The Guilford Press.

Edwards, J. R., and C. L. Cooper. 1988. "The Impacts of Positive Psychological States on Physical Health: A Review and Theoretical Framework." *Social Science Medicine* 27(12): 1447–1459.

Friedman, H. S., and S. Booth-Kewley. 1987. "The Disease-Prone Personality." *American Psychologist* 42:539–555.

Gerdes, E. P. 1995. "Women Preparing for Traditionally Male Professions: Physical and Psychological Symtoms Associated with Work and Home Stress." *Sex Roles* 32:787–805.

Glass, D. C. 1982. "Psychological and Physiological Responses of Individuals Displaying Type A Behavior." *Acta Med Scand (Suppl)* 660: 193–202.

Goldberg, P. 1978. *Executive Health: How to Recognize Health Danger Signals and Manage Stress Successfully*. New York: McGraw-Hill Publications Company.

Gottman, J., C. Notarius, J. Gonso, and H. Markman. 1976. *A Couple's Guide to Communication*. Illinois: Research Press Co.

Hanson, P. G. 1989. *Stress for Success*. Toronto, Canada: Collins Publishers.

Husaini, B., J. Neff, J. R. Newbrough, and M. C. Moore. 1982. "The Stress-Buffering Role of Social Support and Personal Competence among the Rural Married." *Journal of Community Psychology* 52:409–426.

Jacobson, E. 1938. *Progressive Relaxation* (2nd ed.). Chicago: University of Chicago Press.

Johnson, K. 1991. *Trusting Ourselves: The Complete Guide to Emotional Well-Being for Women*. New York: The Atlantic Monthly Press.

Kanner, A. D., J. C. Coyne, C. Schaefer, and R. S. Lazarus. 1981. "Comparison of Two Modes of Stress Measurement: Daily Hassles and Uplifts versus Major Life Events." *Journal of Behavioral Medicine* 4(1):1–39.

Karasek, R. A. 1979. "Job Demands, Job Decision Latitude and Mental Strain: Implications for Job Redesign." *Admimistrative Science Quarterly* 24:285–308.

Kessler, R. C., and J. D. McLeod. 1984. "Sex Differences in Vulnerability to Undesirable Life Events." *American Sociological Review* 49:620–631.

Kobasa, S. O. 1987. "Stress Responses and Personality." In *Gender & Stress*, edited by R. Barnett, L. Biener, and G. Baruch. New York: The Free Press.

LaCroix, A. Z., and S. G. Haynes. 1987. "Gender Differences in the Health Effects of Workplace Roles." In *Gender & Stress*, edited by R. Barnett, L. Biener, and G. Baruch. New York: The Free Press.

Lakein, A. 1973. *How to Get Control of Your Time and Your Life.* New York: New American Library.

Larsen, R. J., E. Diener, and R. S. Cropanzano. 1987. "Cognitive Operations Associated with Individual Differences in Affect Intensity." *Journal of Personality and Social Psychology* 53(4):767–774.

Long, B. C., S. E. Kahn, and R. W. Schutz. 1992. "Causal Model of Stress and Coping: Women in Management." *Journal of Counseling Psychology* 39:227–239.

Long, B. C. 1984. "Aerobic Conditioning and Stress Inoculation: A Comparison of Stress-Management Interventions." *Cognitive Therapy and Research* 8:517–542.

Long, B. C. 1985. "Stress-Management Interventions: A 15-month Follow-up of Aerobic Conditioning and Stress Inoculation Training." *Cognitive Therapy and Research* 9:471–478.

MacDougall, J. M., T. M. Dembroski, and D. S. Krantz. 1981. "The Effects of Types of Challenge on Pressor and Heart Rate Responses in Type A and B Women." *Psychophysiology* 18:1–19.

Machac, M., L. Machacova, and R. Hampi. 1987. "Changes in Cortisol Level in Saliva Following Relaxation-Activation Autoregulative Intervention." *Activitas Nervosa Superior* 29(3):159–163.

Mallinckrodt, B., F. T. Leong, and M. M. Kraij. 1989. "Sex Differences in Graduate Student Life-Change Stress and Stress Symptoms." *Journal of College Student Development* 30:332–338.

Maltz, D., and R. Borker. 1982. "A Cultural Approach to Male-Female Miscommunications". In *Language and Social Identity*, edited by J. J. Gumperz. Cambridge, England: Cambridge University Press.

Martin, D. J., L. Y. Abramson, and L. B. Alloy. 1984. "Illusion of Control for Self and Others in Depressed and Nondepressed College Students." *Journal of Personality and Social Psychology* 46:125–136.

Matthews, K. A. 1982. "Psychological Perspectives on the Type A Behavior Pattern." *Psychological Bulletin* 91:293–323.

McCann, I. L., and D. S. Holmes. 1984. "Influence of Aerobic Exercise on Depression." *Journal of Personality and Social Psychology*. 46:1142–1147.

McKay, M., M. Davis, and P. Fanning. 1981. *Thoughts & Feelings: The Art of Cognitive Stress Intervention*. Oakland, CA: New Harbinger Publications.

McKinney, M. E., and H. White. 1985. "Dietary Habits and Blood Chemistry Levels of the Stress-Prone Individual: The Hot Reactor." *Comprehensive Therapy*. 11:21–28.

Meichenbaum, D. 1985. *Stress Inoculation Training*. New York: Pergamon Press.

Miller, J. 1980. "Individual and Occupational Determinants of Job Satisfaction: A Focus on Gender Differences." *Sociology of Work and Occupations*. 7:337–366.

Miller, S., and N. Kirsch. 1987. "Sex Differences in Cognitive Coping with Stress." In *Gender & Stress*, edited by R. Bamett, L. Biener, and G. Baruch. New York: The Free Press.

National Institute of Mental Health. The Office of Scientific Information and the Depression Awareness, Recognition, and Treatment (D/ART) Program. National Institute of Mental Health, Room 10-85, 5600 Fishers Lane, Rockville, MD 20857.

Nuemberger, P. 1985. *Freedom From Stress: A Holistic Approach*. Pennsylvania: The Himalayan International Institute of Yoga Science and Philosophy of the U.S.A.

Ornstein, R., and D. Sobel. 1987. *The Healing Brain: Breakthrough Discoveries about How the Brain Keeps Us Healthy*. New York: Simon & Schuster.

———. 1989. *Healthy Pleasures*. Reading, MA: Addison-Wesley Publishing Company.

Padus, E., and the Editors of Prevention Magazine. 1986. *The Complete Guide to Your Emotions & Your Health*. Pennsylvania: Rodale Press.

Palos, S. 1972. *The Chinese Art of Healing*. New York: Bantam Books.

Pearlin, L. I., and C. Schooler. 1978. "The Structure of Coping." *Journal of Health and Social Behavior*. 19:2–21.

Polefrone, J., and S. B. Manuck. 1987. "Gender Differnces in Cardiovascular and Neuroendocrine Response to Stressors." In *Gender and Stress*, edited by R. C. Barnett, L. Biener, and G. K. Baruch. New York: The Free Press.

Porter, L., and A. A. Stone. 1995. "Are There Really Gender Differences in Coping?: A Reconsideration of Previous Data and Results from a Daily Study." *Journal of Social and Clinical Psychology* 14(2):184–202.

Reich, J. W., and A. Zautra. 1981. "Life Events and Personal Causation: Some Relationships with Satisfaction and Distress." *Journal of Personality and Social Psychology* 41(5): 1002–1012.

Robertson, J. C., and T. Monte. 1996. *Peak-Performance Living*. San Francisco: HarperSanFrancisco.

Ruble, T. L. 1983. "Sex Stereotypes: Issues of Change." *Sex Roles* 9:397–401.

Schneider, K. June 1996. "Mission Impossible." *People* Magazine 45:65–74.

Selye, H. 1967. *In Vivo: The Case for Supramolecular Biology*. New York: Liveright Publishing Corporation.

Siegel, B. S. 1986. *Love, Medicine & Miracles*. New York: Harper & Row.

Siebert, A. 1996. "The Survivor Personality." Berkley/Perigee.

Striegel-Moore, R. H., L. R. Silberstein, and J. Rodin. 1986. "Toward an Understanding of Risk Factors for Bulimia." *American Psychologist* 41:246–263.

Swedo, S., and H. Leonard. 1996. *It's Not All in Your Head*. San Francisco: HarperSanFrancisco.

Taylor, S. E. 1991. "Health Psychology: The Science and the Field." In *Stress and Coping: An Anthology*, edited by A. Monat and R. S. Lazarus. New York: Columbia University Press.

Thomas, C. B., and K. R. Duszynski. 1974. "Closeness to Parents and the Family Constellation in a Prospective Study of Five Disease States: Suicide, Mental Illness, Malignant Tumor, Hypertension and Coronary Heart Disease." *John Hopkins Medical Journal* 134(5):251–270.

Vanfossen, B. E. 1986. "Sex Differences in Depression: The Role of Spouse Support." In *Stress, Social Support, and Women*, edited by S. E. Hobfoll. New York: Hemisphere.

Wethington, E., J. D. McLeod, and R. C. Kessler. 1987. "The Importance of Life Events for Explaining Sex Differences in Psychological Distress." In *Gender & Stress*, edited by R. Barnett, L. Biener, and G. Baruch. New York: The Free Press.

Woody, E. Z., and P. R. Costanzo. 1981. "The Socialization of Obesity-prone Behavior." In *Developmental Social Psychology: Theory and Research*, edited by S. S. Brehm, S. M. Kassin, and F. X. Gibbons. Oxford: Oxford University Press.

Zautra, A., and J. Reich. 1980. "Positive Life Events and Reports of Well-being: Some Useful Distinctions." *American Journal of Community Psychology* 86:657–670.